Make That Grade Economics Revision

James O'Leary

Gill & Macmillan

Gill & Macmillan Ltd
Goldenbridge
Dublin 8
with associated companies throughout the world

0 7171 2666 8

Index compiled by Helen Litton
Print origination by Mathematical Composition Setters Ltd, Salisbury, Wiltshire
Printed by ColourBooks Ltd, Dublin

A catalogue record is available for this book from the British Library.

5 4 3 2 1

CONTENTS

CHAPTER 1

WHAT IS ECONOMICS?

1.1 *The economic problem*

The fundamental economic problem is one of ***relative scarcity***. There is an insatiable desire for goods and services in society but only a finite quantity of ***economic resources*** available to satisfy these desires.

Some societies may suffer from *absolute scarcity* due to underdevelopment, famine, etc. However even those societies with the most highly developed economies, such as the USA and Japan, are subject to the fundamental problem of relative scarcity.

Relative scarcity means that ***choices*** have to be made. For example, if at budget time the government decides to increase teachers' pay the cost might be measured in terms of poorer facilities in schools, or poorer hospital care, etc. Or, an individual taking a foreign holiday may do so at the expense of a new car or some other desired item.

Making choices implies the existence of a ***scale of preferences*** on the part of the decision-taker. Typically the choices made will represent a ***trade-off***: extra units of good *X* at a cost of fewer units of good *Y*. Having made the choice the next best alternative in the scale of preferences must be forgone. The ***opportunity cost*** of a particular use of scarce resources is the forgone alternative.

Examples:

- an individual with £10 to spend is faced with the choice of either buying a book or going to the cinema;
- the government with £50m to spend is faced with the choice of purchasing military equipment for the defence forces or improving the roads.

For the individual, the opportunity cost of the book is going to the cinema and vice versa; for the government the opportunity cost of the military equipment is the improved roads and vice versa.

Adam and Eve in their Garden of Eden with all its abundance might conceivably have studied physics, biology, ethics, etc., but economics would never have occurred to them.

Economics as an intellectual discipline results from this basic problem of relative scarcity. Economics can be defined as: **the study of human behaviour regarding the optimum use of scarce resources which have alternative uses.**

Optimum is here defined in terms of the achievements of the goals of those with control over the scarce resources.

1.2 *Economic resources and production possibilities*

A society's economic resources can be grouped under four broad headings (sometimes referred to as the ***factors of production***):

- Land;
- Labour;
- Capital;
- Enterprise.

Land is broadly defined as the natural resources (the 'gifts of nature') available such as minerals, the soil, the climate, etc. The labour available can be measured in terms of the quantity and quality of the society's labour force. The stock of capital refers to the plant and equipment (tools, machinery, factories, offices, etc.) available for use in the production of goods and services. Enterprise is the function, essential to a deregulated market economy (Section 1.3), of co-ordinating and activating the other resources with a view to producing goods and services.

At any given point in time a society will have a given quantity of economic resources and this 'endowment' will set an upper limit to what can be produced. However, over time the resources available can be changed in terms of both quantity and quality. Expenditure on education can improve the quality of the labour force and thereby increase the **productivity of labour**. The educational system can also influence the level of enterprise in a society by the degree of emphasis it places on an enterprise culture. Investment expenditure (Section 8.6) can alter the quantity and quality of the capital stock. Over time, therefore, a society's capacity to produce goods and services can be enhanced resulting in improved living standards.

A **production possibility curve** (PPC) is a means of illustrating the capacity of an economy to produce goods and services, given its available resources. The PPC indicates the choices available by representing the **feasible** combinations of output. For diagrammatic purposes (two-dimensional) it is assumed that a society wishes to use its resources to produce two distinct goods, X and Y (Figure 1.1).

If all resources are allocated to the Y industry y_0 is the maximum quantity of Y that can be produced. Likewise x_0 is the maximum output of good X that can be produced. If all resources are allocated between both industries the PPC represents the maximum achievable output of one good given the level of output of the other. For example if x_1 of X is being produced then y_1 of Y is the maximum achievable output of Y.

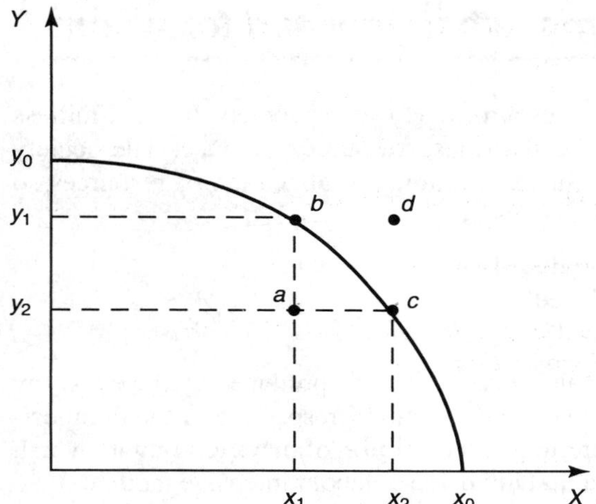

Figure 1.1: *Production possibility curve*

Combinations inside the curve (or frontier) are feasible but not efficient. Inefficient combinations are ones such that output of one good can be increased without reducing the output of the other. For example at point *a* more output of *X* can be produced for the given output of *Y* (move to point *c*) or for the given level of *X* more *Y* can be produced (move to point *b*). Combination on the PPC such as *b* or *c* are both feasible and efficient. An efficient utilization of resources implies that output of one good cannot be increased without reducing the output of the other.

Combinations outside the curve such as point *d* are not feasible given the existing resources. While y_1 of *Y* or x_2 of *X* could be produced separately they cannot be produced in combination. However, an increase in the quantity or quality of resources (e.g. technological progress) ***shifts*** the PPC outward so that points such as *d* may be feasible in the future.

The concept of opportunity cost can be illustrated with the PPC. Assume starting at point *b* more *X* is required and resources are reallocated so that *c* is the new combination of output. *X* output has increased by $x_2 - x_1$ but *Y* output has been reduced by $y_1 - y_2$ in order to achieve the increased output of *X*. The forgone output of *Y* represents the opportunity cost of the extra output of *X*.

The slope of the PPC at any point represents the rate at which one good can be ***transformed*** into the other at that point. The ***concave*** shape of the PPC reflects the assumption that as, say, more and more *X* is produced then larger amounts of *Y* will have to be sacrificed to get even further units of *X* (a ***diminishing marginal rate of transformation***) and vice versa. Not all resources are deemed to be equally productive in both sectors (if they were a straight line PPC would be appropriate).

1.3 Economic systems: what how and for whom

A society's economy has limited resources. However society has a limitless capacity for the goods and services that these resources produce. The society therefore needs some mechanism for determining the allocation of resources so that the following key issues can be resolved:

- What goods are actually to be produced?
- How are these goods to be produced?
- For whom are they to be produced?

What actual combination of goods and services is to be produced by the economy (e.g. balance between luxuries and necessities, etc)? Irrespective of the composition of output there are typically alternative **techniques of production** with which to produce particular goods (e.g. capital intensive or labour intensive methods). So which technique is to be adopted? Finally how are the goods and services to be distributed among the population?

Different economic systems exist depending on the mix between decentralized free markets on the one hand and centralized regulation on the other (Figure 1.2).

In a pure **laissez faire** system the allocation of resources is completely determined by the unregulated interplay of the forces of supply and demand. The ***price mechanism*** indicates to firms the goods and services it is most profitable to produce and the most profitable techniques to employ. When determining the goods and services they wish to purchase consumers will consider the prices to be paid. Furthermore, their ability to buy the goods and services will largely depend on the wages they can earn supplying their labour to labour markets.

The price mechanism plays a co-ordinating role regarding the countless decisions being taken by firms, consumers and workers. The price mechanism also acts as a ***rationing*** device: items whose supply is low relative to demand will tend to have high or rising prices whereas items whose supply is high relative to demand will tend to have low or falling prices.

While the price mechanism operates like an ***invisible hand*** the method of the command economy is more intrusive. What to produce and how to produce them is decided by a central planning agency. Firms are given output targets in conformity with the plan and the necessary resources to meet the targets. Distribution might in principal be determined communally, however in practice consumers may exercise some personal preferences as they spend their incomes. Although prices may exist they are purely for accounting purposes rather than indicators of relative scarcity.

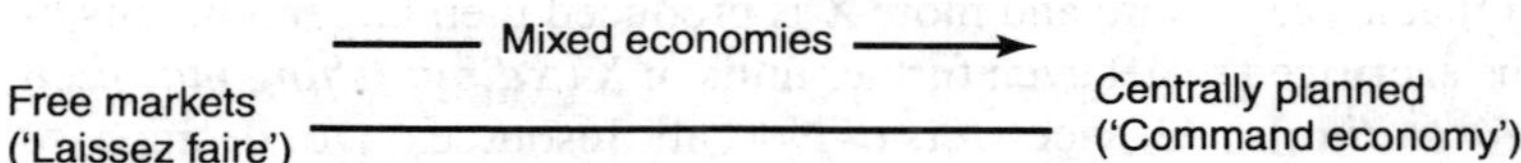

Figure 1.2: *Economic systems*

In practice all modern economies are a mixture of relatively free markets with some element of state regulation to influence resource allocation. Economies differ according to the balance that is struck. Some societies like Hong Kong or the USA have economies firmly tipped in favour of free markets, while others such as Ireland or France traditionally reserve a greater role for the state.

Evaluation of the strengths and weaknesses of alternative systems raise important issues. Ideally all societies wish to have efficient economies, i.e. an economy operating on or at least close to its production possibility frontier (Figure 1.1). However, some societies may wish to forgo a degree of efficiency if this means achieving a greater degree of equality.

The former Soviet Union had an economy based on a high degree of central planning with the scope for market relations severely restricted. This system proved to be highly inefficient largely due to its lack of flexibility and effectively collapsed in the late 1980s due to its inherent inertia. Modern Russia and the former 'Soviet Bloc' countries of Eastern Europe are currently attempting to rebuild their economies with much greater scope for free markets.

A free market system has the advantage of being highly flexible and therefore less wasteful of resources. The trend in the 1990s has been to shift economies closer to the free market end of the spectrum (Figure 1.2). **Privatization** – the practice of transferring resources from the state sector to the private sector – is gaining in popularity (Section 18.3). However free markets are efficient because they operate on the principal of ***the pursuit of self interest***. Gains in efficiency may be at the expense of greater social inequality and insecurity.

1.4 *The methodology of economics*

Economics is an intellectual discipline which attempts to discover and understand the laws governing the behaviour of modern economies. However, unlike many of the natural sciences, economics does not provide opportunities for ***controlled experiments*** in laboratories. The ability to undertake a controlled experiment, and for others to be able to duplicate it, has enabled the natural sciences to choose between competing theories and thereby continue to progress.

The economy is continuously evolving and changing, refusing to stand still for the economists benefit. It follows that the economy is never quite the same from one period to another. Contrast this with the solar system. Planetary motion is repetitive and once the astronomer discovers the laws of motion of the planets this knowledge holds good indefinitely. But a theory which explained some aspect of the economy of the 1930s may be of little relevance to the 1990s.

The absence of controlled experiments is of particular significance for ***macroeconomics*** which looks at the behaviour of the economy as a whole. ***Microeconomics*** studies the behaviour of individual ***economic agents*** (the firm, the consumer, the worker) and the strategies they pursue in particular markets. The big issues about which economists continue to disagree are mainly in the area of macroeconomics.

Economics aims to discover ***causal relationships*** of the form: 'if event A occurs then event B will follow as a consequence'. For example a simple prediction would be: if the price of a good rises the quantity purchased will fall. Controlled experiments enable the natural scientist to isolate the causal relationship between particular variables. In the absence of this the economist must rely heavily on the ***ceteribus paribus*** (or 'all else being equal') assumption. For example, the price of foreign holidays might be rising, but if disposable incomes are also rising this latter event may result in ***increased purchases*** despite the rising price.

Because of the difficulty regarding the (non) use of experiments economics relies heavily on abstract reasoning. According to our definition economics is simply a particular intellectual approach to a certain set of problems. The aim is to formulate general assumptions regarding the behaviour of economic agents which enable testable predictions to be made. For example the general assumption that firms seek to maximize profits enables predictions to be made regarding the response of firms to events such as the imposition of taxes (Section 3.2) etc. Economic analysis relies heavily on the construction of **economic models** which attempt to replicate key features of particular markets, the whole economy or some aspect of economic behaviour.

Normative and positive

Economics concerns itself with **positive** rather than **normative** propositions. A positive proposition entails some empirical content the truth of which can be tested. For example, the proposition: 'it is raining outside', may be true or false but its accuracy can be tested enabling the proposition to be clearly accepted or rejected. On the other hand a normative proposition reflects the value judgement of the person concerned and regarding which the best that might be achieved is an agreement to disagree 'Mozart is better than Beethoven' is such a proposition.

There are issues in economics such as poverty, unemployment, etc that can give rise to strongly held value judgements. Propositions of the form: 'governments should always treat unemployment as a greater evil than inflation' are normative rather than positive. Economists may have various personal views on such issues but economics as an intellectual discipline cannot resolve them. The best that economics can hope to achieve is to be able to explain the cause(s) of unemployment, inflation, etc. Understanding the cause may lead to prescriptions regarding remedies. But policy makers such as elected politicians rather than economists must be left to resolve the normative issues.

The analysis in the following text is referred to as 'comparative static' analysis. It focuses on equilibrium situations and considers the nature of a new equilibrium following a specified disturbance to some initial equilibrium. The actual process of adjustment – the dynamics of adjustment – are not primarily the focus of the analysis. Comparative statics facilitates the use of diagrams which, because of their two-dimensional nature, often require a high degree of simplification (or focus) on the part of the analysis.

REVISION FOCUS CHAPTER ONE

Key Areas

- Fundamental economic problem
  → relative scarcity → choices → scale of preferences
- Economic resources
  → land, labour, capital, enterprise → production possibilities
  → feasible and efficient combinations of output → opportunity cost
- Allocation of resources
  → what, how, for whom → the price mechanism → central planning
- Normative and positive statements
  Microeconomics and macroeconomics

Self Test

(1)	Increasing prosperity will remove the fundamental economic problem	T/F
(2)	Opportunity cost and price are the same thing	T/F
(3)	The production possibility curve indicates what combinations of output are possible, given existing resources	T/F
(4)	Only if the economy is operating outside its production possibility curve can it be operating efficiently	T/F
(5)	Positive statements must be true	T/F
(6)	Normative statements reflect value judgements	T/F
(7)	If economic resources have no alternative use then the opportunity cost of using them for a given purpose is zero	T/F
(8)	The price mechanism is a means of rationing resources according to ability and willingness to pay	T/F

Discussion Topics

- Explain why the production possibility curve is likely to shift outwards over time.
- The price mechanism allocates resources like an *invisible hand*. Explain.
- If an economy is operating inside its production possibility curve (Figure 1.1) resources are not being used efficiently. Explain why.

CHAPTER 2

SUPPLY AND DEMAND

2.1 *Supply and demand curves*

To understand how a modern economy works it is necessary to understand the nature of markets. To understand markets it is necessary to understand **supply** and **demand**. Supply and demand presupposes the existence of self-interested agents whose aim is to maximize their own benefits. Firms supplying markets are typically assumed to have as their objective the **maximization of profits** (Section 6.3). Consumers are assumed to have as their objective **the maximization of utility** (Section 4.1). The assumption of **rational behaviour** implies that agents can be expected to pursue these objectives systematically.

The theory (developed in Chapters 4 to 7) suggests that in competitive markets firms would be more willing to supply a product the higher the price that can be charged but by contrast consumers would be more willing to purchase the lower the price to be paid. We can illustrate these basic features of market behaviour by way of demand and supply schedules. (The following discussion outlines the main features of supply and demand analysis without being overconcerned with the underlying theory which is left for later chapters).

Demand schedule

A demand schedule specifies the quantity that consumers would be willing to purchase over a given time period at various prices. Table 2.1 represents a typical demand schedule.

Note at higher prices consumers are less willing to purchase the product and vice versa. This **inverse relationship** between price and the quantity demanded is known as the **law of demand** (Section 4.1). By multiplying the price and the corresponding quantity we can calculate the **total revenue**, i.e. the total amount of money that consumers would be willing to spend at that price. The demand schedule indicates the intentions of consumers (what they would be willing to do at various prices) not their actual behaviour. To know this we need to know the actual price that prevails in the market. The determination of the actual market price will depend on the interaction of the forces of supply and demand.

Table 2.1: *Demand schedule*

Price (P)	Quantity (Q)	Total Revenue (TR = PQ)
£1.50	100	£150
£1.40	110	£154
£1.30	120	£156
£1.20	130	£156
£1.10	140	£154
£1.00	150	£150
£0.90	160	£144

Demand curve

The information in the demand schedule can be easily represented by a demand curve as in Figure 2.1

The inverse relationship between price and quantity demanded means that the demand curve will slope downward from left to right. The actual slope (i.e. how steep) will depend on how responsive quantity demanded is to price changes. The degree of response will vary from good to good and can be measured by the **price elasticity of demand** (Section 2.5).

The total revenue (TR) at any given price can be illustrated by drawing a line horizontally from the price to the curve and vertically down to the corresponding quantity. The area of the resulting rectangle measures the total revenue at that price. For example, in Figure 2.1, when price is £1.30 quantity demanded is 120 per period and TR equals £1.30 × 120 = £156.

A change in the price of the product leads to a change in the quantity consumers wish to purchase. The effect of a change in price can be illustrated by a **movement**

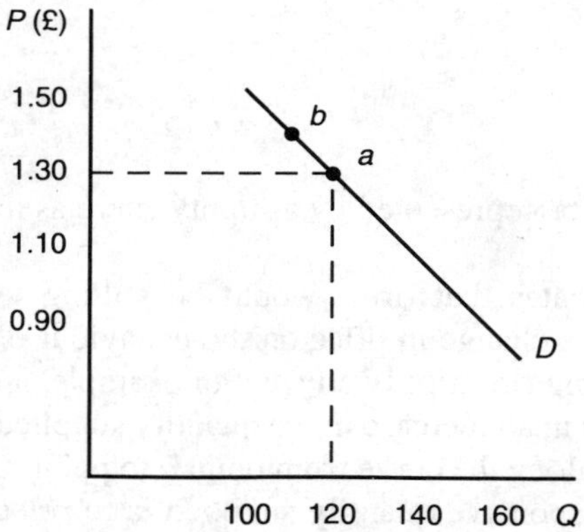

Figure 2.1: *Demand curve*

along the demand curve. For example, if price rises from £1.30 to £1.40 and quantity demanded falls from 120 to 110 this implies a movement along the demand curve from point *a* to point *b* (Figure 2.1).

Supply schedule

The supply schedule indicates the quantity that sellers would be willing to supply at various prices over a given time period. Like the demand curve it represents the intentions of those in the market rather than their actual behaviour. The following figures represent a typical supply schedule.

Table 2.2: *Supply schedule*

P(£)	Qs
1.50	160
1.40	150
1.30	140
1.20	130
1.10	120
1.00	110
0.90	100

Where markets are competitive, the higher the price that firms can charge for the product the greater the quantity they are likely to supply, all else being equal. This **positive relationship** between price and the quantity firms are willing to supply is reflected in the supply schedule.

Supply curve

The information in the supply schedule can be represented by a supply curve as in Figure 2.2.

The upward sloping supply curve indicates that firms would be willing to supply more at higher prices. The effect of a change in price on the behaviour of firms can be illustrated by a **movement along the supply curve**. For example, an increase in price from £1.20 to £1.40 results in an increase in the quantity supplied from 130 to 150, indicated by a movement along the curve from point *a* to point *b*. The slope of the curve depends on how responsive quantity supplied is to price changes. The responsiveness can be measured by the **price elasticity of supply** (Section 2.7).

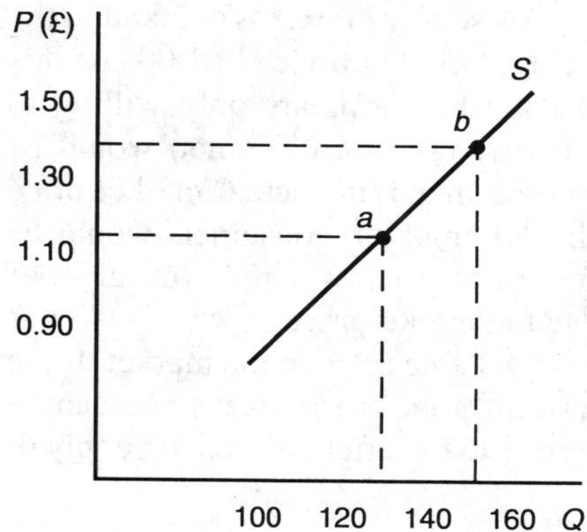

Figure 2.2: *Supply curve*

2.2 Determination of market price

In a competitive market the actual price that emerges will be determined by the interaction of the forces of supply and demand. By bringing the supply and demand curves together in the same diagram we can see this quite clearly.

Given the negatively sloped demand curve and the positively sloped supply curve we can expect to find a point of intersection (there will be only one point of intersection for well behaved S&D curves). In Figure 2.3 this is at point *a* with a price of £1.20 and corresponding quantity of 130. This is the equilibrium price/quantity combination. It is important to realize that there is only one **market-clearing price**. At any price other than the equilibrium price there will be either excess supply or excess demand in the market.

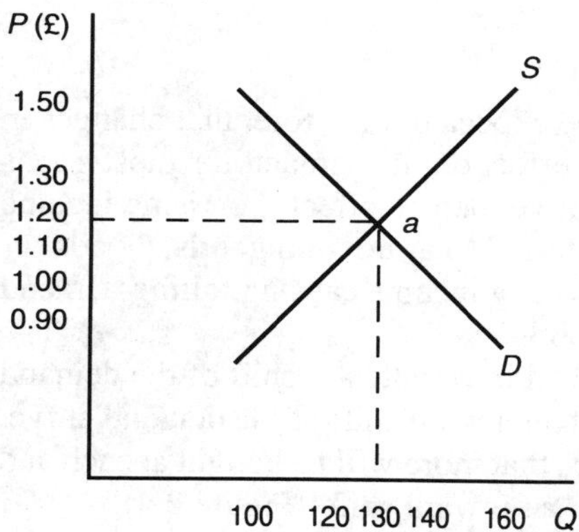

Figure 2.3: *Market equilibrium*

What is likely to happen if there is either excess supply or excess demand in the market? For example let us assume that the actual market price is £1.00. At this price consumers are attempting to buy 150 units but firms are only willing to supply 110 units for sale. The effect of the excess demand (40 units) would be to drive up the price in the market. If on the other hand, the actual market price was £1.50 firms would be attempting to sell 160 units but consumers would be only willing to purchase 100 units. The effect of the excess supply (60 units of accumulating unsold stocks) would be to drive the market price down.

The market-clearing price is therefore the only stable price in the market. If the actual market price is other than this equilibrium price the market price can be expected to converge on the equilibrium price due to the effect of excess supply or excess demand.

2.3 Conditions of demand

If the equilibrium price is to change then either the demand curve or the supply curve (or both) must shift. The factors determining the position (as opposed to slope) of the demand curve are referred to as the **conditions of demand**. Changes in these conditions will cause the demand curve to shift. Some of the more obvious conditions of demand are:

- income of consumers;
- prices of other goods;
- consumer tastes;
- seasonal factors;
- population changes.

Consumers' income

Income determines ability to spend. It can be expected, therefore, that changes in consumers disposable incomes will have an effect on the demand for most goods and services. Goods for which there is a positive income effect (i.e. rising income causing rising demand and vice versa) are referred to as **normal goods**. Goods for which there is a negative income effect (i.e. rising income causing falling demand and vice versa) are referred to as **inferior goods.**

For normal goods rising incomes is reflected in an outward shift of the demand curve whereas falling incomes is reflected in an inward shift of the demand curve. An outward shift in the demand curve implies that more will be bought at each and every price while the opposite is the case for an inward shift. (Figure 2.4).

Figure 2.4 indicates how rising income causes the demand curve to shift outward from D_0 to D_1 resulting in a higher equilibrium price ($p_0 \rightarrow p_1$) and quantity ($q_0 \rightarrow q_1$). Falling income would cause the demand curve to shift inward

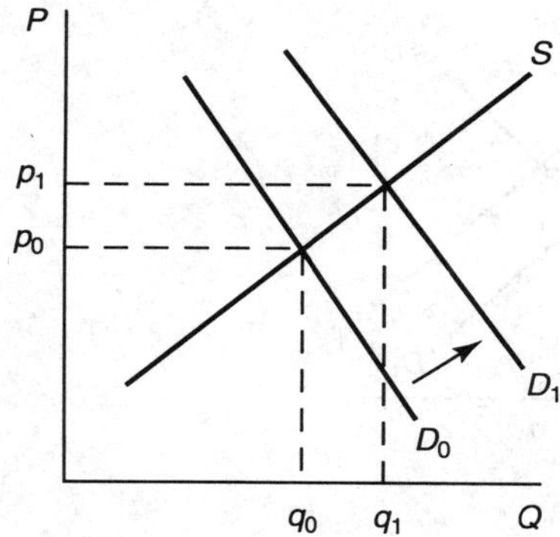

Figure 2.4: *Change in demand*

resulting in a lower equilibrium price and quantity. For **inferior goods** the effect on the demand curve of changing income is the opposite to that of normal goods. Rising income causes the demand curve to shift inwards and falling income causes it to shift outwards.

The extent of the impact of changing income on demand can be measured by the **income-elasticity of demand** (Section 2.6).

The price of other goods

To understand how the demand for a product is affected by changes in the prices of other goods it is necessary to be aware of the different relationships that can exist between goods. Two cases are of interest: **substitute goods** and **complementary goods.**

Complementary goods are goods that are bought together. Examples would be gin and tonic or tea and milk. Substitute goods are 'either/or' type goods and are less likely to be bought together. Examples would be gin and whiskey or tea and coffee.

The impact of a change in the price of one good on the quantity demanded of another good will depend on whether the goods in question are substitutes or complements. A rise in the price of one good will cause the demand for another good to rise if the goods in question are substitutes. However if the goods in question are complements a rise in the price of one will cause the demand for the other to fall. These relationships are illustrated in Figure 2.5.

Assume, for whatever reason, that the price of gin rises from $p_0 \rightarrow p_1$ as illustrated in Figure 2.5 (a). This will cause the quantity of gin demanded to fall from $q_0 \rightarrow q_1$ (a movement along the demand curve). There will be a fall in the demand for tonic, tonic being a complement to gin. This is illustrated by an inward shift in the demand curve for tonic in Figure 2.5 (b) with the equilibrium price and quantity of tonic falling. The rise in the price of gin will cause an increase in the

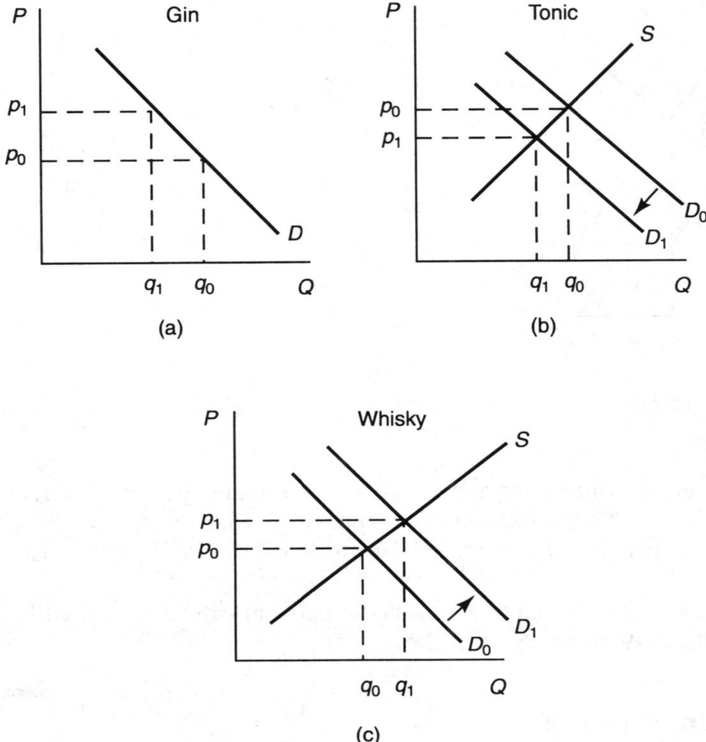

Figure 2.5: *Substitutes and complements*

demand for whiskey, whiskey being a substitute for gin. This is illustrated by an outward shift in the demand curve for whiskey in Figure 2.5 (c) with the equilibrium price and quantity of whiskey rising.

What we are analysing here are the **cross-effects** from one market to another. The extent of the cross effect can be measured by the **cross-elasticity of demand** (Section 2.6).

Consumers' tastes

Consumers' tastes are clearly an important influence on the demand for products. Consumers tastes can change over time to the benefit of some goods and the disadvantage of others. A whole industry (advertising) exists the purpose of which is to influence consumers tastes. A successful advertising campaign shifts consumers tastes in favour of the particular product. (Figure 2.6).

Figure 2.6 illustrates how a change in consumers tastes in favour of the good

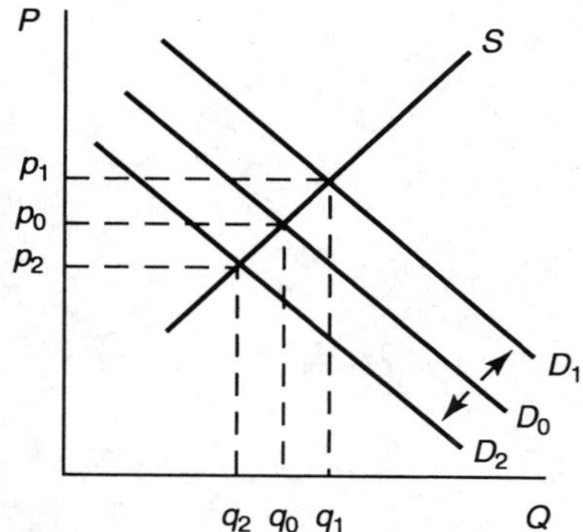

Figure 2.6: *Changing tastes*

shifts the demand curve outwards ($D_0 \rightarrow D_1$). The equilibrium price and quantity increase. A change in consumers tastes away from a good shifts the demand curve inwards ($D_0 \rightarrow D_2$) resulting in a fall in equilibrium price and quantity.

A change in any factor which influences the demand for the good, other than the price of the good itself, will have the effect of shifting the demand curve in a predictable way.

2.4 Conditions of supply

The **conditions of supply** determine the position of supply curves and changes in these conditions will cause supply curves to shift. The conditions of supply are related to the **costs of production** (Chapter 5). Changes in the costs of production relative to the price that can be charged will influence the willingness of firms to supply products. Conditions of supply include the following:

- technology (improvements leading to lower costs);
- labour costs;
- raw material costs;
- indirect taxes (Section 3.2);
- interest rates.

An increase in costs, by making it less profitable to supply, will cause supply curves to shift inwards and vice versa (Figure 2.7). An increase in costs of production (e.g. raw material prices) will cause the supply curve to shift inwards from S_0 to S_1. The result is an increase in equilibrium price ($p_0 \rightarrow p_1$) and a fall in equilibrium quantity ($q_0 \rightarrow q_1$).

An increase in the cost of an important raw material (e.g. oil) may have serious consequences for output and employment throughout the economy. By contrast a

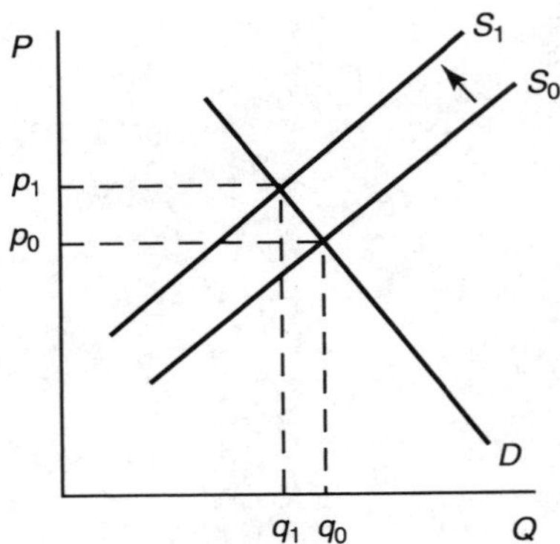

Figure 2.7: *Conditions of supply*

fall in an important cost (e.g. interest rates), by shifting supply curves outward can have beneficial effects on output and employment throughout the economy.

2.5 *Price elasticity of demand (PED)*

Elasticity is concerned with the responsiveness of one variable to changes in some other variable, all else being equal.

PED measures the responsiveness of quantity demanded to changes in the price of the product, all else being equal. Figure 2.8 illustrates two demand curves, D_0 and D_1.

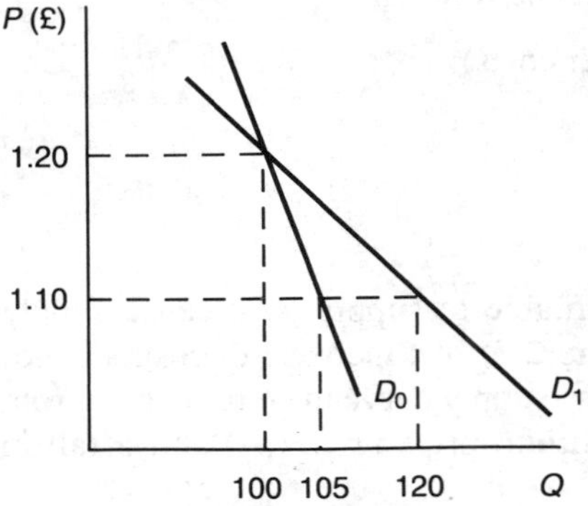

Figure 2.8: *Price-elasticity of demand*

At the *initial* price of £1.20 the quantity demanded is 100 on both demand curves. When price falls to £1.10 quantity demanded increases to 120 along D_1, but only to 105 along D_0. The response of quantity demanded to the price change is greater along D_1. PED is defined as:

$$\text{PED} \equiv \frac{\text{\% change in quantity demanded}}{\text{\% change in price}} \quad \text{or} \quad \frac{\%\Delta Qd}{\%\Delta P}$$

Example 1 (D_0):

$$\%\Delta Qd = \frac{\Delta Q \times 100}{q_0} = \frac{5 \times 100}{100} = 5\%$$

$$\%\Delta p = \frac{\Delta P \times 100}{p_0} = \frac{-10 \times 100}{120} = -8.3\%$$

$$\text{PED} = \frac{\%\Delta Qd}{\%\Delta P} = \frac{5\%}{-8.3\%} = -0.6$$

Example 2 (D_1):

$$\%\Delta Qd = \frac{20 \times 100}{100} = 20\%$$

$$\%\Delta P = -8.3\%$$

$$\text{PED} = \frac{\%Qd}{\%\Delta P} = \frac{20\%}{-8.3\%} = -2.41$$

For calculation purposes the formula can be expressed as:

$$\frac{\%\Delta Qd}{\%\Delta P} = \frac{\dfrac{\Delta Q \times 100}{q_0}}{\dfrac{\Delta P \times 100}{p_0}} = \left[\frac{\Delta Q}{\Delta P} \times \frac{p_0}{q_0}\right]$$

The formula inside the brackets is known as the 'point' measure of elasticity. To calculate simply divide the change in quantity (ΔQ) by the change in price (ΔP) and multiply by the *original* price (p_0) divided by the *original* quantity (q_0).

Interpreting PED

Firstly the PED coefficient has a *negative sign*. This follows from the inverse relationship between price and quantity demanded, for if price is falling quantity demanded will be rising and vice versa. When interpreting the coefficient it is necessary to focus on its *magnitude* (the negative sign is often ignored).

In terms of the magnitude three possibilities are of interest (ignoring the negative sign):

PED > 1 (price-elastic)

PED < 1 (price-inelastic)

PED = 1 (unitary elasticity)

If demand is **price-elastic** (PED > 1) the % quantity change is greater than the % price change but in the opposite direction. This implies that total revenue (TR = PQ) will fall if there is a price rise or rise if there is a price fall. For example, along D_1 demand is price-elastic for the relevant prices (PED = 2.41). When price falls from £1.20 to £1.10 total revenue increases from £120 (i.e. £1.20 × 100) to £132 (i.e. £1.10 × 120).

If demand is 'price-inelastic' (PED <1) the % quantity change is less than the % price change. In this case the total revenue (PQ) will rise if price rises but fall when price falls. For example, along D_0 demand is price-inelastic (PED = 0.6) over this price range. When price falls from £1.20 to £1.10 total revenue falls from £120 (i.e. £1 × 120) to £115.50 (i.e. £1.10 × 105).

If demand is of 'unitary' elasticity (PED = 1) the % change in price and the % change in quantity are **equal** but in opposite directions. This means that the effect of a price change on total revenue (PQ) will be exactly cancelled by the opposite change in quantity. Therefore if PED = 1 a change in price will have no effect on total revenue.

INTERPRETING PED MEASURES

PED > 1	(Elastic)	P↑	⇒	TR↓
		P↓	⇒	TR↑
PED < 1	(Inelastic)	P↑	⇒	TR↑
		P↓	⇒	TR↓
PED = 1	(Unitary)	P↑ or ↓	⇒	TR no change

Unfortunately there is a slight problem with our 'point' measure of elasticity. Consider the following figures from the demand schedule (Table 2.1). Total revenue remains constant as price changes, we conclude that PED must be unitary (PED = 1).

P(£)	*Qd*	*TR(£)*
1.30	120	156
1.20	130	156

However if we use the point measure to calculate PED for these figures not only will this not be so, but the PED measure will be different depending on whether price is rising or falling.

For example if price rises from £1.20 to £1.30:

$$\text{PED} = \frac{\Delta q}{\Delta p}\frac{p_0}{q_0} = \frac{-10}{+10}\frac{120}{130} = -0.92$$

To overcome these problems there is an 'arc' measure of PED. Instead of taking the *original* price and quantity to work out the percentage change the arc measure takes the *average* of the two prices and two quantities:

$$\text{PED} = \frac{\dfrac{\Delta q \times 100}{1/2(q_0+q_1)}}{\dfrac{\Delta p \times 100}{1/2(p_0+p_1)}} = \left[\frac{\Delta q}{\Delta p} \times \frac{(p_0+p_1)}{(q_0+q_1)}\right]$$

The formula in brackets simply divides the change in quantity by the change in price and multiplies by the sum of the prices divided by the sum of the quantities. This measure is consistent with the interpretations given above.

Special cases

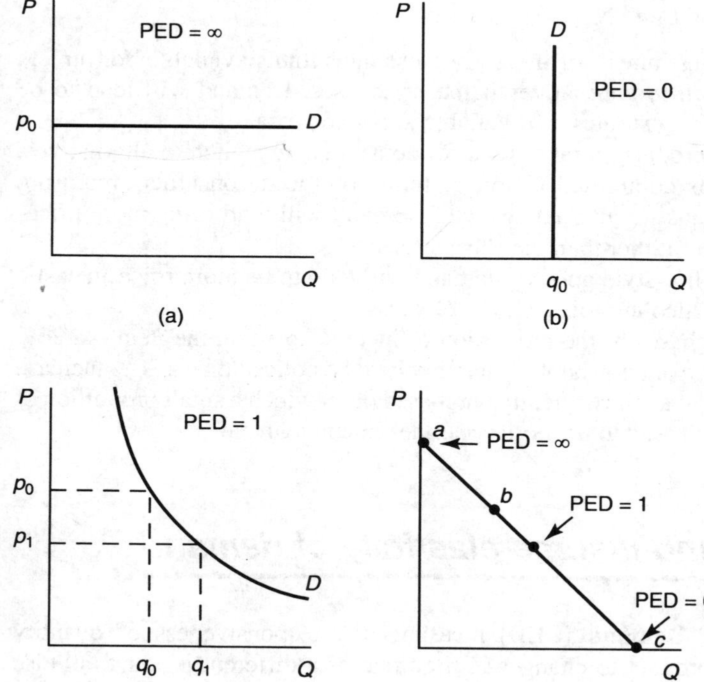

Figure 2.9: *Price-elasticities of demand*

For a horizontal demand curve (Figure 2.9(a)) demand is 'perfectly elastic' at the given price. If the price were to rise even slightly above p_0 demand would fall to zero.

For a vertical demand curve (Figure 2.9(b)) demand is 'perfectly inelastic' over the relevant price range. If the price were to rise even slightly above p_0 demand would fall to zero.

Whatever the change in price, the quantity demanded remains fixed at q_0.

A **rectangular hyperbole** (Figure 2.9(c)) is a curve such that the area of two rectangles drawn for any two price-quantity combinations is equal (e.g. $p_0q_0 = p_1q_1$). This implies that TR is the same for all prices in which case PED = 1 over the whole price range.

For a straight line demand curve (Figure 2.9(d)), the price elasticity at any point is given by the ratio of the distance along the line from the point to the horizontal axis to the distance to the vertical axis. For example PED at point b is given by bc/ab. It follows that PED = 1 midway along the line, approaches infinity towards the vertical axis and approaches zero towards the horizontal axis.

Determinants of PED

PED depends on how consumers respond to a price change. The following assumptions will tend to hold:

- Availability of substitutes – if there are close substitutes available consumers are likely to switch to alternatives if the price rises. Demand will tend to be price-elastic when substitutes are available and vice versa.
- Time – for some products it takes time for consumers to switch to alternatives. For example firms committed to longer term contracts, consumers requiring time to find or adjust to alternatives, etc. Demand will tend to be more price-elastic in the longer rather than the shorter term.
- Habit-forming or life-style goods – demand will tend to be more price-inelastic for goods such as alcohol, tobacco, petrol, etc.
- Frequency of purchases or the proportion of income spent on the item – a 20% increase in the price of door-knobs is less likely to be noticed than a 20% increase in petrol. Goods that are infrequently purchased or on which a small proportion of income is spent will tend to be more price-inelastic in demand.

2.6 *Cross and income-elasticity of demand*

Cross-Elasticity of Demand (CED) measures the responsiveness of quantity demanded for one product to changes in the price of a different product, all else being equal. For example a firm providing coach-transport may be concerned with the change in demand for its service following a change in the price of rail-transport.

$$\text{CED} \equiv \frac{\%\text{ change in quantity demanded of good } X}{\%\text{ change in price of good } Y}$$

We saw (Figure 2.5) that when the price of gin *increased* the demand for the complement (tonic) *decreased* but the demand for the substitute (whiskey) *increased.* In general the coefficient of CED will have a negative sign (CED < 0) for complementary goods but a positive sign (CED > 0) for substitute goods. So unlike the PED coefficient the sign of the CED conveys important information indicating whether the goods in question are complements (–sign) or substitutes (+sign).

Goods that are close substitutes will have strong positive cross-effects (highly 'cross-price elastic'). It follows that the demand for these goods is likely to be highly price elastic (PED > 1) due to the available substitute.

Income-elasticity of demand (YED) measures the responsiveness of quantity demanded for a product to a change in consumes' income, all else being equal.

$$\text{YED} \equiv \frac{\%\text{ change in quantity demanded}}{\%\text{ change in income}}$$

Consumers expenditure on goods and services will clearly be influenced by changes in income. At its very simplest rich people spend a lot while poor people spend little. As your income rises you will tend to spend more. If when income **rises** the demand for a particular product **rises** (YED > 0) the good in question is defined as a **normal good**. The positive income effect for the normal good may be strong or weak. In general the demand for luxuries is likely to be **income-elastic** (YED > 1) whereas the demand for necessities is likely to be **income-inelastic** (0 < YED < 1).

If when income **rises** the demand for a particular product **falls** (YED < 0) the good in question is defined as an **inferior good**. This **negative income effect** is likely to be due to the availability of a more expensive substitute. With rising prosperity consumers switch to the preferred alternative. Tyre-remoulds, local holiday resorts (Butlins?), low quality cars (LADA?) are likely to be inferior.

When interpreting YED both the sign ('normal' or 'inferior') and the maxnitude ('elastic' or 'inelastic') are important. With rising prosperity over time the industries providing luxuries are likely to experience significant expansion. However in recessions, when incomes are being squeezed, the demand for inferior goods may temporarily increase.

2.7 *Price elasticity of supply (PES)*

The PES measures the responsiveness of quantity supplied of a product to changes in the price of that product, all else being equal.

$$\text{PES} = \frac{\%\text{ change in quantity supplied}}{\%\text{ change in price}}$$

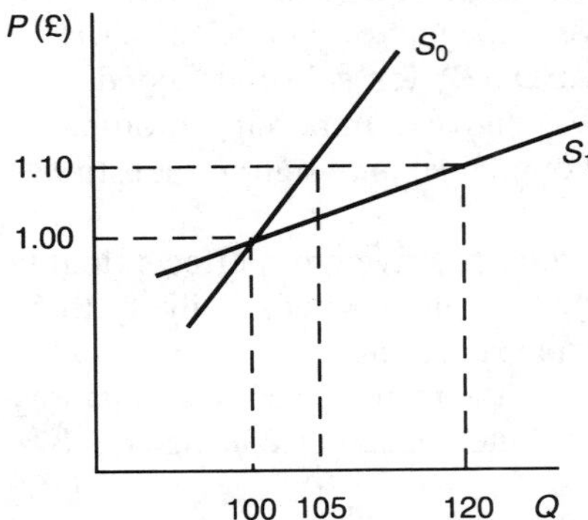

Figure 2.10: *Price-elasticity of supply*

In Figure 2.10 when price rises from £1 to £1.10 (+10%) quantity supplied increases form 100 to 105 (+5%) along S_0 and from 100 to 120 (+20%) along S_1. Clearly supply is more price-elastic over this price range along S_1.

$$\text{PES }(S_0) = \frac{5\%}{10\%} = 0.5$$

$$\text{PES }(S_1) = \frac{20\%}{10\%} = 2$$

When interpreting the PES coefficient the sign will typically be positive due to the **positive** relationship between price and quantity supplied. Of interest is the magnitude.

$0 < \text{PES} < 1$ 'price-inelastic'

$\text{PES} > 1$ 'price-elastic'

In general it is in the interest of consumers that the supply of goods be elastic rather than inelastic. If the demand for a product rises (outward shift in demand curve) elastic supply means that the impact on the market will be for output to expand rather than for price to rise. Elasticity means flexibility whereas inelasticity means inflexibility.

Any straight line supply curve, going through the origin (Figure 2.11) has a PES equal to one (PES = 1) over the whole price range.

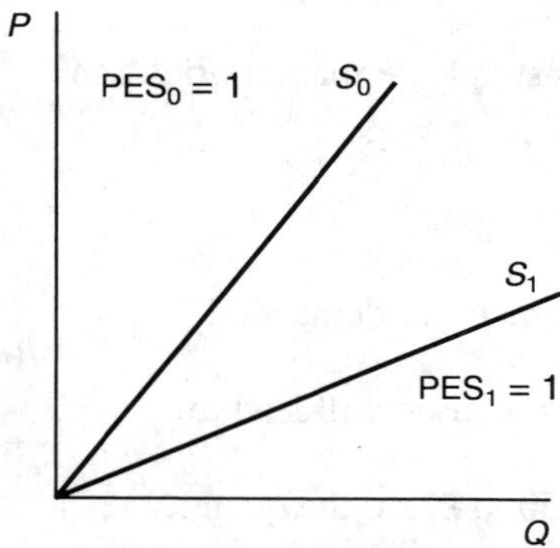

Figure 2.11: *Unit-elasticity of supply*

Determinants of PES

PES depends on how quickly resources can be transferred to the production of the good in question. The quicker resources can be employed producing the good the more elastic supply will be and vice versa. The following will have an influence:

- Technology – production processes using sophisticated or highly-skilled resources typically require a longer period of time for output to be increased than less sophisticated processes
- Capacity utilization – industries working with spare capacity can usually increase output quicker than industries working at full capacity
- Stock levels – some industries work with higher stock levels than others in which case supply to the market can be adjusted more easily
- Time – clearly in the longer term supply is likely to be more elastic than in the shorter term.

REVISION FOCUS CHAPTER TWO

Key Areas

- Demand schedule
  → law of demand → demand curve → conditions of demand → movement along and movements of the curve → price-elasticity of demand ('elastic' and 'inelastic') → cross-elasticity of demand ('substitutes' and 'complements') → income-elasticity of demand ('normal' and 'inferior' goods)
- Supply schedule
  Supply curve → conditions of supply → movement along and movement of the curve → price-elasticity of supply

- Equilibrium price
  → determination of → market price and excess supply → market price and excess demand

Self-Test

(1) The law of demand is a relationship between quantity demanded and consumers income T/F
(2) If demand for a product is price-elastic, a rise in price will lead to a rise in total revenue T/F
(3) If when the price of a product rises from £1.50 to £2.50 the quantity demanded falls from 625 to 575, PED(arc) = (a) −2 (b) −0.17 (c) −0.5
(4) If the cross-elasticity of demand for two goods is positive, the goods in question are substitutes T/F
(5) As incomes fall the demand for inferior goods rise T/F
(6) The price elasticity of supply is likely to be more elastic in the short rather than the longer term T/F
(7) An improvement in the technology of a production process will usually cause equilibrium price to fall T/F
(8) A rise in the price of a substitute will cause the equilibrium price of a product to fall. T/F

Discussion Topics

- A change in any factor influencing demand, other than the price of the good itself, will cause the demand curve to shift. Explain.
- The availability of substitutes will be an important determinant of the PED. Explain.
- Explain how price-, cross- and income-elasticity of demand are measured and how the results are to be interpreted.

CHAPTER 3

APPLICATIONS OF SUPPLY AND DEMAND ANALYSIS

3.1 *Consumers' surplus*

It is not uncommon for consumers to purchase items at prices below the price they would have been willing to pay. The difference between the maximum price the consumer would be willing to pay rather than go without the item and the price actually paid is known as the **consumer's surplus.**

For example, if you would be willing to pay £20 to attend a particular concert but can purchase a ticket for £15 there is a consumer surplus of £5 in this transaction.

Consumers' surplus can be illustrated using supply and demand curves. The market demand curve indicates the value that consumers attach to additional units of a product. If consumers are to be enticed to purchase additional units then typically the selling price must be lowered. In Figure 3.1 for example nobody is willing to purchase at a price of p_0 or above. As price falls below p_0 consumers are willing to purchase q_1 at p_1, q_2 at p_2 etc. A feature of a competitive market in equilibrium is the fact that all consumers pay the same price for the product. In Figure 3.1 all consumers will pay p_3 and total consumers' expenditure is p_3q_3 per period. However the segment of the demand curve from point a to p_0 indicates that many

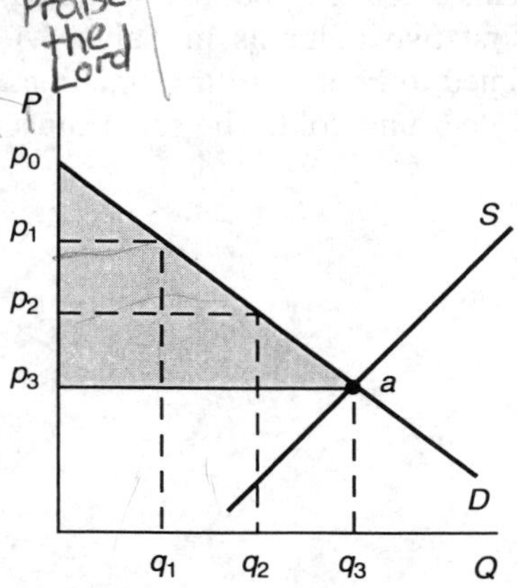

Figure 3.1: *Consumer's surplus*

of these consumers would have paid more than p_3 rather than go without the product. The shaded triangle p_3p_0a, is a measure of the total consumers' surplus in this market. The consumers surplus in any market is measured by the area below the demand curve but above the equilibrium price.

A perfect system of **price discrimination** (Section 6.5) whereby each consumer was charged the maximum price they would be willing to pay, would turn the consumer's surplus into revenue for the sellers and thereby increase their profits.

3.2 *Indirect taxes*

Governments impose a range of taxes for various reasons. Two of these reasons are:

- the need to raise revenue to finance expenditures on schools, hospitals, defence, etc.;
- to discourage certain types of trade by making it more costly.

Taxes may be **direct** or **indirect**. A direct tax is typically a tax on the income or profit of a specific individual or firm. The **burden** of the tax is clear. With an indirect tax, however, the burden of the tax may be shared between different taxpayers. Taxes on expenditure (e.g. VAT, excise taxes) are examples of indirect taxes.

A tax on sales is effectively a penalty on trade. The seller incurs a tax liability at the point of sale thereby raising the sellers costs. However the seller will try to recoup this cost by passing it on to the buyer in the form of a higher price. The extent to which the seller can pass on the burden in the form of a higher price will determine the **incidence of the tax**, i.e. how the burden is shared.

As with any increase in the cost of supplying a product, the effect of the tax will be to shift the market supply curve to the left. This effect can be demonstrated using the following hypothetical figures. The first two columns in Table 3.1 represent a typical supply schedule which is assumed to be the pre-tax situation. Assume the government imposes a sales tax of £1 per unit sold. The seller must

Table 3.1: *A supply schedule before and after a tax*

P (£)	Q_s	Q_s^t
20	150	140
19	140	130
18	130	120
17	120	110
16	110	100
15	100	

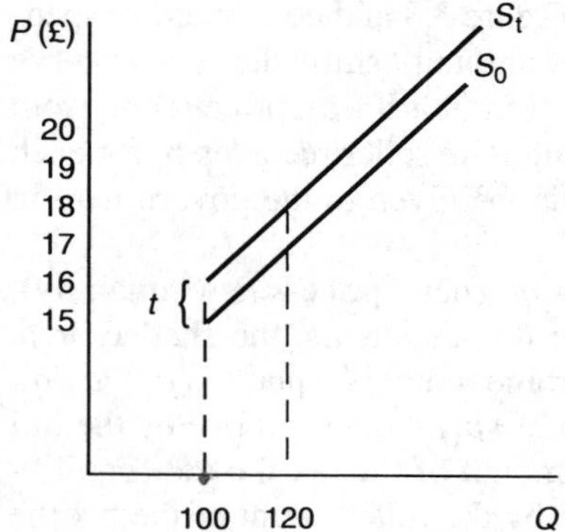

Figure 3.2: *Per unit tax*

now pay £1 to the government from whatever price is charged to the consumer. The column Q_s^t represents the quantities sellers would be willing to supply following the imposition of the tax. If the sellers were willing to supply 140 units at a price of £19 with no tax, then consistency of behaviour would lead them to require a price of £20 for that same quantity when this price includes a £1 tax. Likewise they will only supply 130 units when the £19 price includes a £1 tax and so on.

The effect of the per unit tax is to shift the supply curve parallel to itself as illustrated in Figure 3.2 ($S_0 \rightarrow S_t$). The vertical distance between the curves corresponds to the amount of the tax.

Assuming there is a normal downward-sloping demand curve for this product the effect of the tax will be to **increase price** and **decrease quantity** traded. However the price will not increase by the full amount of the tax as illustrated in Figure 3.3.

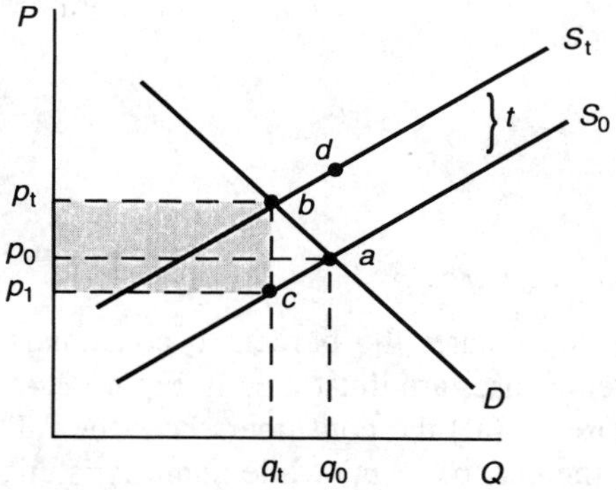

Figure 3.3: *Incidence of tax*

Prior to the tax the equilibrium price is p_0 in Figure 3.3 and consumer's expenditure is p_0q_0. The imposition of a per unit tax of amount t shifts the supply curve from S_0 to S_t. The equilibrium shifts from point a to point b with price rising from p_0 to p_t and quantity falling from q_0 to q_t. Although the seller receives p_t for each unit sold only p_1 is kept as the difference (t) must be given to the government in tax.

Consumers' expenditure after the tax is p_tq_t (new price × new quantity), however the sellers only keep p_1q_t of this. The remainder, i.e. the shaded area, represents the tax revenue received by the government and is equal to $(p_t - p_1)q_t$.

It should be noted that although price rises ($p_0 \rightarrow p_t$) it does not rise by the full amount of the tax. If price did rise by the full amount of the tax the new equilibrium would be at point d. As price does not rise by the full amount of the tax the consumer does not bear the full burden of the tax, it is shared with the sellers.

The effect of the tax is to transfer what was previously consumers surplus (upper part of shaded area) and what was previously sellers revenue (lower part of shaded area) to the government in the form of tax revenue. Those transfers indicate how the tax revenue is being financed and represent the burden to consumes and sellers respectively. The triangle cba represents a **deadwright loss** – a loss to consumers and sellers with no corresponding gain to government in tax revenue.

The **incidence of the tax** (distribution of the burden) depends on the slopes of the supply and demand curves which in turn depend on the price-elasticities of supply and demand. The ratio of the consumer's burden to the seller's burden is **inversely** related to the ratio of PED to PES:

$$\frac{\text{PED}}{\text{PES}} = \frac{\text{seller's burden}}{\text{consumer's burden}} = \frac{p_0 - p_1}{p_t - p_0}$$

Example:

a per unit tax of 6p is levied

PED = –2

PES = 1

$$\frac{\text{seller's burden}}{\text{consumer's burden}} = \frac{2}{1}, \text{ i.e. } \frac{4\text{p}}{2\text{p}}$$

sellers lose 4p per unit. consumers pay an extra 2p

The more inelastic demand is (low PED) the greater the burden to consumers relative to sellers and vice versa. Two extreme cases are illustrated in Figure 3.4.

With a perfectly inelastic demand [Figure 3.4(a)] the consumers bear the full burden as price rises by the full amount of the tax ($p_0 \rightarrow p_t$) while quantity is unaffected. With a perfectly elastic demand [Figure 3.4(b)] the sellers bear the full burden as market price (p_0) is unaffected while quantity falls from q_0 to q_t.

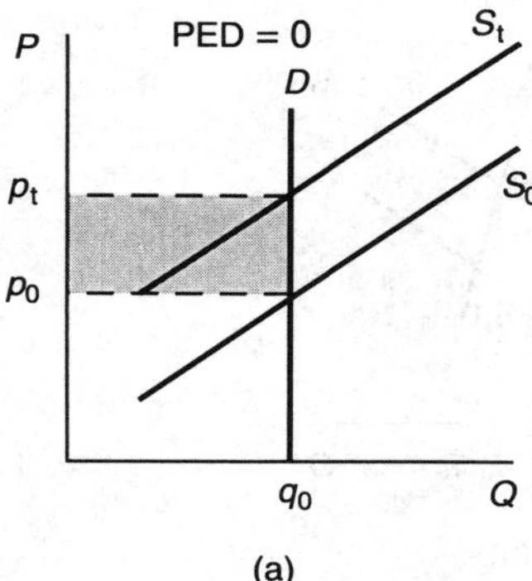

(a)

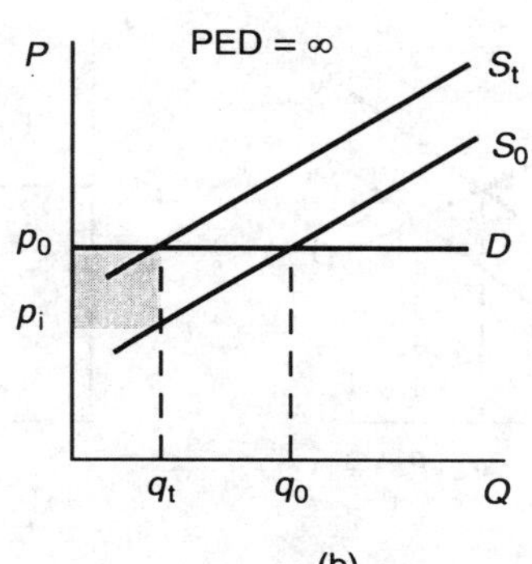

(b)

Figure 3.4 *Incidence of tax*

Clearly if the government is primarily concerned to raise revenue it should tax goods the demand for which is price-inelastic. In this case there will be a relatively small fall in quantity purchased resulting in a relatively large tax yield. Whereas if the government taxes items, the demand for which is price-elastic, there will be a relatively large decline in quantity traded resulting in little tax revenue. When the government taxes tobacco, alcohol and petrol it does so primarily with a view to raising tax revenue rather than reducing consumption.

Occasionally governments impose lump-sum taxes on firms. For example a once-off **windfall tax** might be levied on the supernormal profits (Section 6.2) of financial institutions or privatized public utilities (water, gas, etc.). A lump sum tax is equivalent to an increase in the *fixed costs* rather than the *variable costs* (Section 5.3) of production. In this case the supply curve (which depends on variable costs) would not be affected so that price and quantity should also remain unaffected.

3.3 *Subsidies*

Indirect taxes may be used to reduce the quantity traded, however if the government wants to increase the quantity traded the use of subsidies might be appropriate. A subsidy works in the opposite way to an indirect tax by **reducing the cost** of production to the supplier. Subsidies may contribute to the fixed costs (e.g., lump sum subsidy) or the variable costs (e.g., per unit subsidy).

A per-unit subsidy will cause a parallel shift of the supply curve to the right. The effect is the opposite to that of the per-unit tax.

Where the demand for the product is relatively price-elastic (Figure 3.5(a)) the effect of the subsidy will be a relatively large increase in consumption ($q_0 \rightarrow q_s$) for a relatively small reduction in price ($p_0 \rightarrow p_s$). On the other hand, where

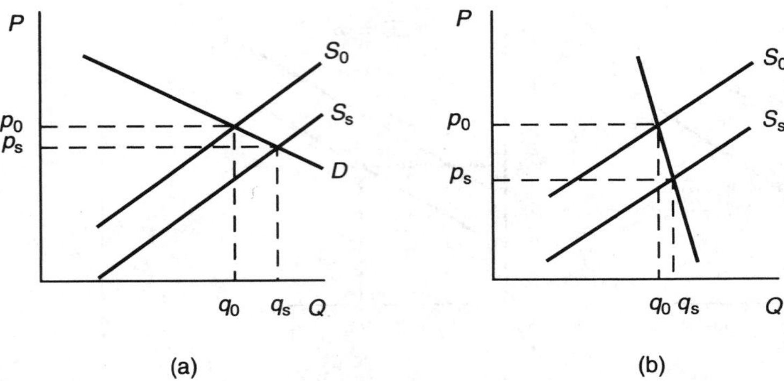

Figure 3.5: *Subsidies*

demand is relatively inelastic (Figure 3.5(b)) there will be a relatively small increase in consumption for a relatively large reduction in price.

Governments may subsidise the supply of a range of items (cultural, educational, some necessities, etc.). If the object is to increase consumption, the analysis suggests that to subside goods the demand for which is price-inelastic will not have the desired effect. The actual effect will be a significant reduction in price for those consumers concerned, (i.e. an increase in their consumer's surplus) with little increase in consumption.

On the other hand, if demand is elastic there will be a relatively large increase in consumption, which in turn implies a relatively high cost to the government in terms of the subsidy paid out.

3.4 Price controls

The price mechanism is a means of rationing scarce resources. In a competitive environment prices emerge through the interaction of supply and demand. Those who are both willing and able to purchase at the relevant price will receive the scarce resources.

All governments seek to influence the allocation of resources in society. One of the more obvious methods is through social welfare systems whereby income is redistributed to the poor, unemployed, etc. Another method is through **price controls.** For example governments might legislate for maximum prices for certain necessities to ensure that the poor have access to them or establish minimum prices for goods in an effort to guarantee a certain income to their producers.

Maximum prices

Assume the government fixes a maximum price for a product which is otherwise supplied under competitive conditions. The situation is illustrated in Figure 3.6.

In a competitive market the equilibrium price p_0 and equilibrium quantity q_0

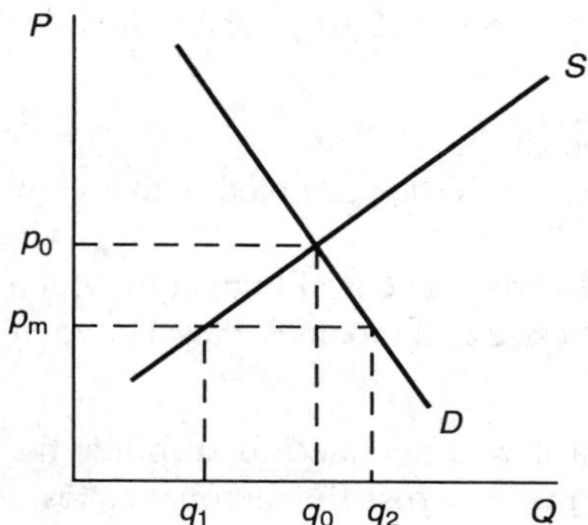

Figure 3.6: *Maximum price*

would emerge. However, the government regards a price of p_0 as unacceptable and makes it illegal for sellers to charge above p_m. The maximum price will discourage supply which will fall to q_1 and encourage demand which will rise to q_2. If the government sets a maximum price which is below the free market equilibrium price there will be excess demand ($q_2 - q_1$ in Figure 3.6).

The following features are likely to emerge in this market:

- As not all these wishing to purchase at p_m can be catered for, suppliers must decide which consumers to do business with. It may be on a first-come-first-served basis but it might enable suppliers to discriminate between consumers according to their own set of preferences or prejudices.
- As there are many consumers in this market willing to pay above p_m an illegal black-market is a likelihood.

It should be obvious from the diagram that a maximum price only makes sense if it is below the equilibrium price. In an unregulated market the market price would not be above p_0 anyway so to set a maximum price above p_0 would be a meaningless exercise.

3.5 *Minimum prices – the Common Agricultural Policy*

Governments sometimes set minimum prices for products, usually with a view to guaranteeing a minimum income to the suppliers. To set a minimum price below the equilibrium price will have no effect as the market price will tend to the (higher) equilibrium price anyway. **If governments set a minimum price above the equilibrium price there will tend to be excess supply in the market resulting in unsold stocks.**

One of the early 'successes' of the European Union (then known as the EEC) was the establishment of a common agricultural policy (CAP). The principles underlying CAP were:

- A single market for agricultural produce in the EU.
- Community preference – agriculture in the EU was to be promoted with a view to self-sufficiency where practicable.
- Fiscal solidarity – the CAP was to be financed from a central budget to which all member states contributed (in proportion to size and income) irrespective of which members benefited.

The single market envisaged was one in which it was intended to **stabilize** the price of agricultural produce and to **harmonize** prices across the member states.

Unregulated markets for agricultural products

Unregulated agricultural markets have traditionally a tendency to be **unstable**. This instability results from two features:

- *planned supply* and *actual supply* frequently diverge due to weather conditions, pestilence, etc.;
- demand for staple agricultural produce tends to be **price-inelastic** (Section 2.5).

These two conditions can lead to wide fluctuations in price from harvest to harvest.

In Figure 3.7 D represents the market demand for a given agricultural product, S represents the planned supply, i.e. the quantities farmers would wish to supply at different prices, S_B represents the actual supply following a *bumper harvest* and S_p the actual supply following a *poor harvest*.

If everything goes to plan the equilibrium outcome in Figure. 3.7 will be a price of p_0 and a quantity of q_0. However a bumper harvest (S_B) will cause price to fall to p_2 whereas a poor harvest (S_p) will cause prices to rise to p_1. If demand is price-

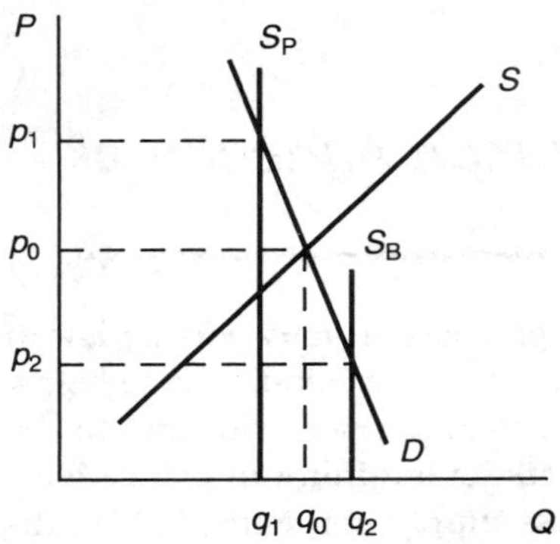

Figure 3.7: *Agricultural markets*

inelastic over this price range the price fall (bumper harvest) will result in a **fall** in consumers expenditure (Section 2.5) and therefore reduced farm incomes. On the other hand the rise in price (poor harvest) will result in increased consumer expenditure and therefore increased farm incomes. (Diagramatically $p_1q_1 > p_0q_0 > p_2q_2$).

The result is that fluctuations in harvests translate into wide fluctuations in price and farm incomes. Also farm incomes will tend to *rise with poor harvests* and *fall with good harvests*. It was, and (to a lesser extent) still is, common for governments to intervene in agricultural markets with **stabilization programmes**, the CAP being the EU's particular version.

A stabilization programme can be designed to stabilize either the market price or farm incomes but typically not both. The following simple *buffer stocks* system is designed to stabilize price. The CAP is a more complicated variation on this scheme.

Assume the government intends to stabilize price at p_0 in Figure 3.8. When there is a bumper harvest a government agency buys $q_2 - q_0$ of the harvest at a unit price of p_0. By removing this portion of the harvest from the market and placing it in storage the market price remains at p_0. The cost to the government is $(q_2 - q_0)p_0$ plus *storage costs*. When there is a poor harvest, to prevent price rising the government releases $q_0 - q_1$ of the product from storage receiving $(q_0 - q_1)p_0$ in revenue. The effect of the buffer stocks is to stabilise the *actual supply* to the market at q_o and thereby stabilise price at p_0.

Provided harvests tend to fluctuate around q_0 the cost to the government will be modest as intervention stocks will not tend to increase over time. Although market price is stabilized farm incomes continue to vary. However, farm incomes are now positively related to the harvest (farmers can always sell what they produce at p_0) rather than inversely related to it.

Major problems arise if the authorities stabilize price but choose a price above the equilibrium price to be stabilized as illustrated in Figure 3.9.

Assume the authorities (the EU Council of Agriculture Ministers) guarantee a

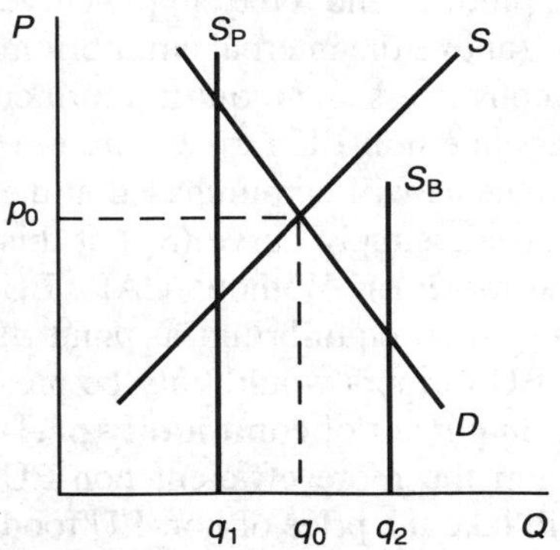

Figure 3.8: *Buffer stocks*

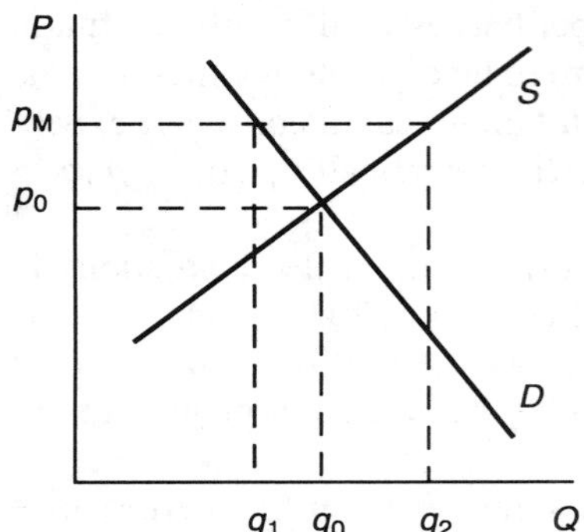

Figure 3.9: *CAP and excess supply*

minimum price of p_m to farmers. The effect will be to *discourage consumption* (which will fall from q_0 to q_1) but to *encourage production* (as farmers will now wish to produce q_2 rather than q_0). If there is a tendency for supply to fluctuate it will now fluctuate about q_2 rather than q_0. The result is an inbuilt tendency for *excess supply* each and every harvest.

This simple analysis explains the notorious butter mountains, beef mountains, wine lakes, etc. which brought the CAP into disrepute. Costwise the scheme will become a nightmare. Consumers will only purchase q_1 spending $p_m q_1$ in total. This means the authorities will be obliged to purchase $q_2 - q_1$ on average each and every harvest at a cost of $(q_2 - q_1)p_m$. Furthermore, the cost of storage will become a major problem due to the inbuilt tendency for excess supply each period.

There will also be a distorting effect on international trade in agricultural produce. Assume (correctly) that for at least some produce farmers outside the EU are more efficient than EU farmers and are willing to supply at a lower price than EU farmers. It will be necessary to erect high tariffs (Section 16.6) on the importation of this food into the EU as Figure 3.10 illustrates.

Let D represent the demand in the EU for some produce and S the supply curve representing EU farmers. Under CAP a price of p_1 (above the internal equilibrium of p_0) is fixed resulting in purchases of q_1 by EU consumers and requiring further intervention purchases by the authorities. If we assume non-EU farmers are prepared to supply the EU with as much of this produce as will be purchased at the lower world price (p_w), the result is a perfectly elastic supply curve (S_w) at this price (this is known as the **small country assumption**). Without CAP, EU consumers would buy the cheap imports resulting in an equilibrium at point *a*, with q_3 purchased at p_w. At this price, however, EU farmers would only be prepared to supply q_2 resulting in imports of $q_3 - q_2$. In pursuit of **community preference** it is necessary to protect EU farmers from the more efficient non-EU farmers. The way this is done is by a tariff that will take the price of non-EU food above p_1 so that EU consumers will not be inclined to purchase it.

A further distorting effect on world trade comes from the EU's growing inter-

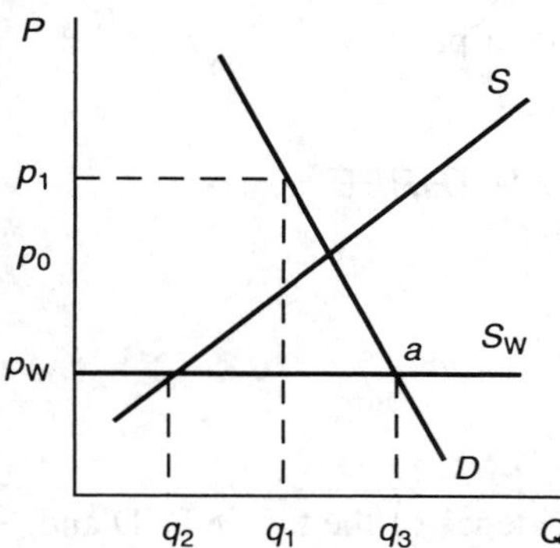

Figure 3.10: *CAP and international trade*

vention stocks. One solution is to subsidize EU farmers to **export (outside EU)** the surplus at a price below the world price. If EU farmers sell at below p_w to non-EU countries the difference between the price charged and p_1 can be made up from the CAP budget. Export subsidies might help to keep intervention stocks under control but they will undermine **more efficient** non-EU farmers in world markets.

Inevitably there is going to be internal and external pressure to reform CAP:

- from EU consumers who are paying above world prices for many foodstuffs;
- dissatisfaction with the proportion of the EU budget that is taken by CAP (at one time it was over 80%, in 1997 it was approximately 50%) to the neglect of other deserving causes;
- as subsidies were traditionally linked to production the large (richer) farmers got the lions share at the expense of small (poorer) farmers, hence a lack of **equity** in the operation of CAP;
- from Member states who are making major contributions to the EU budget (fiscal solidarity) but getting relatively little back by way of CAP, e.g. UK;
- from non-EU producers (e.g. USA) unhappy with the tariffs and the export subsidies which distort world trade.

Quotas have long been used by the EU as a means of limiting the output of individual farmers in an attempt to solve the problem of excess supply.

The (Irish) EU Commissioner for Agriculture, Ray McSharry, introduced further reforms (1991) aimed at cutting surpluses and bringing EU prices closer to world prices. An important innovation in these reforms was to **de-couple** subsidies from production i.e. pay farmers not to produce. The Uruguay Round of the GATT talks resulted in the EU having to agree to reduce tariffs and export subsidies. The prospects of an enlarged EU is creating further pressure to reform CAP.

With increased use of pesticides and technology in farming in the post-war period the tendency for harvest fluctuations is much diminished. Furthermore, with much greater international trade in foodstuffs, a poor harvest in one region may well be compensated by a good harvest in some other region. The deregulation of agricultural markets is likely to gather pace.

REVISION FOCUS CHAPTER THREE

Key Areas

- Consumers' surplus
- Indirect taxes
  → impact on the supply curve →
  impact on equilibrium price and quantity → incidence of the tax → PED and tax yield
- Subsidies
  → impact on supply curve → impact on equilibrium price and quantity
- Price controls
  → maximum prices → minimum prices
- Common agricultural policy

Self-Test

(1)	The imposition of an indirect tax has the effect of shifting the supply curve to the right	T/F
(2)	All else being equal, the higher the PED the greater the impact of an indirect tax on price rather than quantity	T/F
(3)	All else being equal, the burden of the tax will be borne more by suppliers the higher the PED is	T/F
(4)	All else being equal, a per-unit subsidy will have a greater effect on equilibrium output the higher the PED is	T/F
(5)	A maximum price will have no effect if it is set below the equilibrium price	T/F
(6)	Minimum prices are imposed with a view to protecting the consumers	T/F
(7)	The imposition of an indirect tax will have the effect of reducing consumers' surplus	T/F
(8)	All else being equal, the tax yield from an indirect tax will be greater the higher the PED is	T/F

Discussion Topics

- If government is mainly concerned to raise tax revenue rather than discourage consumption it should tax goods the demand for which is price-inelastic. Explain.
- Explain why the EUs Common Agricultural Policy is so unpopular (except among farmers).
- The incidence of a per-unit tax can be calculated if the PED and the PES are known. Explain.

CHAPTER 4

CONSUMER THEORY

4.1 *Indifference curves*

The purpose of consumer theory is to provide a theoretical foundation for the *law of demand*. This law predicts an inverse relationship between changes in the price of a good and changes in the quantity consumers would be willing to purchase, all else being equal. This relationship is illustrated in the familiar downward sloping demand curve.

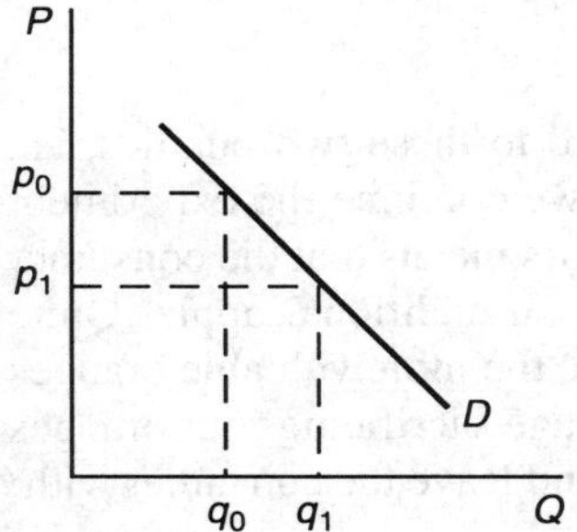

Figure 4.1: *The law of demand*

In Figure 4.1 the fall in price from p_0 to p_1 leads to an increase in the quantity purchased from q_0 to q_1. There is overwhelming empirical evidence for this inverse relationship, however, as we shall see, there may be exceptions to the rule.

There are different theoretical approaches to consumer theory but they all have the same objective, i.e. to derive a downward sloping demand curve from plausible theoretical assumptions. What follows is one approach using indifference analysis.

We require some behavioural assumptions regarding consumers behaviour. These assumptions are the foundation stones for the theory and are accepted without proof.

Assumptions

1. Consumers behave so as to *maximize utility* subject to a budget constraint.
2. Consumers preferences are such that there is a *diminishing marginal rate of substitution* (dmrs) between goods.

3. A feature of consumers preferences is *non-satiation*.
4. Consumers preferences are *transitive*.

The first assumption simply means that consumers wish to get as much satisfaction from a given level of expenditure. It implies that behaviour is purposeful rather than random and that consumers will adapt their behaviour in pursuit of this objective. The second assumption is easily explained by way of an example. Imagine a consumer with a liking for two goods, say apples and oranges. To begin with assume the consumer has a large number of oranges and few apples, e.g.

30 O + 1 A

Now given that the consumer enjoys both apples and oranges this combination represents a particular level of satisfaction. Assume now that the consumer is offered an additional apple in exchange for oranges such that the new combination of apples and oranges will leave the consumer with the same level of satisfaction as before. We need some rate of exchange here to begin our experiment, so let us assume that the consumer will swap five oranges for the apple (a rate of substitution of five for one). The new bundle is now:

25 O + 2 A

By assumption the consumer is indifferent with regard to these two bundles, i.e. they represent the same level of satisfaction. Now if we continue the experiment and offer apples in exchange for oranges as before a dmrs means that the consumer is now less willing to sacrifice as many oranges for an additional apple. Quite simply the fewer oranges and the more apples available the more valuable oranges become and the less valuable apples become. At this stage sacrificing four oranges for an additional apple would be consistent with dmrs and leave the consumer with:

21 O + 3 A

By assumption the consumer is indifferent with regard to these three bundles as they each represent the same level of satisfaction.

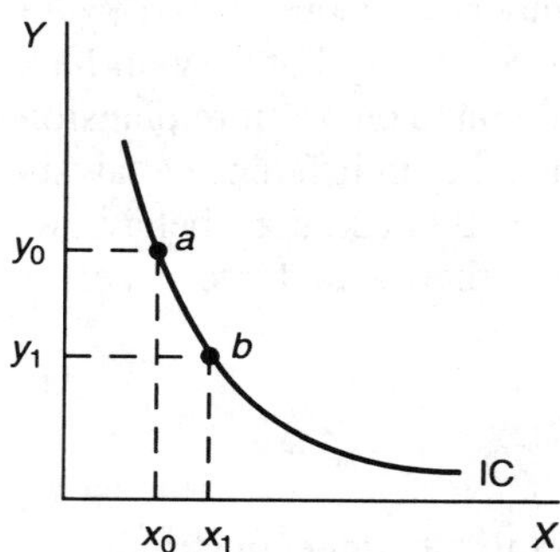

Figure 4.2: *Indifference curve*

An implication of dmrs is that if we plot bundles of goods (good x and good y) regarding which the consumer is indifferent the resulting curve will be **convex** to the origin (Figure 4.2). This curve is referred to as an **indifference curve**.

An indifference curve represents combinations of two goods giving the same level of satisfaction to the consumer. The consumer is therefore indifferent with regard to combinations on the same indifference curve. For example, given a choice between bundle a or b (Figure 4.2) the consumer is indifferent.

The **non-satiation** assumption simply means that the consumer, if given a free choice, would always prefer more to fewer goods. The **transitivity** assumption simply means that if the consumer prefers some bundle a to some bundle b and is indifferent between bundle b and some bundle c then for consistency the consumer also prefers bundle a to bundle c.

With these assumptions it is possible to represent the consumer's preferences by way of an indifference map (Figure 4.3). If we repeated the previous experiment but started off with the consumer having 40 oranges and 1 apple the principle of dmrs would still hold but the consumer would be on a higher indifference curve with a higher level of satisfaction due to non-satiation (40 oranges preferred to 30).

Higher indifference curves represent combinations of two goods giving higher levels of satisfaction. In Figure 4.3 the consumer would prefer any combination on IC_2 to any combination on IC_1 and so on. It is also possible to demonstrate that indifference curves may not intersect or there would be a contradiction with our assumptions.

Assume two indifference curves did intersect such as IC_0 and IC_1 in Figure 4.4. How are we to interpret this? b is preferred to c due to non-satiation (more of both goods); the consumer is indifferent between b and a (both on IC_0); the consumer is also indifferent between c and a (both on IC_1). However given the transitivity

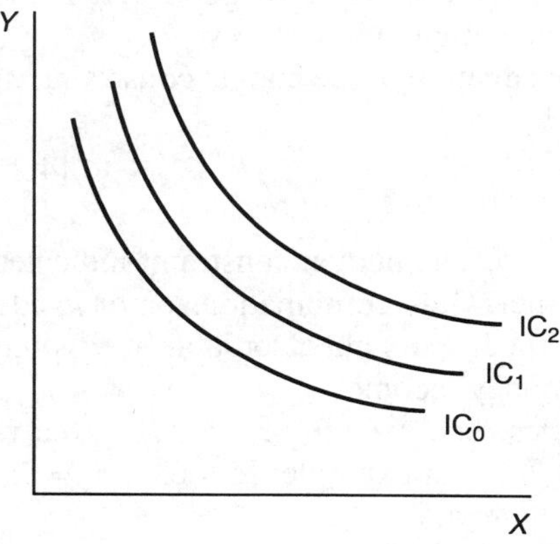

Figure 4.3: *Indifference map*

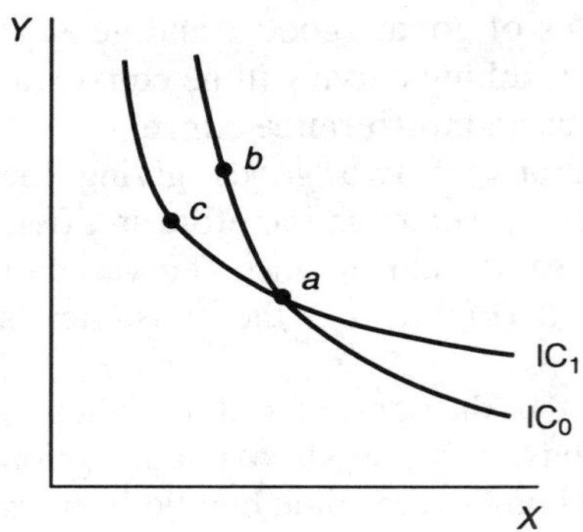

Figure 4.4: *Intersecting indifference curves*

assumption the consumer should prefer *b* to *a* if *c* and *a* are equal and *b* is preferred to *c*. Hence we have a contradiction.

4.2 The budget constraint

So far we have discussed consumers preferences without any reference to prices. However in a market economy goods must be paid for. We will proceed by focusing on a consumer with a given money income (*M*) considering how to spend this money on quantities of two goods *X* and *Y*.

Assuming there is no savings the consumer's expenditure must satisfy the following equation:

$$M = yp_y + xp_x \qquad [4.1]$$

where y is the quantity of good Y purchased, p_y is the price of good Y, x is the quantity of good X purchased and p_x is the price of good X.

This equation can be rearranged to give the equation of the budget constraint as:

$$y = \frac{M}{p_y} - \frac{p_x X}{p_y} \qquad [4.2]$$

The budget constraint is illustrated in Figure 4.5. The budget constraint indicates the affordable choices available to the consumer. Only combinations on or inside the line are affordable. Combinations outside the line are not affordable at existing prices given the consumers current level of money income.

The budget line has the following properties. The y – intercept is M/p_y, the x-intercept is M/p_x and the slope is equal to $-p_x/p_y$. For example: $M = £20$, $p_y = £1$, $p_x = £0.50$ gives the values in the brackets (Figure 4.5).

The budget constraint will shift if either price or money income changes. If money income changes the line will move parallel to itself; outward for an

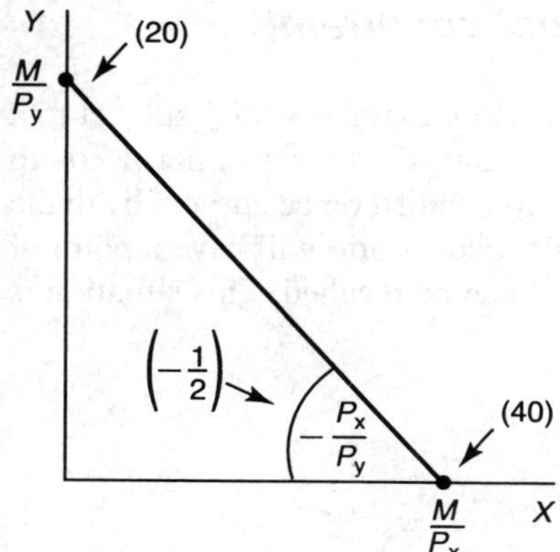

Figure 4.5: *Budget constraint*

increase in income and inward for a decrease in income. If either one of the prices change the line will pivot on the other axis and move outward for a fall in price and inward for a rise in price.

It is important here to be aware of the distinction between real income and money income. Real income is concerned with the consumer's purchasing power. Purchasing power can be affected if either money income or prices change. A fall in prices with money income held constant will mean a rise in real income and vice versa. A rise in money income may mean no increase in real income if prices rise by a sufficient amount. Figure 4.6 illustrates with respect to a fall in the price of X.

Following the fall in the price of X the budget constraint moves from BC_0 to BC_1. This represents an increase in the real income of the consumer. The shaded area represents combinations of goods X and Y that were unaffordable before the price fall.

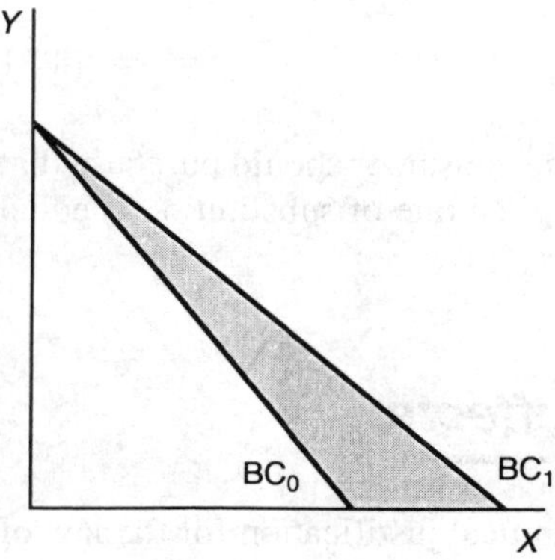

Figure 4.6: *Price changes and real income*

Maximizing utility subject to a budget constraint

The basic assumption is that the consumer wishes to maximize utility subject to a budget constraint. In terms of indifference curve analysis the consumer needs to choose some bundle of goods on the highest possible indifference curve. Given the convex shape of the indifference curves the budget constraint will have a point of tangency with the highest indifference curve that can be reached. This situation is illustrated in Figure 4.7.

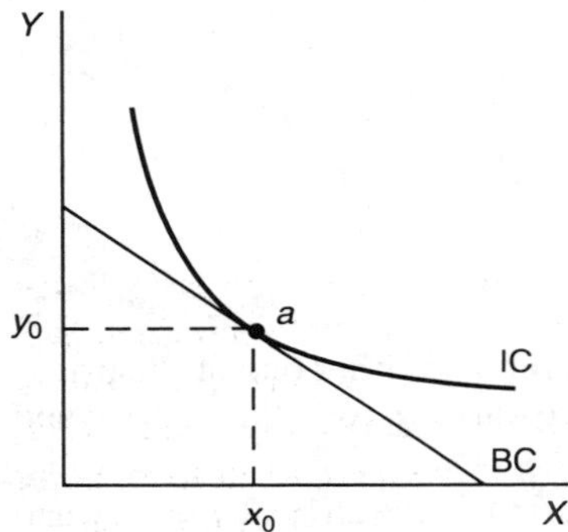

Figure 4.7: *Maximizing utility subject to a budget constraint*

The utility maximizing combination of goods *X* and *Y* is at a point of tangency between the budget constraint and the highest possible indifference curve. This is at point *a* in Figure 4.7. The slopes of the budget constraint and the indifference curve are equal at this point. The slope of the budget constraint is determined by the relative prices of the goods while the slope of the indifference curve is determined by the marginal rate of substitution at that point. For the consumer to be maximizing utility, therefore, the following condition must hold:

$$\text{MRS}_{xy} = \frac{p_x}{p_y} \quad [4.3]$$

What this equilibrium condition implies is that the consumer should purchase that combination of goods *X* and *Y* such that the marginal rate of substitution is equal to the relative prices prevailing in the market.

4.3 Income and substitution effects

The whole point of the analysis is to give a theoretical justification for the law of demand. We need now to focus on how the consumer will respond to a price change. Assume starting at point *a* in Figure 4.8 the price of *X* was to fall.

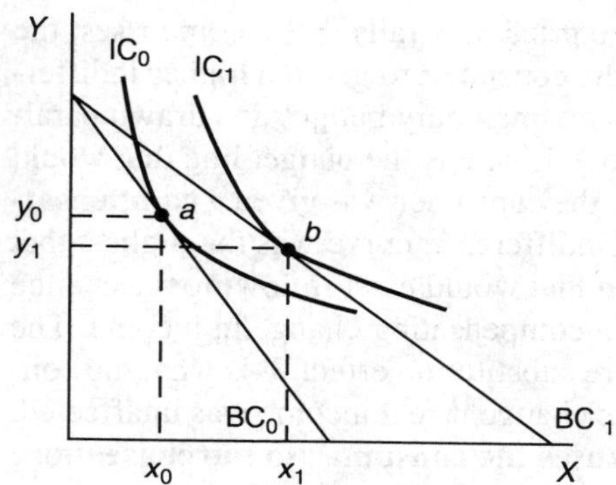

Figure 4.8 *Consumer's response to a change in price*

The fall in the price of *X* shifts the budget constraint from BC_0 to BC_1 which enables the consumer to reach a higher indifference curve. The new equilibrium is at point *b*. As Figure 4.8 has been drawn the consumer has responded to the fall in the price of *X* by increasing the quantity of *X* purchased from x_0 to x_1 and reducing the quantity of *Y* purchased from y_0 to y_1. However the movement from point *a* to *b* needs to be analysed in some depth rather than simply taken for granted. When the price of *X* changes relative prices are affected as illustrated by the different slopes of the budget constraints. However the consumer's real income is also affected, in this case it has risen. The change in relative prices and the change in real income have distinct effects which need to be analysed separately. These effects are known as the substitution effect and the income effect. To isolate the pure substitution effect we wish to know what the consumer would have done if the relative prices had changed but the consumer's real income was unaffected. This is illustrated in Figure. 4.9.

The initial equilibrium is at point *a* where the original budget constraint is

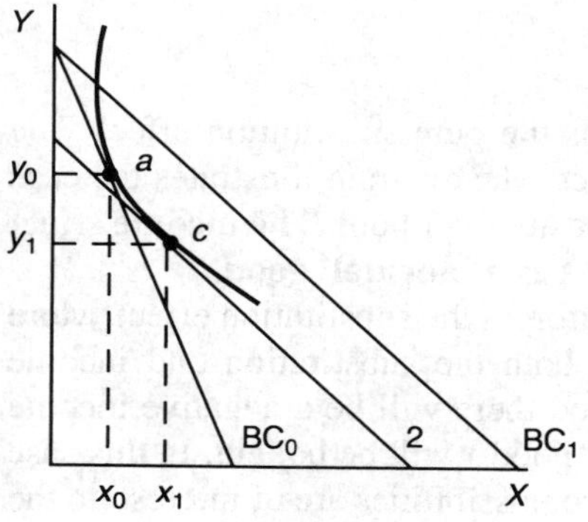

Figure 4.9: *The substitution effect*

tangent to the indifference curve. When the price of *X* falls real income rises; the budget line shifts ($BC_0 \rightarrow BC_1$) enabling the consumer to get to a higher indifference curve (not indicated). Budget line 2 is an imaginary budget line drawn parallel to BC_1 (it reflects the new relative prices). Line 2 is the budget line that would prevail if after the change in relative prices the consumer was given a **compensating change in income** so that the original indifference curve was the highest that could be reached. Point *c* is the equilibrium that would exist following the change in the price of *X* if the consumer received a compensating change in income. The movement from point *a* to point *c* is the pure substitution effect. It is what the consumer would have done following the price change if real income was unaffected. **Note that the pure substitution effect causes the consumer to purchase more of the relatively cheaper *X* and less of the relatively dearer *Y*.** We have here our law of demand: as the price of *X* falls the consumer buys more of good *X*.

In reality of course the consumer does not receive a compensating change in income and is in fact at some point (*b*) on BC_1. Where this point is depends on the nature of the income effect. If *X* is a **'normal' good** there will be a positive income effect (Section 2.3). A positive income effect means that the rise in real income will cause more *x* to be bought. This implies that point *b* will be located to the right of point *c* as illustrated in Figure 4.10.

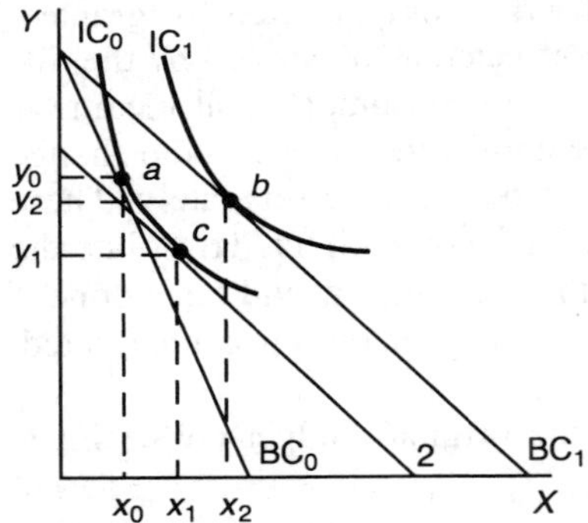

Figure 4.10: *Income and substitution effect*

In Figure 4.10 the movement from *a* to *c* is the pure substitution effect. The movement from *c* to *b* is the pure income effect. The diagram illustrates the case of two 'normal' goods as the income effect is positive for both. **The income effect reinforces the substitution effect on *X* when *X* is a 'normal' good.**

If *x* is a 'normal' good the income effect reinforces the substitution effect. More of the cheaper good is being bought due to both the substitution and income effects. However if good *X* is an 'inferior' good there will be a negative income effect which means that as income rises less of good *x* will be bought. In this case point *b* will be located to the left of point *c*. Two possibilities are of interest, to the left of *c* but to the right of *a* or to the left of *c* and also to the left of *a*. These two cases are illustrated in Figure 4.11.

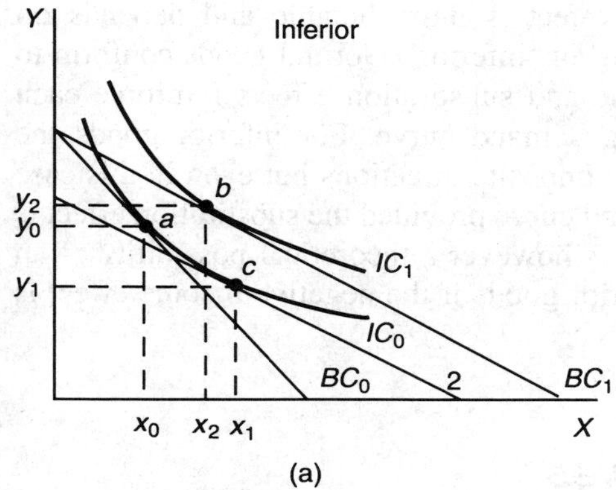

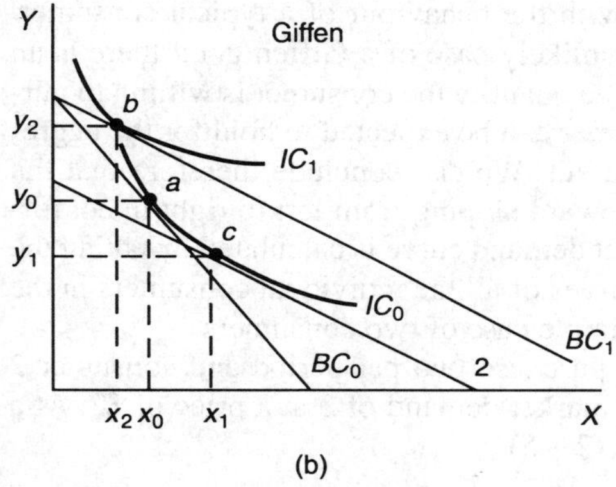

Figure 4.11: *Inferior and Giffen goods*

For both diagrams in Figure 4.11 the substitution effect is the movement from x_0 to x_1 and the income effect is the movement from x_1 to x_2. In diagram (a) X is an inferior good but the negative income effect is not enough to dominate the substitution effect. The overall effect is for the consumer to buy more of the good ($x_0 \rightarrow x_2$) when the price falls. It follows that inferior goods can have the usual downward sloping demand curve. In diagram (b) X is an inferior good and the negative income effect is such that it reverses the impact of the substitution effect. This theoretical possibility is known as a **'Giffen' good.** Giffen goods are an exception to the law of demand as there is a positive relationship between price and the quantity demanded resulting in an upward sloping demand curve. In Figure 4.11(b) the overall effect of the fall in the price of X is for the quantity purchased to fall from x_0 to x_2.

To conclude, the substitution effect is always such that the consumer will buy more of a good whose price has fallen and vice versa. When relative prices change the consumer adjusts the quantities purchased so as to equate the mrs with the new relative prices. However the income effect is unpredictable and depends on whether the good in question is 'normal' or 'inferior'. Normal goods conform to the law of demand because the income and substitution effects reinforce each other resulting in a downward-sloping demand curve. For inferior goods the income and substitution effects work in opposite directions but even in this case there will be a downward-sloping demand curve provided the substitution effect is stronger than the income effect. There is however a theoretical possibility of an upward-sloping demand curve for inferior goods if the negative income effect is stronger than the substitution effect.

4.4 Market demand curves

The previous analysis was concerned with the behaviour of a typical consumer. We have concluded that except in the unlikely case of a Giffen good there is an inverse relationship between price and the quantity the consumer is willing to purchase. What holds for the typical consumer can be expected to hold for the aggregate behaviour of consumers in the market. We can conclude therefore that the market demand curve will also be downward sloping from left to right in conformity with the law of demand. The market demand curve is calculated by taking the horizontal summation of the demand curves of all the individual consumers in the market. Figure 4.12 illustrates for the simple case of two consumers.

At a price of £2 consumer 1 would purchase two per period and consumer 2 would purchase one. This gives a total market demand of 3 at a price of £2. At a price of £1.50 total market demand is 7 (2 + 5).

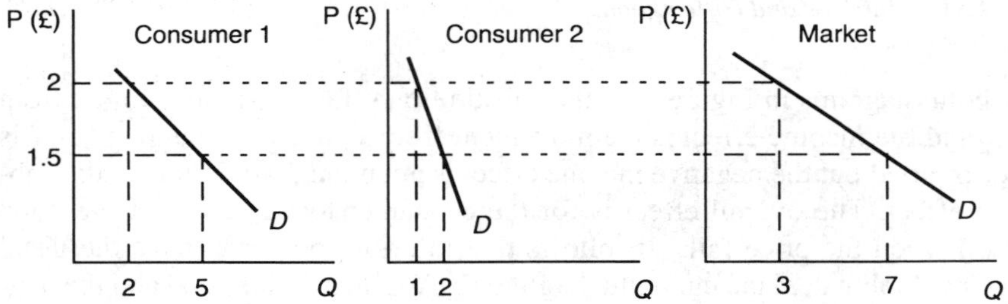

Figure 4.12: *Individual and market demand curves*

REVISION FOCUS CHAPTER FOUR

Key Areas

- The law of demand

- Indifference curves
  → diminishing marginal rate of substitution
- The budget constraint
  → real income and money income → slope of the budget constraint
- Maximizing utility subject to a budget constraint ($MRS_{xy} = px/py$)
- Income and substitution effects of price change
  → normal goods → inferior and Giffen goods
- Individual and market demand

Self-Test

(1)	The slope of the indifference curve at any point corresponds to the marginal rate of substitution at that point	T/F
(2)	The slope of the budget constraint depends on the consumer's money income	T/F
(3)	If the consumer is maximizing utility the slopes of the budget constraint and indifference curve will be equal.	T/F
(4)	A change in price causes a substitution effect but leaves real income unaffected	T/F
(5)	The pure substitution effect always leads to more of the good whose price has fallen being bought	T/F
(6)	The income effect reinforces the substitution effect for normal goods.	T/F
(7)	Inferior goods must have upward-sloping demand curves	T/F
(8)	All Giffen goods are inferior but not all inferior goods are Giffen	T/F

Discussion Topics

- The quantity demanded of normal goods will *increase* when price *falls* and vice versa. Explain.
- Inferior goods can be expected to have downward-sloping demand curves but in the rare case of a Giffen good the curve will be upward-sloping. Explain.
- Using a diagram to illustrate, distinguish between the income and substitution effects of a price change.

CHAPTER 5

COSTS OF PRODUCTION

5.1 The production function

In a market economy firms produce goods or services with a view to selling them for profit. To produce goods or services firms require factor inputs. Typically these *factor inputs* can be classified as *fixed capital* (plant and equipment), *working capital* (raw materials) and *labour* (different skills). Production is the process of transforming these various inputs into the *output* the firm wishes to achieve. The firm will usually have a choice regarding the technique of production: whether to use more or less capital or labour, the quality of the inputs to be used, etc.

The firm's *production function* is composed of all the alternative *technically efficient* techniques of production from which the firm must choose. Technically efficient techniques simply mean that no more of any input than is necessary is being used. The choice of technique will depend on the cost of the factor inputs.

In less developed economies where capital is scarce and expensive and labour is plentiful and cheap, low-technology labour-intensive techniques will predominate. If the cost of labour rises in any economy then, all else being equal, there will be an incentive to switch to more capital-intensive techniques and vice versa. The *economically efficient* technique is the one that enables the firm to produce a given output at the lowest cost. It is this technique that the profit-maximizing firm will seek to employ.

With advances in technology the production function itself changes as the firm has a wider range of techniques to choose from. However, it should be clear that technological efficiency and economic efficiency are not the same thing. For example, when Concorde was developed it represented the most advanced form of civil aviation from a technology point of view. But from an economics point of view it was a waste of resources (other than Air France and British Airways, no airline was interested in using it, with the result that it hardly got beyond the prototype stage).

5.2 *Short-run and long-run adjustments*

If the firm wishes to increase the level of output it is producing it will need to increase the factor inputs being used. However it may not be possible to adjust all the inputs at short notice. While various types of labour may be employable at short notice and increased raw materials may be available it is unlikely that the stock of fixed capital can be quickly changed. If the firm wishes to make *short-run* adjustments in production it must do so within its existing capacity, i.e. with the given level of the fixed factors.

- Fixed factors of production: those inputs which cannot be varied at short notice, typically plant and equipment.
- Variable factors of production: those inputs which can be varied at short notice, typically labour and raw materials.
- The short run: that time period within which at least one factor of production is fixed and cannot be adjusted.
- The long run: the length of time it takes for the firm to vary all its factors of production. In the long run all factors of production become variable.
- The very long run: in the very long run the technology of the industry changes so that the firms production function itself changes.

The above concepts will mean different things in different industries depending on the level of skill and technology. In some industries the shortage of highly skilled labour may represent the principal obstacle to expansion and therefore labour could be a fixed factor. In low-technology industries (e.g. textiles) the 'long run' may be a relatively short period of time compared to others (e.g. nuclear fuel). In modern hi-tech sectors with almost continuous changes in technology the 'very long run' is becoming a relatively short period of actual time.

5.3 *Costs of production*

Various measures of cost exist.

- Total Cost (TC) – TC refers to the total cost of producing a given level of output over a given time period, e.g. the firm's annual costs. Total costs can be subdivided into total fixed costs (TFC) and total variable costs (TVC).

$$TC = TFC + TVC \quad [5.1]$$

  Fixed costs are those costs which are not directly linked to the level of output. They will have to be paid even if the firm produces no output and will not change in the short-run as output changes. Interest repayments on borrowed finance, rent, rates, insurance are typical examples of fixed costs. Variable costs are those costs which are directly linked to the level of output. Total variable costs will tend to rise as output rises and fall as output falls. Typical variable costs would be for raw materials, labour, energy, transport etc.
- Average Total Cost (AC) – The average total cost (or unit cost) is simply the total cost divided by the corresponding level of output (*Q*). As total costs can

be subdivided into total fixed and total variable, so also can average cost be subdivided into average fixed cost (*AFC*) and average variable cost (AVC).

$$AC = \frac{TC}{Q} = \frac{TFC}{Q} + \frac{TVC}{Q} \quad [5.2]$$
$$= AFC + AVC$$

- Marginal Cost (MC) – The marginal cost is the change in total cost resulting from the production of an additional unit of output. However as fixed costs do not change in the short run marginal cost is in fact *marginal variable cost*. The marginal cost of the nth unit of output can be calculated in the following way:

$$MC_n = TC_n - TC_{n-1} \quad [5.3]$$

So, for example, if we wish to calculate the marginal cost of the 10th unit we subtract the total cost of producing nine units form the total cost of producing 10 units.

5.4 Behaviour of costs in the short run

To develop an understanding of the short-run behaviour of firms we need to know how the various measures of cost respond to short-run changes in output.

The behaviour of the fixed cost measures is unambiguous as by assumption total fixed costs do not change in the short run. It follows from this that AFC must continuously fall as output increases as Figure 5.1 illustrates.

If we assume for example that TFC = £1000 then AFC must decline as illustrated. In fact the AFC curve is a rectangular hyperbole (see Figure 2.9(c), page 19).

The behaviour of the variable cost measures (TVC, AVC, MC) is less straight forward and requires a theoretical approach. The theory underlying the analysis of these costs is known as *the law of diminishing marginal returns.*

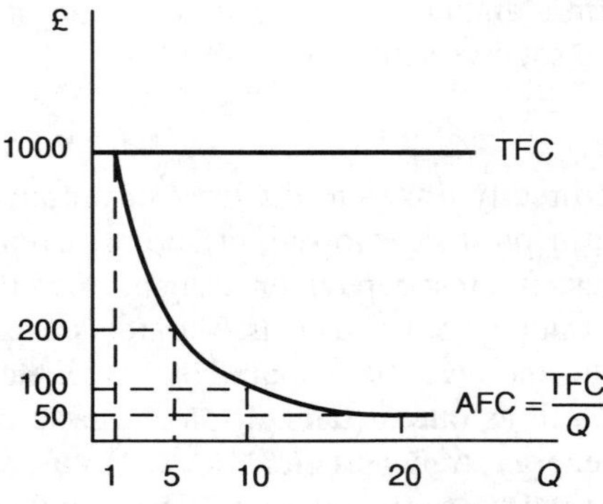

Figure 5.1: *Total and average fixed cost*

The law of diminishing returns: as extra units of a variable factor input are combined with a fixed quantity of other factor inputs the marginal product of the variable factor will eventually decline.

The law of diminishing returns is only relevant to short-run changes in output. In the short run there is at least one fixed factor whereas in the long run all factor inputs are variable.

Example

Assume a well equipped and well stocked McRonalds fast food outlet in a busy urban area. McRonalds specializes in burgers and french fries. If there is only one worker having to perform all tasks (stock control, cooking, wrapping, serving, etc.) there is limited scope for increased efficiency. A second worker, by enabling a degree of specialization to occur, is likely to lead to a more than doubling of meals being served. A third worker, by enabling even further specialization, is likely to increase the number of meals served by more than the second worker. This rising marginal product of labour (MP_L) may continue for a further number of workers but it cannot continue indefinitely. Eventually there will be a degree of congestion behind the counter due to the limited stock of fixed capital (cookers, sale points etc.). The result will be an eventual decline in the marginal and the average product of labour. The following table illustrates this.

Table 5.1: *Total, average and marginal products of labour*

Number of workers (L)	Total product (meals) Q	Marginal product of labour (MP_L)	Average product of labour (AP_L)
1	20	20	20
2	50	30	25
3	90	40	30
4	140	50	35
5	180	40	36
6	204	24	34
7	217	13	31
8	224	7	28

Provided the marginal product of the next worker is above the existing average, the average must rise if the worker is employed. As the marginal eventually falls and continues to do so the average must also eventually fall.

If we assume (for simplicity) that wages represent the only variable cost and that the rate is £20 per worker per shift we get the costs illustrated in Table 5.2 on the next page.

TVC is simply the wage rate (£20) times the number of workers; AVC is simply TVC divided by the corresponding quantity of meals; the MC is simply the change in TVC (£20 per each extra worker) divided by the marginal product of

Table 5.2: *Production and costs*

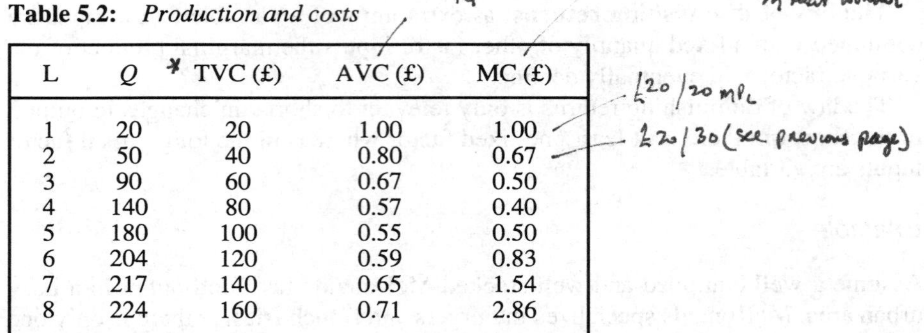

L	*Q*	TVC (£)	AVC (£)	MC (£)
1	20	20	1.00	1.00
2	50	40	0.80	0.67
3	90	60	0.67	0.50
4	140	80	0.57	0.40
5	180	100	0.55	0.50
6	204	120	0.59	0.83
7	217	140	0.65	1.54
8	224	160	0.71	2.86

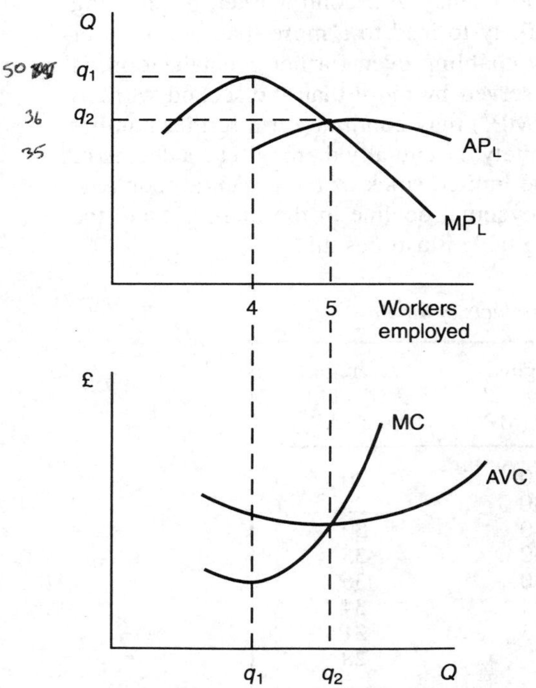

Figure 5.2: *Product curves and cost curves*

that worker. (This *MC* represents an approximation to the theoretical definition which strictly speaking requires a change in output of only *one* extra meal for its calculation).

The relationship between the product curves and the variable cost curves are illustrated in Figure 5.2.

Where the MP_L is at a maximum the marginal cost of production will be at a minimum. Where the AP_L is at a maximum the average variable cost will be at a

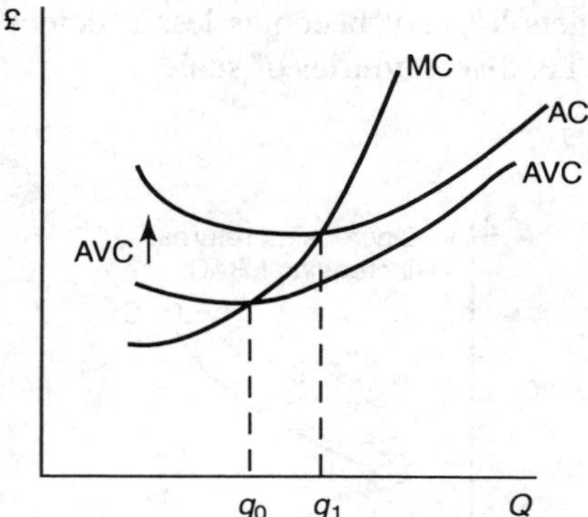

Figure 5.3: *The theoretical short-run costs*

minimum. The MP_L cuts the AP_L at its maximum point, the MC cuts the AVC at its minimum point.

To determine the behaviour of the average total cost recall that AC = AFC + AVC. The AC is higher than the AVC by an amount equal to AFC. We have seen that the AFC gets smaller and smaller as output increases. It follows then that the difference between the AC curve and the AVC gets narrower and narrower as output expands as illustrated in Figure 5.3.

The MC curve cuts the AC and the AVC curves from below at their minimum points. Provided the MC is below the average, the average must be falling whereas if the marginal is above the average the average must be rising. The AVC reaches a minimum (q_0) at a lower level of output than AC (q_1).

5.5 *Behaviour of costs in the long run*

In the long run all factor inputs become variable (though the state of technology remains given). In the long run the firm can adjust all inputs so as to achieve the optimum combination whereby the lowest possible unit cost of production can be achieved. In the long run the firm can produce a given level of output in the most economically efficient way.

The behaviour of long-run costs depends on **returns to scale** in the industry in question. Returns to scale is concerned with the relationship between the *scale of production* and *efficiency in production*. Three possibilities exist:

- Increasing returns to scale – as the firm gets larger (increasing all inputs) it becomes more efficient resulting in lower costs per unit of output, i.e. **economies of scale.**
- Constant returns to scale – as the firm gets larger it retains the same level of efficiency resulting in constant costs per unit of output.

- Decreasing returns to scale – as the firm gets larger it becomes less efficient resulting in higher costs per unit of output, i.e. **diseconomies of scale**.

Figure 5.4 illustrates these three possible cases.

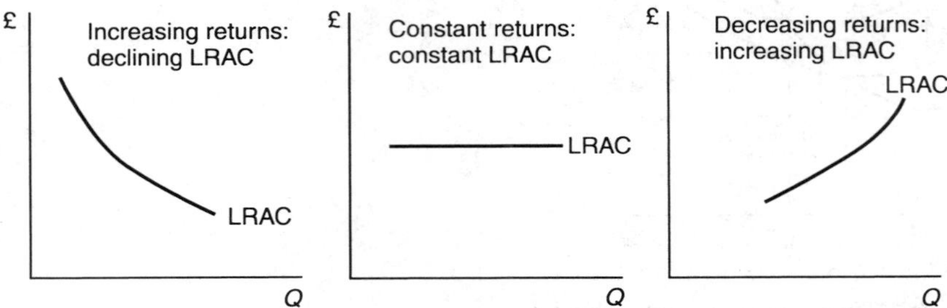

Figure 5.4: *Returns to scale and long-run average cost (LRAC)*

There are many sectors of modern economies where significant *economies of scale exist* up to a relatively high level of output. Much of manufacturing industry (aircraft, cars, pharmaceuticals, etc.), banking, telecommunications, public utilities (water, gas electricity), etc. all display significant economies of scale. To be efficient in these sectors firms must operate on a large scale.

Other sectors such as personal services (doctors, lawyers, dentists, etc.) building, restaurants, consultancy, specialist retailers, etc. can achieve maximum efficiency at relatively low levels of output. The ability to identify and cater for niche markets can also enable relatively small firms to prosper.

Where significant economies of scale do exist the causes tend to include the following:

- the opportunity for division of labour and specialization in large organizations which leads to improvements in labour productivity;
- opportunities for the mechanization of simplified processes;
- the opportunities for low cost bulk buying in large organizations (in effect the suppliers are passing on the advantages of the economies they achieve dealing with large customers);
- the use of expensive capital equipment that can only be justified at high levels of output (i.e. the 'indivisibility' of capital);
- economies of 'increased dimensions' resulting from the fact that building costs do not increase in proportion to volume (e.g. oil-supertankers, hypermarkets etc.);
- financial economies can arise as larger firms are typically perceived as being a lower risk than smaller ones resulting in a lower cost of capital;
- marketing and distribution economies.

Even where economies of scale are significant there must be some limit to their extent for, quite clearly, there must be a (non-zero) lower limit to LRAC. Expansion beyond this limit must result in either constant returns to scale or decreasing returns to scale. Figure 5.5 illustrates these two possibilities.

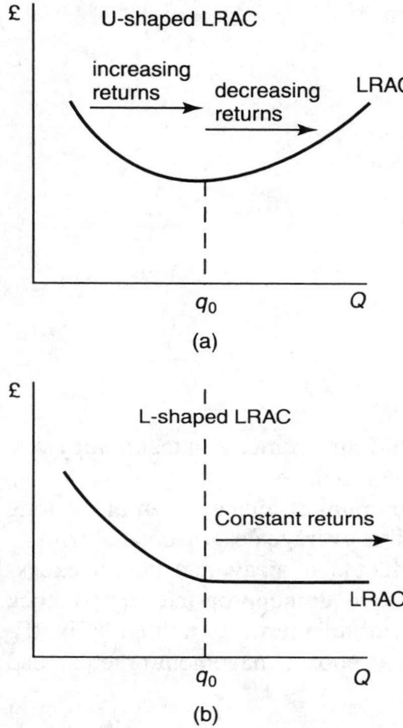

Figure 5.5: *Long run average costs*

If and when diseconomies of scale occur, resulting in rising long-run unit costs the cause has to do with managerial rather than technical problems. Very large organizations can become unwieldy resulting in problems to do with communications, inflexibility, local empire building, staff motivation, etc. The larger the organization the more critical the managerial function becomes.

5.6 *Optimum size and minimum efficient scale*

The *optimum size of the firm* is the level of output that allows the *LRAC* to be minimized. In Figure 5.5(a) the optimum size is q_0. In Figure 5.5(b) there is no optimum as different levels of output (q_0 and higher) enable the LRAC to be minimised. In this case q_0 is referred to as the *minimum efficient scale* (MES).

The long-run average cost curve indicates the lowest possible average cost associated with any given level of output. It represents *what is possible* when the optimum combination of fixed and variable inputs is being used to produce any given level of output. The curve is drawn on the assumption that the pattern of

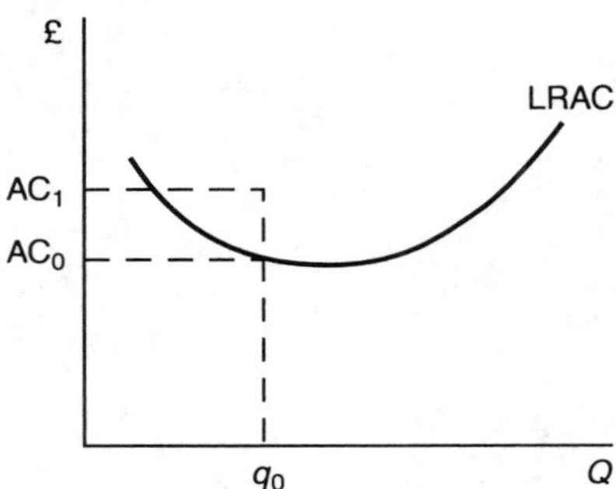

Figure 5.6: *X-inefficiency*

input prices and the state of technology is given. Improvements in technology will tend to lower it while rising input prices will tend to raise it.

In reality firms may not be operating at maximum efficiency even in the long run. For example, in Figure 5.6 the lowest possible average cost associated with an output of q_0 is AC_0. However the firm may in fact have an average cost in excess of this, say at AC_1. This inefficiency may be due to an inappropriate capital stock or simply *X*-inefficiency. *X*-inefficiency is an umbrella term for a range of inefficiencies that can emerge in organizations such as poor management practice, bad industrial relations, overmanning, etc.

5.7 Economies of scale and competition

The extent of economies of scale in an industry will have important implications for the level of competition in that industry. The key issue here is the level of output at which firms reach an optimum size (or MES) relative to the total demand for the product in the market. If there are large economies of scale relative to market size then there will only be room for a small number of firms implying a high degree of **concentration** in the industry. On the other hand, if economies of scale are insignificant relative to market size there will tend to be a highly competitive environment with lots of firms competing. Economies of scale and competition are inversely related.

A special case is that of *natural monopoly* (Section 9.3). This is where efficiency and competition are mutually exclusive. Economies of scale are so large relative to the market size that having a single supplier is the most efficient way to supply the market as illustrated in Figure 5.7.

The LRAC represents the unit costs achievable by a specific firm and D represents the market demand curve. A single supplier could supply the market and achieve unit costs of AC_0, whereas if the market was split between, say two suppliers then higher unit costs (AC_1 for example) would be the result.

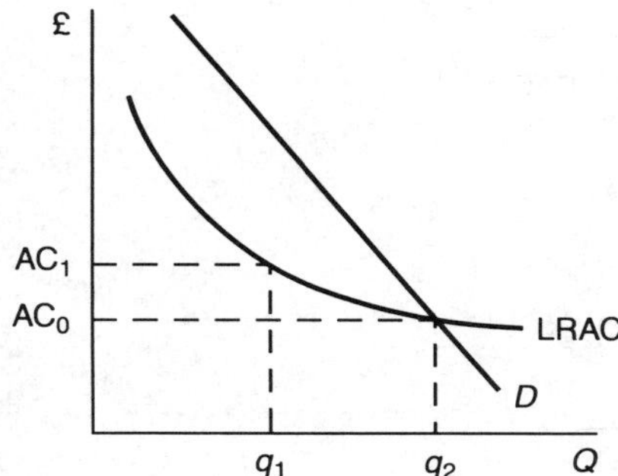

Figure 5.7: *Natural monopoly*

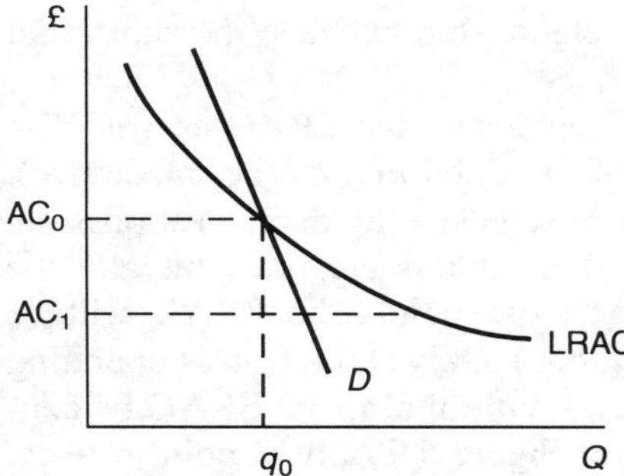

Figure 5.8: *Unexploited economies of scale*

Water supply is a good example of natural monopoly.

On the other hand, it may be that demand for the product or service is too small to enable economies of scale to be exploited. This is often a problem in rural areas where post offices, schools, etc. are often too small for efficiency. This possibility is illustrated in Figure 5.8.

Large economies of scale exist to be exploited but market demand is too small to enable it to happen. The unit costs that can be achieved (AC_0) are significantly higher than what could be achieved (AC_1) if there was greater demand. If this firm is to cover its long-run costs, it must charge a price at least equal to (AC_0) which implies a level of output no more than q_0.

5.8 *Short-run and long-run costs*

The LRAC curve represents a lower boundary for the average costs that are achievable, given the existing state of technology and existing input prices. It follows that the short run average cost curves cannot be lower than the LRAC for

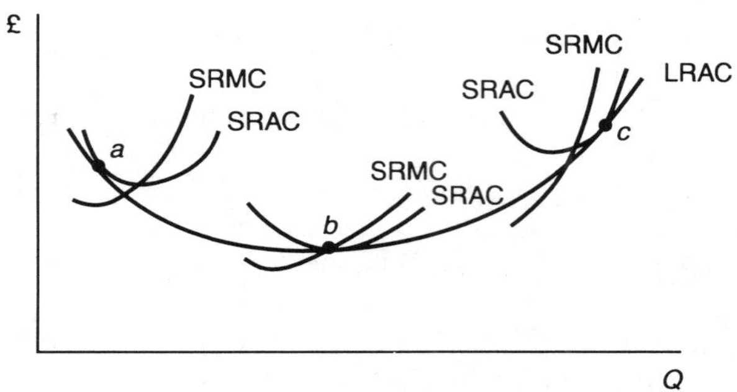

Figure 5.9: *Short- and long-run cost curve*

any level of output. Figure 5.9 illustrates the relationship between the short- and long-run average costs (for a U-shaped LRAC).

The LRAC curve represents an 'envelope' enclosing the SRAC curves. The SRAC curves are drawn for different levels of the fixed factors (i.e. plant size). The LRAC is arrived at by connecting the points representing the lowest possible SRAC for different levels of output. (Note, these points are not generally the minimum points on these SRAC curves.) At these points the LRAC will be tangent to the corresponding SRACs (points *a*, *b*, *c*). Only if the firm is operating at its optimum size (or minimum efficient scale) will minimizing SRAC be consistent with minimizing LRAC. For example in Figure 5.9 only at point *b* is the minimum point of SRAC tangent to the LRAC curve.

REVISION FOCUS CHAPTER FIVE

Key Areas

- Production function
  →fixed and variable inputs→short-term and long-term adjustments
- Short-run costs
  →the law of diminishing returns→total, average and marginal costs→shape of the short-run cost curves
- Long run costs
  →returns to scale→causes of economies and diseconomies of scale →long-run average cost curve→optimum size→minimum efficient scale→*x*-inefficiency→market concentration→natural monopoly

Self Test

(1) If the cost of labour rises relative to the cost of capital this will improve the prospects for labour employment — T/F

(2) The law of diminishing returns is of relevance when all factor inputs are variable T/F
(3) If average costs are falling then the corresponding marginal costs must be less than the average costs T/F
(4) The law of diminishing returns implies an eventually rising marginal cost of production T/F
(5) For the long-run average cost curve it is assumed that at least one factor input is fixed in supply T/F
(6) A U-shaped LRAC curve implies decreasing returns to scale at some levels of output but not so for the L-shaped LRAC curve T/F
(7) If a firm is minimizing short-run average costs then it must be operating on its LRAC curve T/F
(8) If a firm is operating at its optimum size then SR and LR average costs can be minimized simultaneously T/F

Discussion Topics

- The law of diminishing returns impacts on short-run costs whereas returns to scale impact on long-run costs. Explain.
- The scope for economies of scale in an industry will determine the extent of competition in that industry. Explain.
- Distinguish between the short run, long run and very long run regarding the firm's production function.

CHAPTER 6

PROFIT AND THE BEHAVIOUR OF THE FIRM

6.1 *Total, average and marginal revenues*

Firms exist to supply markets with goods or services for sale. Key issues to be determined are:

(i) the quantity to be supplied and
(ii) the price to be charged.

Supplying the market will impose **costs** on the firm while the sale of goods will lead to **revenue** for the firm. How costs and revenues interact will determine the optimum price–quantity combination.

Three aspects of revenue are of relevance when analysing the behaviour of firms:

- Total Revenue (TR)
- Average Revenue (AR)
- Marginal Revenue (MR)

Total revenue (ignoring taxes) for a given period depends simply on the price charged (P) and the quantity purchased (Q):

$$\text{TR} = \text{PQ} \qquad [6.1]$$

Average revenue is simply the total revenue divided by the number of units sold:

$$\text{AR} = \text{TR}/Q \qquad [6.2]$$

Assuming there is no price discrimination (Section 6.5) the AR and P are equivalent ($\text{AR} = \text{TR}/Q = \text{PQ}/Q = P$).

Marginal revenue is the change in total revenue resulting from the sale of an extra unit of output. The marginal revenue associated with the nth unit sold is:

$$\text{MR}_{(n)} = \text{TR}_{(n)} - \text{TR}_{(n-1)} \qquad [6.3]$$

For example if TR increases from £20 to £21 when quantity increases from 10 to 11,

$$\text{MR}_{(11)} = \text{TR}_{(11)} - \text{TR}_{(10)} = £21 - £20 = £1 \qquad [6.3]$$

Table 6.1: *Hypothetical revenue figures*

P(AR)	Q	TR(PQ)	MR
£2.00	10	£20.00	
£1.90	11	£20.90	£0.90
£1.80	12	£21.60	£0.70
£1.70	13	£22.10	£0.50
£1.60	14	£22.40	£0.30
£1.50	15	£22.50	£0.10
£1.40	16	£22.40	–£0.10

The specific effect of a rising quantity of sales on revenues will depend on whether or not the firm is a **price-taker** in the goods market.

Price-taker: *a firm is a price-taker in the goods market if it can always sell additional units without having to lower the price it charges.*

A price-taker can sell as much as it wishes at the prevailing market price. The alternative case is where the firm would have to reduce the price it charges in order to increase the quantity of sales.

The figures in Table 6.1 illustrate the situation for a firm when, not being a price taker, it is forced to reduce price to increase the quantity purchased by consumers. The first two columns represent the **demand schedule** facing the firm. Not being a price-taker, the firm is faced with a downward-sloping demand curve. TR is not increasing in proportion with Q, it will therefore peak and eventually decline. Because the firm must reduce price to generate additional sales the MR is less than the corresponding price charged. The reason for this is, when the firm reduces price to sell the additional unit it loses revenue on the existing sales as it must also reduce the price of these.

The general shape of the revenue curves when the firm is not a price-taker are as illustrated in Figure 6.1 on the next page.

Not being a price-taker the firm's TR curve slopes upward, peaks and thereafter declines. MR will be zero for the same level of output where TR is at a maximum (q_0 in Figure 6.1). MR is lower than AR and the slope of the MR line is twice as steep as the AR line.

The AR line, as it is a relationship between price and quantity sold, is none other than the firm's demand curve. In Figure 6.1 p_0 is the price to charge if q_0 is the quantity the firm wishes to sell. A firm faced with a downward-sloping demand curve for its product has a degree of **market power**. Unlike the price-taker it may choose the price at which it is willing to trade. However, if a particular price is chosen by the firm, it is the consumers and not the firm who will decide the quantity that will be sold.

The price-taker on the other hand can always sell additional units at the prevailing market price. Therefore TR continues to increase in proportion with the quantity sold. As an additional unit can always be sold for the prevailing price, the

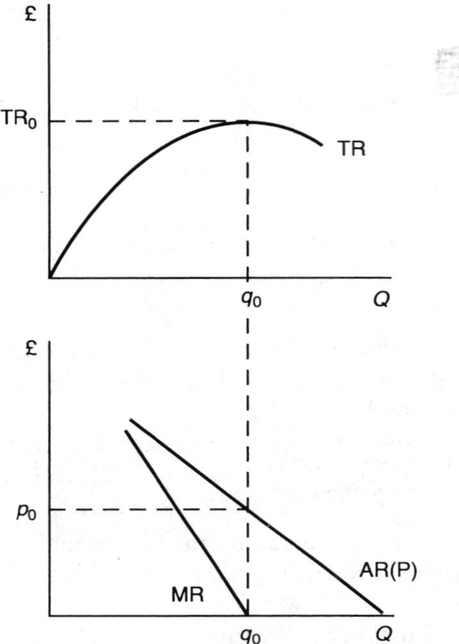

Figure 6.1: *The price-makers revenue curves*

marginal revenue from additional units and the prevailing price must be equivalent.

The general shape of the revenue curves when the firm is a price-taker are as illustrated in Figure 6.2.

The *P*, AR and MR are all equivalent and represented by the same horizontal line. This horizontal line also represents the demand curve facing the firm. At the prevailing price (p_0) any quantity the firm wishes to supply to the market will be purchased. The TR is an upward sloping straight line.

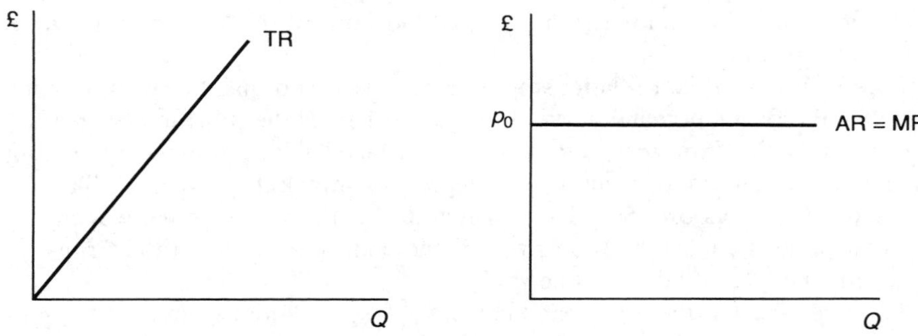

Figure 6.2: *Revenue curves for the price-taker*

6.2 *Measuring profit*

The profit (Π) made over a given period is the difference between the total revenue from sales and the total cost of generating those sales

$$\Pi = TR - TC \qquad [6.4]$$

In practice however the measurement of profit is not as straightforward as the above equation might suggest.

Consider the following simple example:

- £1m which is earning interest at 10% pa (£100,000) is withdrawn from the bank and invested in a commercial project. This project subsequently generates 8% annual return (£80,000).
- From the point of view of the **tax authorities** (who will want to tax all profits) there is an £80,000 profit here to be taxed., The **accountant** can be expected to calculate an equivalent amount of profit to that of the taxman. From the point of view of the **economist** (who is primarily concerned with the efficient use of scarce resources) this project is generating a loss of £20,000. The £1m would have been better employed left in the bank.

When measuring costs the economist is concerned with the opportunity cost (Section 1.1) of resources. The return the resources would earn in the next best activity of **similar risk** is to be included as a cost when measuring profit. For the investor in the previous example if the choice is between leaving the money in the bank or some alternative, the £100,000 interest forgone should be included as a cost when evaluating the alternative. When projects of different risk are being compared, high-risk projects will be expected to generate a higher return than lower-risk projects. This **risk-premium** is to compensate for the additional risk and is included as a cost.

This approach to the measurement of costs leads to the following definitions of **normal profit, supernormal profit** and **losses**:

- Normal profit is being earned when total revenue is just sufficient to cover all costs (TR = TC).
- Supernormal profit is being earned when total revenue is greater than all costs incurred (TR > TC).
- Losses are being incurred when less than normal profit is being earned (TR < TC).

Normal profit may vary from industry to industry, depending on the risk involved. Investments of similar risk have equivalent rates of normal profit. The rate of return on government bonds (Section 13.4) is generally taken as a measure of the **risk-free rate of return**.

If the typical firm in an industry is earning normal profits it is doing as well as it could do in any alternative similar-risk activity. This firm has no incentive to leave this industry, nor have outside firms an incentive to enter it.

If the typical firm in an industry is earning supernormal profits it is doing better than in any alternative similar risk activity. This firm certainly has no incentive to leave this industry but outside firms will have an incentive to enter it.

If the typical firm is making losses it could be doing better in some alternative activity. Clearly there is an incentive for this firm to leave the industry for the alternative.

6.3 *Profit-maximizing strategies*

To maximize profits it is necessary that TR be greater than TC by as large an amount as possible. To maximize the difference between TR and TC it is necessary that MC and MR are equal.

$$MC = MR \qquad [6.5]$$

This represents a necessary condition for profit maximization. By bringing the cost curves (Chapter 5) together with the revenue curves (Section 6.1) we can illustrate the profit-maximizing strategy diagramatically. Figure 6.3 illustrates with respect to a firm which is assumed to be a price-taker.

The profit maximizing strategy is to produce that level of output such that MC = MR. This is at point *a* with an output level of q_0. Assume in Figure 6.3 that the firm produces some level of output less than q_0, say q_1. At this level of output MR exceeds MC. If the firm was to increase output beyond q_1 the addition to revenue from the sale of extra units (MR) would be greater than the addition to costs due to those additional units (MC), therefore profit must increase. Beyond q_0 extra units of output add more to costs than to revenue (MC > MR) and therefore to produce in excess of q_0 has a negative effect on profits. Figure 6.3 illustrates a firm making supernormal profits because at an output of q_0 TR > TC. TR is represented by the larger rectangle (p_0q_0), TC is represented by the lower rectangle (AC_0q_0) the difference between them (the shaded area) represents the supernormal profit.

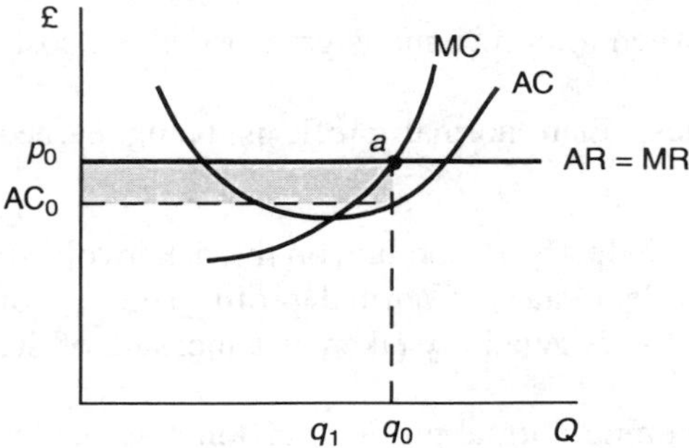

Figure 6.3: *Price-taker making supernormal profits*

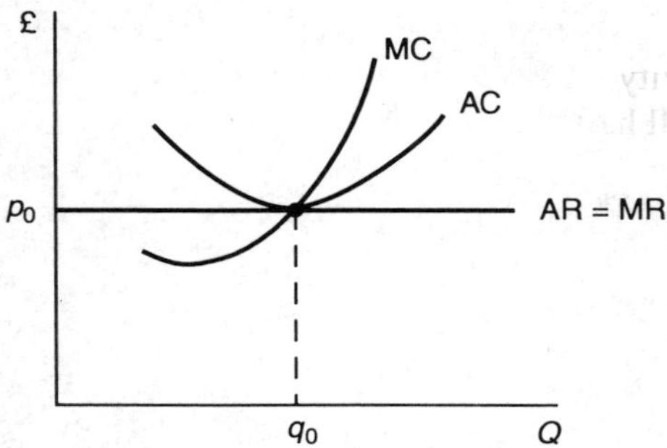

Figure 6.4: *Price-taker making normal profits*

Figure 6.4 represents a price-taker maximizing profits but only able to make normal profits. At an output of q_0 profits are being maximized (MC = MR) however only normal profits are being earned as total revenue equals total cost (or AC = AR).

Figure 6.5 illustrates the profit-maximizing strategy of a firm faced with a downward-sloping demand curve. In Figure 6.5 (a) MC = MR at an output level of q_0. This is the profit-maximizing level of output. The demand curve indicates the price (p_0) consumers would be willing to pay to purchase q_0. Supernormal profits equal to the shaded area are being made. In Figure 6.5(b) q_0 is the profit maximizing level of output (MC = MR) but only normal profits are being earned (TR = TC).

Although MC = MR is a necessary condition for profit maximization it may not be a sufficient condition. Figure 6.6 illustrates a situation where losses would be incurred at all levels of output. AC is greater than AR (i.e. TC > TR) at all levels of output. Even if the firm produces where MC = MR (i.e. q_0) losses will be incurred. Although profits cannot be made under the conditions illustrated in

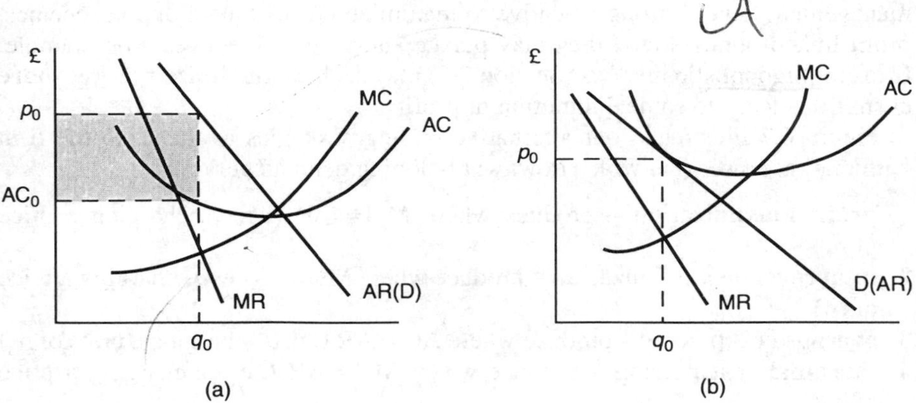

Figure 6.5: *The price-maker and profit maximization*

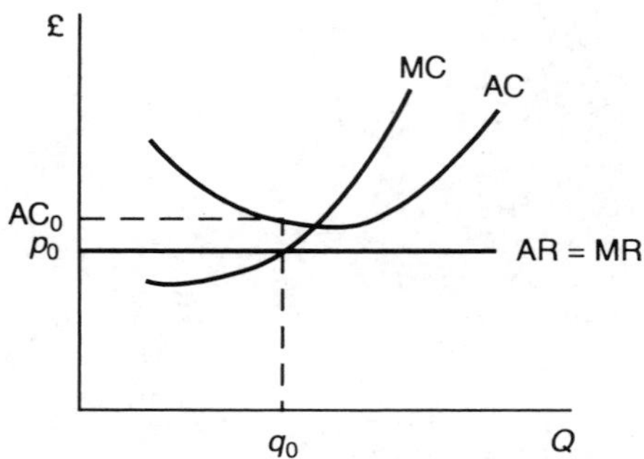

Figure 6.6: *Losses at all levels of output*

Figure 6.6, producing q_0 might represent a **loss minimizing** strategy. If so to continue in production in the short run is preferable to immediate closure (see Figure 7.3).

6.4 Alternative pricing strategies

In a market economy the survival of firms depends on their ability to generate profits. They will not survive in the long run unless they at least earn normal profits. Because of the importance of profit it is usual to assume that the typical firm has as its objective the **maximization of profits**.

However, it would be unrealistic to assume that all firms at all times are exclusively concerned with profit maximizing. Most large firms in advanced economies are public limited companies (PLCs) in which there is a dichotomy between ownership of the firm (shareholders) and the running of the firm (directors). Unless management have a strong incentive to maximize profits (share option schemes, profit linked bonuses etc.) they may pursue alternative objectives. For example, firms in oligopolistic markets (Section 7.5) may seek to **maximize market share** even if this leads to some diminution of profit.

Figure 6.7 illustrates four alternative pricing strategies available to the firm with market power (i.e. with a downward-sloping demand curve):

1. **profit maximization** – produce where MC = MR (i.e. q_0 charging a price of p_0)
2. **total revenue maximization** – produce where MR = 0 (i.e. q_1 charging a price of p_1)
3. **average cost pricing** – produce where AC = AR (i.e. q_3 charging a price of p_3)
4. **marginal cost pricing** – produce where MC = AR (i.e. q_2 charging a price of p_2)

Average cost pricing might be attractive to a firm wanting to maximize sales

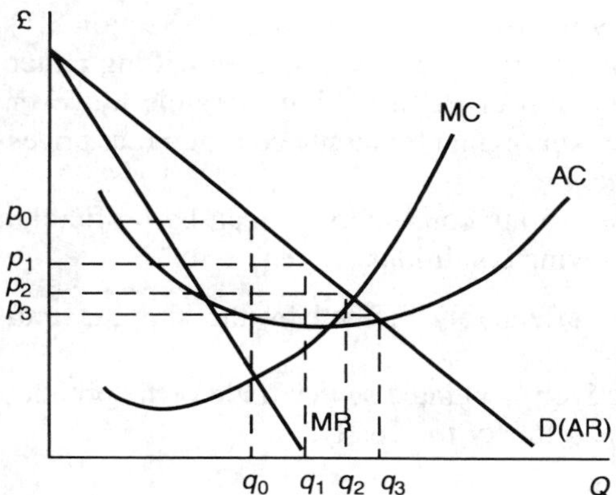

Figure 6.7: *Alternative pricing strategies*

subject to earning a normal rate of profit. Maximizing total revenue (in isolation of costs) could in fact lead to losses (if the AC curve was above the AR at q_1).

The marginal cost pricing rule (MC = P) is the appropriate strategy if the maximization of consumers' welfare is the objective. This is not likely to be an objective of private sector firms but could be the policy of public sector firms (nationalized, semi-state) should the government wish it. In Figure 6.7 the profit-maximizing firm would produce q_0 and no more. However, consumers are willing to pay a price for additional units of output (up to q_2) that is greater than the marginal cost of producing them. This can be seen diagramatically as the AR curve lies above the MC curve up to an output of q_2. An economy that was sensitive to consumers' preferences would produce those extra units. Beyond q_2 marginal cost is higher than the price consumers are willing to pay. To produce in excess of q_2 would be a sub-optimal use of resources from a consumers perspective.

The marginal cost pricing rule has implications for public policy. If the marginal cost of using existing public assets such as art galleries, parks, roads, etc. is zero then the appropriate price to charge is also zero. If resources are not relatively scarce why ration them? The argument here assumes no problem regarding congestion. Where congestion is a problem resources need to be rationed and a zero price would not be appropriate. The government is left with the problem of financing the fixed costs of providing these assets. The possibility of charging a *two-part tariff* is discussed in Section 9.3 in the context of *natural monopoly*.

6.5 *Price discrimination*

Price discrimination (PD) is the practice of charging different prices to different consumers for the same product for reasons unrelated to costs of production. A perfect system of PD would completely remove consumers surplus (Section 3.1) by getting each consumer to pay the maximum price they would be willing rather than go without the good. A perfect system of PD is seldom possible however charging different prices in different market segments is quite common (car prices in different countries, student travel, etc.).

Where the willingness to pay differs among consumers PD can be profitable. However for PD to be possible the following conditions are required:

1. The market for the product can be effectively divided by the supplier into distinct market segments.
2. These market segments can be effectively separated so that trade in the product between the segments is either not possible or too costly.

For PD to be profitable it is necessary that:

3. The willingness to pay is different in the market segments, in particular the price elasticity of demand is different.

Price discrimination is only possible where the firm has a degree of market power. The price-taker is obliged to trade at the prevailing market price or not al all, thus precluding PD. Condition (2) is necessary or else purchasers in the low-priced segment could profitably under cut the original supplier in the high-price segment.

Assume a firm supplying a product to a market that can be effectively divided into segments A and B, and that the cost of supplying these segments is similar. If price discrimination is to be profitable then the price elasticity of demand in A differs from that in B ($PED_A \neq PED_B$). We can think of the firm as having two decisions to make:

1. what quantity to supply in total
2. how to distribute this total between the segments so as to maximize profits

Taking the second point first, the firm should supply both segments in such a way that the marginal revenue from the last unit sold in both segments is the same:

$$MR_A = MR_B \qquad [6.6]$$

If this were not the case the firm could increase total revenue by switching supply from the segment with the lower marginal revenue to the segment with the higher. This increase in total revenue would represent an increase in profits as, by assumption, total costs would be unaffected.

A definite relationship exists between marginal revenue, price and the price elasticity of demand given by the following formula:

$$MR = P(1 + 1/PED) \qquad [6.7]$$

From equation [6.7] it follows that the marginal revenue for the two market segments (A and B) can be expressed as:

$$MR_A = P_A(1 + 1/PED_A)$$

$$MR_B = P_B(1 + 1/PED_B)$$

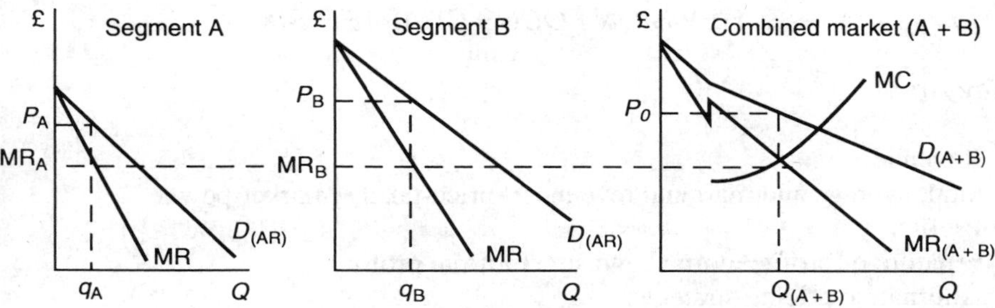

Figure 6.8: *Price discrimination*

If the firm supplies both segments so as to equate the marginal revenue in both then a different price must be charged. By equating marginal revenues it follows:

$$P_A(1 + 1/\text{PED}_A) = P_B(1 + 1/\text{PED}_B)$$

But as by assumption $\text{PED}_A \neq \text{PED}_B$ it follows that P_A cannot equal P_B.

Example

$\text{PED}_A = -2$ and

$\text{PED}_B = -3$

then

$P_A(1 + 1/{-2}) = P_B(1 + 1/{-3}) \Rightarrow P_A = 1.33P_B$.

Profit maximization therefore leads to price discrimination. Also the price will be higher in the segment where demand is more inelastic. So, students get cheaper flights than business-class passengers, not through the generosity of the airline but because students are not prepared to pay the same price as business class passengers.

The total output to produce, if profits are to be maximized, is where the marginal cost of production is equal to the marginal revenue in the combined market as illustrated in Figure 6.8 above.

$Q_{(A+B)}$ is the total output determined in the combined market. Without price-discrimination p_0 would be the single price. However if p_0 was charged in both A and B the marginal revenues would differ. It is more profitable to distribute $Q_{(A+B)}$ in such a way as to equate the marginal revenues, i.e. sell q_B in B at a price of p_B and q_A in A at a price of p_A.

Profits are maximized where:

$$\text{MC} = \text{MR}_A = \text{MR}_B \qquad [6.8]$$

i.e. profit maximization is occurring separately in both segments.

REVISION FOCUS CHAPTER SIX

Key Areas

- Revenue
  total, average and marginal revenues→price-taker→market-power
- Profit
  →nature of profit→normal and supernormal profit
- Alternative pricing strategies
  →profit-maximizing strategy (MC = MR)→revenue-maximization (MR = 0)→average-cost pricing (AC = AR)→marginal-cost pricing (MC = P)
- Price-discrimination
  →nature of→necessary conditions for PD to be possible and profitable→$MC = MR_A = MR_B$

Self Test

(1) The firm with market power can determine *either* the price to charge or the quantity to sell but not both. T/F

(2) If a firm is a price-taker it will be faced with a horizontal demand curve for its product. T/F

(3) The average revenue curve and the demand curve are equivalent for both the firm as price-taker and with market power T/F

(4) To make normal profit a firm must earn more than in the next best (similar-risk) activity T/F

(5) The profit-maximizing rule (MC = MR) also requires that the MC curve cuts the MR curve from below. T/F

(6) If a firm is a price-taker the marginal revenue curve and the demand curve are equivalent T/F

(7) If a firm wishes to maximize total revenue it should produce where (a) AC = AR (b) MR = MC (c) MR = 0

(8) Price-discrimination is due to the different costs of supplying different market segments. T/F

Discussion Topics

- Using a diagram to illustrate, explain the alternative pricing strategies that firms might adopt.
- Explain the conditions that are required if price-discrimination is to be both possible and profitable.
- Distinguish between profit as measured by the economist and as measured by the accountant.

CHAPTER 7

MARKET STRUCTURES

7.1 *Markets*

A market is any arrangement whereby buyers and sellers of a product are brought into contact. Markets can be based locally (e.g. bread), nationally (e.g. cars) or globally (e.g. oil). Contact between buyers and sellers may be direct or through the medium of modern communications systems, etc. Some markets (stock market, second-hand car dealers, etc.) are based on **market-makers** who undertake to **buy and sell** the product on a spread of prices. Market-makers represent a link between the primary buyers and sellers.

A market may be concerned with a homogeneous product or a range of differentiated products. The important point is that the goods being sold are close substitutes and therefore cross-elasticities of demand (Section 2.6) are high within the boundary of the market. For example the market for transport in a region might include rail, road or air transport as alternatives.

Markets can be distinguished according to the degree of competition that firms supplying the market encounter. The greater the level of competition the more the firm will have to adapt to events rather than influence them.

The following market structures are listed in a descending order of competitiveness:

- perfect competition;
- monopolistic competition (or imperfect competition);
- oligopoly;
- monopoly.

7.2 *Perfect competition*

The term **perfect** should be interpreted to mean *unrestricted* rather than implying some form of approval. A perfectly competitive market is defined in terms of the following conditions:

1. **Many firms** competing, each intending to maximize profits.
2. All firms are selling a **homogeneous product**, i.e. the output of one firm is a perfect substitute for the output of any other firm in the market.

3. **Perfect information**, i.e. all relevant information regarding the market is freely available to all concerned.
4. **Freedom of entry and exit**, i.e. there are no obstacles to new firms entering the market or to existing firms leaving the market.

Implications

The many firms condition precludes the possibility of collusion on the part of suppliers and ensures a competitive environment. A homogeneous product implies that competition will be exclusively based on price; when choosing whom to trade with consumers will be solely concerned with the price being charged. Freedom of entry implies that if existing firms are earning supernormal profits (Section 6.2) new entrants will arrive causing the industry to expand. Losses will cause the industry to contract given freedom of exit. Perfect information simply precludes any complications that could arise (speculation, insider dealing, consumers being mislead, etc.) if less than perfect information existed.

If any firm in this market was to attempt to charge a price even slightly above its competitors it would sell nothing. Therefore, trade will only take place at the prevailing market price. At this price each firm will be faced with a **perfectly elastic demand curve** (i.e. horizontal). In this market all firms are *price-takers*. Given the small size of the firm relative to the industry (i.e. all the firms in the market) if an individual firm was to alter the quantity it supplied it would have no noticeable effect on overall market conditions.

The prevailing market price will be determined by the interaction of the overall supply and demand in the market. The choice facing the individual firm concerns the quantity it wishes to supply at the prevailing market price as illustrated in Figure 7.1.

The equilibrium price and quantity in the market (P_0Q_0) is determined at the intersection of the market supply (S) and market demand (D) in Figure 7.1(a). At

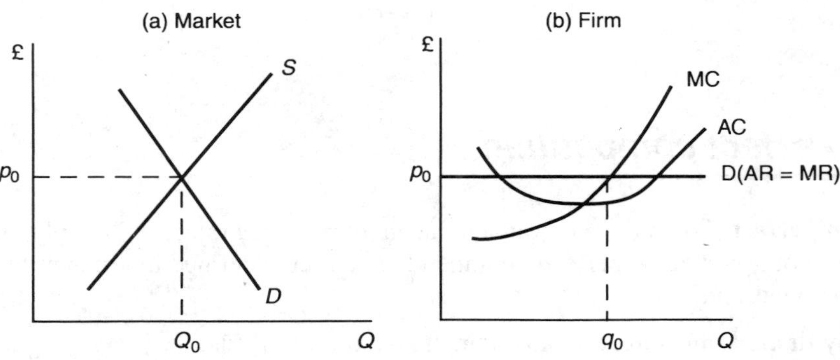

Figure 7.1: *Perfect competition: the market and the firm*

this price the individual firm is faced with a perfectly elastic demand curve (Figure 7.1(b)) and must decide on the quantity it is willing to supply. Given that the firm is a profit-maximizer (by assumption) it will produce that level of output where MC = MR. This is q_0 in Figure 7.1(b) (note Q_0 is assumed to be extremely large compared to q_0).

Short-run and long-run equilibrium of the firm

In the short run it is possible that firms in a perfectly competitive market are making supernormal profits (TR > TC). However, these supernormal profits will entice new firms into the market. The result of this will be for the market supply curve to shift outward and the market price to fall. This process will continue as long as supernormal profits persist as illustrated in Figure 7.2.

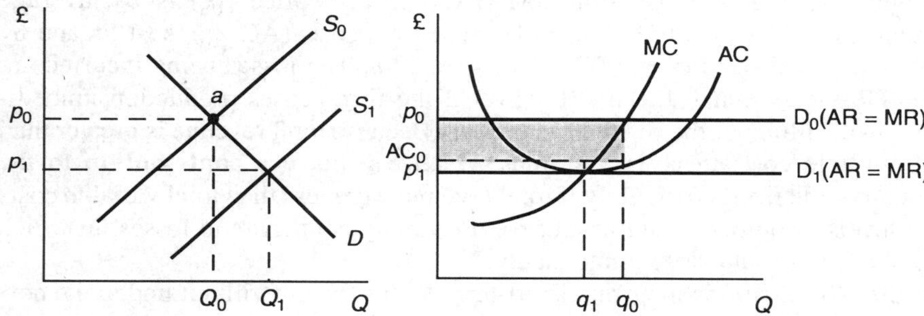

Figure 7.2: *Short-run and long-run equilibrium*

The initial market equilibrium is at point *a* with p_0 and Q_0 the equilibrium price and quantity. At this price the individual firm maximizes profit by producing q_0. However, given that average revenue (p_0) is greater than average cost (AC_0), at this level of output the firm is making supernormal profit (equal to shaded area). The existence of supernormal profits attracts new firms causing the market supply curve to move rightwards ($S_0 \rightarrow S_1$). As the industry expands ($Q_0 \rightarrow Q_1$) the market price falls ($p_0 \rightarrow p_1$) and continues to do so while supernormal profits are available. In the long run no supernormal profits are being earned by the individual firm. The new price is at p_1, the individual firm produces q_1 and at this output AR = AC (i.e. normal profits).

There are no guarantees that firms will make supernormal profits, even in the short run. In fact it may be that firms are incurring losses in the short run but their best option is to continue producing rather than to close as illustrated in Figure 7.3 on the next page.

MC = MR at an output of q_0. At this output average cost is greater than average revenue ($AC_0 > p_0$) implying losses. However, as AR > AVC the **loss-minimizing**

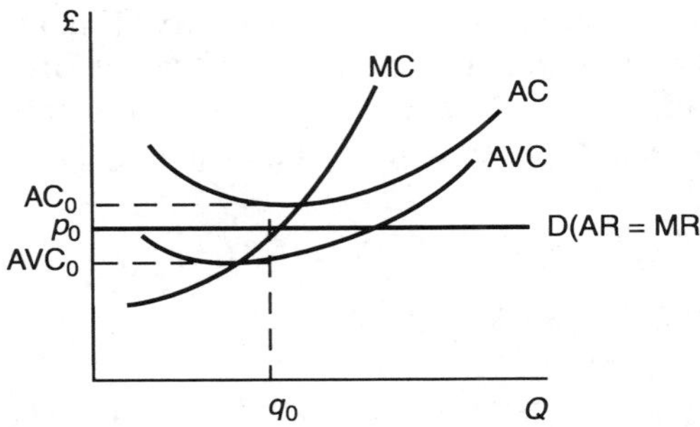

Figure 7.3: *Loss-minimizing strategy*

strategy is to continue producing q_0 in the short run. For example, assume in Figure 7.3 that average total cost (AC_0) is £10, price (p_o) is £9, average variable cost (AVC_0) is £8 and q_0 is 1m. The total costs (AC_0q_0) is £10m and by implication total fixed costs (TC – TVC) are £2m. The losses being incurred are £1m (TR – TC = £9m – £10m). However if the firm ceases production immediately it will still incur the fixed costs of £2m. Because total revenue is greater than total variable costs there is a surplus which can make a **contribution** to the payment of the fixed costs. Only if total revenue were less than total variable costs at all levels of output would production inevitably contribute to losses, in which case, the firm should close immediately.

If the typical firm is incurring short-term losses then it will not undertake new investment in this industry. In the longer term firms will leave the industry, aware that they can do better elsewhere. The industry supply curve will shift to the left causing the price to rise. This process will continue till the remaining firms in the contracted industry are in a position to make normal profits. This is the opposite of the process illustrated in Figure 7.2 but the long-run equilibrium is similar.

The nature of long-run equilibrium

The conditions that prevail in long-run equilibrium in perfect competition are the following:

- MC = MR – firms are maximizing profits;
- AC = AR – firms are only making normal profits;
- MC = *P* – there is an optimum use of resources (Section 6.4);
- LRAC is at a minimum – firms are producing at the economically efficient level;
- *P* = LRAC – consumers are paying a price equal to the lowest possible average cost.

Figure 7.4 illustrates these conditions. At point *a* we have *P* = MR = MC = AC.

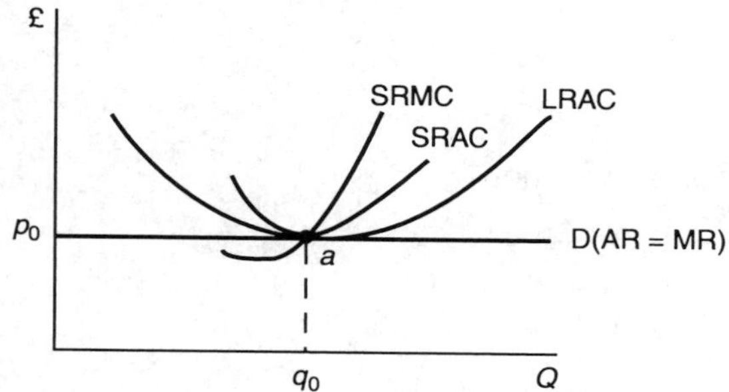

Figure 7.4: *Long-run equilibrium of the firm in perfect competition*

The perfectly competitive model has desirable features from the consumers' perspective. Competition forces firms to be efficient and the benefits of this efficiency are passed on to consumers.

Critics of the model are inclined to dismiss it because of its *unrealistic assumptions* and the difficulty of finding a perfectly competitive industry in the real world. Perfect information rarely exists; economies of scale in many sectors preclude *many firms* competing; most industries are trading **differentiated** rather than homogeneous products, etc.

However some sectors do approximate to the perfectly competitive model and either way it is instructive to discuss the implications if industries fail to satisfy some of the assumptions. Firms hiring videotapes are operating in a highly competitive environment (easy entry, homogenous products, many firms). It is reasonable to assume that supernormal profits will not be a long-term feature of this sector. On the other hand governments have a tendency to restrict entry to certain sectors by reserving the right to licence suppliers (for example, taxis and pubs in Dublin). If supernormal profits exist in these sectors then the absence of freedom of entry will enable them to persist.

The supply curve of the firm and the industry

The profit-maximizing firm produces where MC = MR. However for the firm in perfect competition the marginal revenue and the market price are equivalent so that in fact the firm produces where MC = P. Due to this latter relationship the marginal cost curve is the supply curve of the perfectly competitive firm.

Figure 7.5 illustrates alternative market prices and the corresponding horizontal demand curves facing a firm. At a price of p_0 the firm will produce q_0, at p_1 production is q_1, at p_2 the firm produces q_2 (at least in the short term to minimize losses). However at a price of p_3 the best strategy is to cease production immediately as further production would add to losses.

That segment of the MC curve lying above the AVC curve represents a relationship between market price and the quantity the firm would be willing to

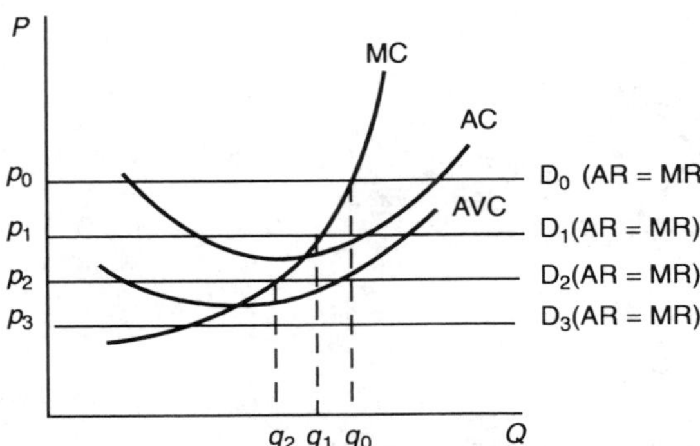

Figure 7.5: *The supply curve of the firm in perfect competition*

produce. In other words, this is the (short run) supply curve of the firm. The (short run) industry supply curve of Figure 7.1(a) is arrived at by taking a **horizontal summation** of the supply curves of the individual firms. The industry supply curve can be regarded as the industry marginal cost curve as it is simply the summation of the MC curves of the individual firms.

The long run industry supply curve

Significant **internal** economies of scale would not be consistent with perfect competition. If there were significant scale economies competitive pressure would force firms to expand in size in order to exploit them. This would result in **concentration** in the industry which would be inconsistent with the **many firms** assumption.

The existence of **external economies of scale**, however, would not be inconsistent with the perfectly competitive assumptions. External economies are efficiency gains that all firms in an industry can benefit from due to the expansion of the industry. The growth of an industry (in this case due to extra firms) can give rise to improvements in support facilities (banking, education, training, infrastructure, etc.).

The nature of external economies (or diseconomies) will determine the shape of the long-run industry supply curve. As the industry expands it might do so with constant unit costs, falling unit costs or rising unit costs. Figure 7.6 illustrates the three possibilities.

It is assumed that the industries are expanding in response to rising demand ($D_0 \rightarrow D_1 \rightarrow D_2$). For example in Figure 7.6(a) the initial equilibrium is at point *a*. The increased demand ($D_0 \rightarrow D_1$) creates a new short-run equilibrium at point *b* where price is higher ($p_0 \rightarrow p_1$). The increase in price results in supernormal profits causing the industry to expand ($S_0 \rightarrow S_1$). The new long-run equilibrium is at point *c*. Further expansion results in a new long-run equilibrium at point *d*.

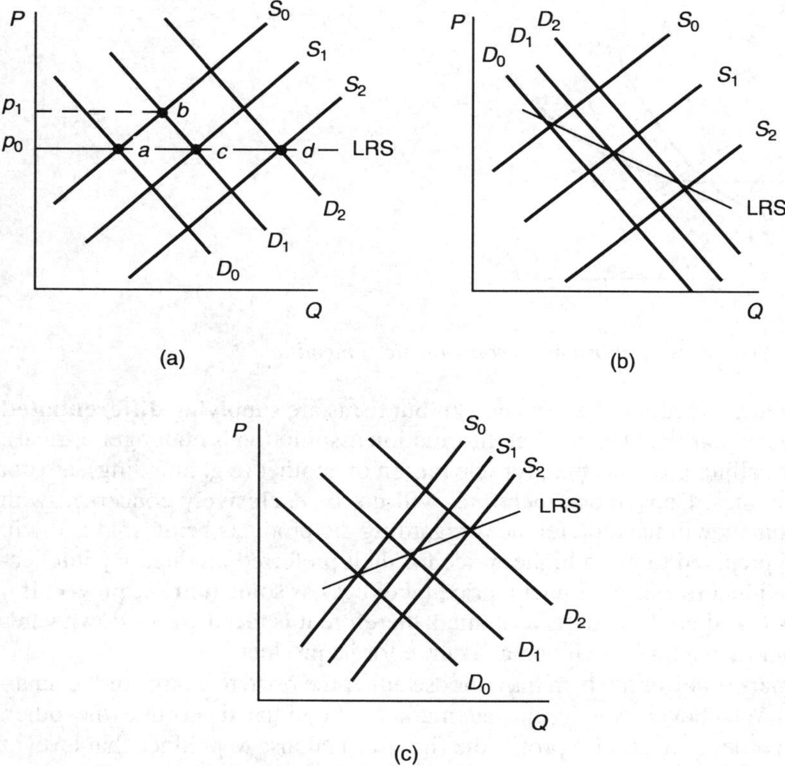

Figure 7.6: *(a) Constant cost expansion; (b) Falling cost expansion; (c) Rising cost expansion*

The long-run supply curve is arrived at by joining up points *a*, *c* and *d*. Figure 7.6(a) represents an industry expanding at constant unit cost implying no external economies or diseconomies. Figure 7.6(b) represents an industry expanding with falling unit costs implying external economies. Figure 7.6(c) represents an industry expanding with rising unit costs implying external diseconomies. External diseconomies might be the result of rising input prices due to increased exploitation of relevant resources.

7.3 Monopolistic competition

To get from perfect competition to monopolistic competition it is sufficient to relax just one of the assumptions of perfect competition, the homogeneous product assumption. This market structure is characterised by **many** profit-maximizing

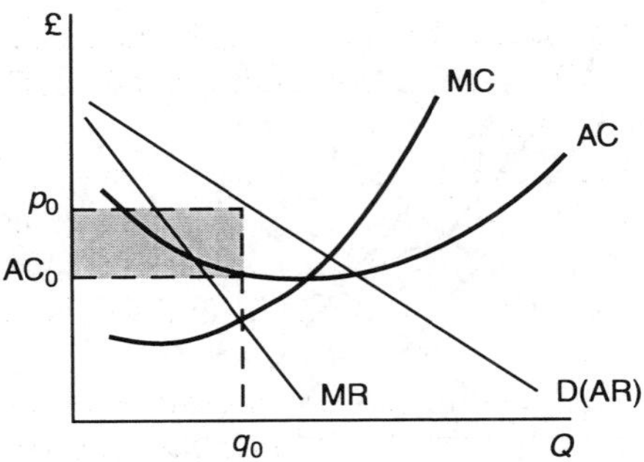

Figure 7.7: *Short-run equilibrium in monopolistic competition*

firms competing, freedom of entry and exit but firms are supplying **differentiated products** to the market. (The perfect information assumption is no longer critical).

Firms are selling products that, for one reason or another (e.g. branding), are not perfect substitutes. Consumers, therefore, will not be exclusively concerned with price. Consumers will have preferences regarding the products being sold and will therefore be prepared to pay a higher price for their preferred product. By implication the individual firm is no longer a price-taker but has some **market power**. If it raises prices it will not lose all its customers therefore it is faced with a downward-sloping rather than a horizontal demand curve for its product.

Having market power the firm may choose either the price to charge or the quantity to sell. Whichever one is chosen market conditions determine the other. However, in order to maximise profits the firm must choose to produce that level of output where MC = MR. In the short run market conditions may allow this firm to make supernormal profits. Figure 7.7 represents a possible short-run equilibrium for a firm in an imperfectly competitive market.

The firm is maximizing profits by operating where MC = MR. The result is an equilibrium quantity of q_0 and price of p_0. Given that total revenue is greater than total cost ($p_0q_0 > AC_0q_0$) the firm is making supernormal profits (shaded area). Given the assumption of freedom of entry these supernormal profits can only exist in the short term.

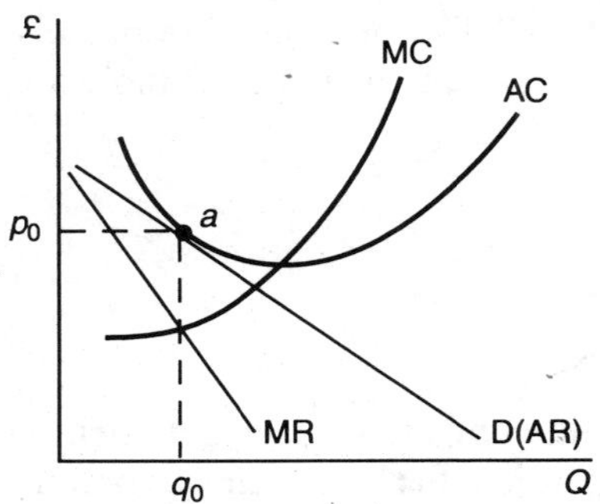

Figure 7.8: *Long-run equilibrium in monopolistic competition*

The existence of supernormal profits attracts new firms to the industry. The long-run conditions for the firm are: MC = MR (profit maximization); TR = TC (normal profits). Figure 7.8 illustrates these conditions.

To interpret Figure 7.8 it is important to realize that the AC curve cannot be below the AR curve at any point for if AR > AC supernormal profits would be possible. However there must be some point where AR = AC (point *a*) to enable normal profits to be earned. For point *a* to be a profit maximizing situation MC must equal MR at the same level of output (q_0).

Getting from the short-run equilibrium of Figure 7.7 to the long-run equilibrium of Figure 7.8 can be explained as follows. As new firms enter the industry consumers are given more choice. Existing firms will lose customers causing their demand curves to move inward to the left. This process continues until supernormal profits no longer exist.

There is an interesting feature of the LR equilibrium as illustrated in Figure 7.8. Given that the firm has a downward-sloping demand curve which is tangent to an U-shaped average cost curve, the point of tangency (point *a*) must be to the left of and above the lowest point on the AC curve. In other words, firms are not using their resources as efficiently as possible. Unit costs would be lower if the firm expanded production, but it is not profitable for the firm to do so. This is referred to as the **excess capacity theorem**.

Consumers have greater choice due to differentiated products but there is a cost in terms of inefficiency in production and consequently higher prices.

7.4 Monopoly

In the case of monopoly there is a **sole supplier** of a particular good or service. Furthermore, the monopolist is protected by **barriers to entry** which prevent new firms entering the industry.

As we saw when discussing monopolistic competition, once we drop the assumption of a homogeneous product all firms become monopoly suppliers of *their product*. The extent of market power depends on the availability of substitutes. When discussing monopolistic competition the assumption was that a wide range of close substitutes did exist. When discussing monopoly it is necessary to assume the absence of close substitutes.

Barriers to entry can take a number of forms. For example they may be legal barriers based on patents or government licences; economies of scale which give the existing firm cost advantages; control over an essential raw material, etc. The important point is that the presence of the barrier means that if supernormal profits are being earned by the monopolist they may persist *even in the long run*.

Where different suppliers are supplying products with high cross elasticities of demand monopoly power is limited. For example the railways may be controlled by a monopoly supplier but there is competition from alternative modes of transport (aircraft, coaches, private transport). So, there is not a monopoly supplier of transport as the consumer has choice.

Under conditions of monopoly the consumer has no choice from whom to pur-

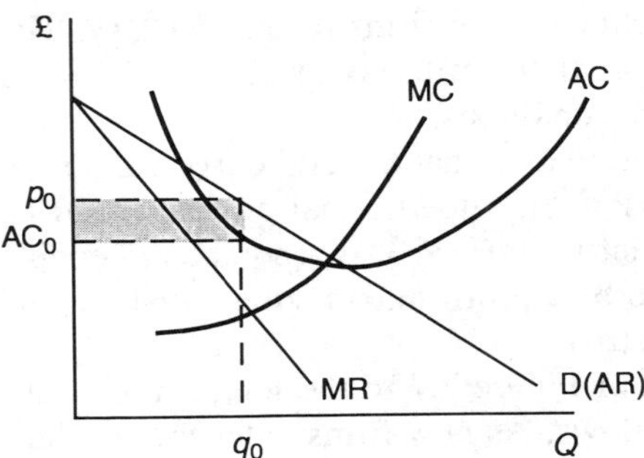

Figure 7.9: *Equilibrium of the monopolist*

chase. The demand curve facing the monopolist is, therefore, the total market demand for the product. Having market power the monopolist may choose the price to charge or the quantity to sell. However if it wishes to maximize profits the monopolist must produce where MC = MR as illustrated in Figure 7.9.

The profit-maximizing equilibrium of the monopolist is where MC = MR resulting in an output of q_0 and a price of p_0. Provided TR > TC at this point monopoly profits will be earned. At an output of q_0 supernormal profits equal to $(p_0 - AC_0)q_0$ exist in Figure 7.9 (the shaded area).

If there were freedom of entry to the market these profits would attract new firms into the industry. Given barriers to entry, however, these supernormal profits will persist into the long run. There is therefore no need to distinguish between the short-run and the long-run equilibrium of the monopolist.

Monopoly profits do not perform the allocative function that profits in a competitive environment play. Where there is freedom of entry supernormal profits act as a signal to firms to allocate more resources to the sector concerned. Under conditions of monopoly however, monopoly profits merely serve to transfer income from consumers to the producer. This is one of the major criticisms of monopoly and is the reason why governments often seek either to prevent or regulate them.

A further criticism is that all else being equal the monopolist when compared to the perfectly competitive industry restricts output and charges a higher price to the consumer. When discussing perfect competition we saw that the supply curve of the industry was equivalent to the marginal cost curve of that industry (see Figure 7.5 and relevant discussion). Equilibrium in perfect competition therefore is where the industry marginal cost curve intersects the market demand curve as illustrated in Figure 7.10.

MC represents the marginal cost curve of the industry. D is the market demand curve and MR the corresponding marginal revenue curve. Under perfectly competitive conditions as the industry marginal cost curve is the same as the industry supply curve equilibrium would be where supply equals demand (point *a*) with a price of p_0 and a quantity of q_0. If we now assume that this industry is turned into

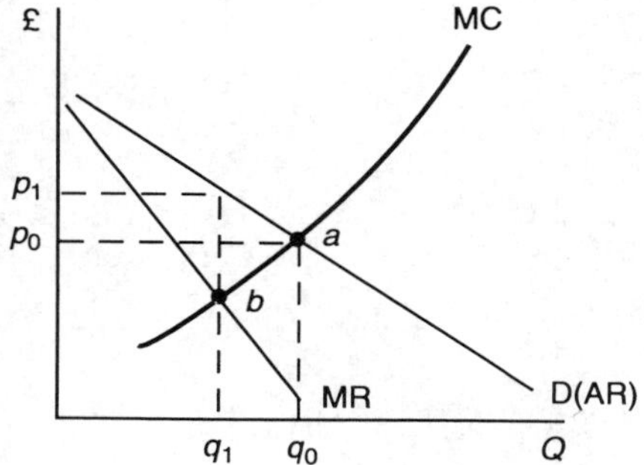

Figure 7.10: *Monopoly and perfect competition compared*

a (multi-plant) monopoly the profit-maximizing strategy is to set MC = MR (point *b*). The resulting equilibrium is a price of p_1 and a quantity of q_1. The monopolist has restricted output ($q_0 \rightarrow q_1$) and charged a higher price ($p_0 \rightarrow p_1$).

The issue here is not one of firms being more or less ethical. It is simply the logical outcome of the same strategy – profit maximization – but in different market conditions. Being price takers the competitive firms expand production up to the point where MC = P (remember $P \equiv$ MR for the firm in perfect competition) whereas the monopolist stops short of this, producing where MC = MR (but for the monopolist MR < P).

This particular criticism of monopoly depends critically on the assumption that the monopolized industry is no more efficient than it would be as an atomized perfectly competitive one. In practice, economies of scale exist in many sectors and a perfectly competitive structure would be inefficient for those sectors. If the monopolist achieves economics of scale the costs would be lower than for the competitive industry and it would be wrong to use the same MC curve to represent both (as we did in Figure 7.10). With economies of scale the monopolized industry could be selling more and at a lower price than would be the case if the industry were perfectly competitive.

The implications of this for public policy is that a blanket opposition to monopolies would be inappropriate. Government have legal powers to prevent monopolies and mergers. However if the potential monopoly can demonstrate that it would be more efficient than the (competitive) alternative, governments are unlikely to stand in the way.

Absence of a supply curve

It is not possible to derive a **supply curve** for a monopolised industry. In a perfectly competitive environment firms are **price-takers**, that is, they respond to market price rather than individually determining it. When market price rises firms in perfect competition respond by supplying more. However, when firms

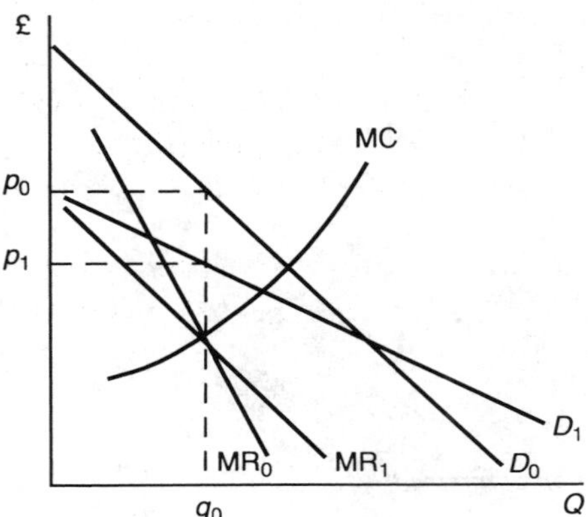

Figure 7.11: *Absence of normal supply curve under monopoly*

have **market power** they need to take account of the effect their own actions will have on market price.

When a firm is faced with a downward sloping demand curve there is not necessarily a unique relationship between market price and the quantity the firm is willing to supply as Figure 7.11 illustrates.

Setting MC = MR does not necessarily result in a unique market price. Depending on whether demand is D_0 or D_1, the market price will be p_0 or p_1 for the same quantity supplied q_0. Put another way, for different prices (p_0 or p_1) the monopolist supplies the same quantity (q_0).

7.5 Oligopoly

Oligopoly is a market structure whereby the market is dominated by a few relatively large firms. These firms are aware of each other and realise that the actions of one (e.g. a price cut) will have an impact on the others (e.g. loss of sales). There is, therefore, a high degree of **interdependence** between oligopolists. When one firm is deciding to change the price it charges it will be obliged to consider the reactions of its competitors.

Despite the prevalence of oligopolistic markets in the real economy (banking, computers, cars, energy, transport, etc.) the economic theory of oligopoly is less robust than for other market structures. The problem has to do with the degree of **uncertainty**. Firms are unsure how competitors will respond to their actions but must try to anticipate. Whatever **strategy** firms adopt it must include a response to the response of competitors and so on.

Oligopolistic markets tend to have the following characteristics:

- Non-price competition – *Price wars* can be mutually damaging so firms may compete on quality, advertising, service, etc. However new entrants may rock the boat by competing aggressively on price.

- Price leadership – Prices have to be changed in response to industry-wide changes in costs so a price-leader may emerge to signal such price changes.
- Cartels – One way to reduce uncertainty and to maximize joint profits is to collude either formally or informally.
- Protection of market share – Success in these markets is often measured in terms of market share. Defence of market share is likely to be a primary concern.

The kinked-demand curve

Consider a small number of firms supplying differentiated products to a particular market. The model makes the following assumptions regarding behaviour:

- If one firm **lowers price** competitors will regard this as a threat (to market share) and respond by lowering their prices by a similar amount.
- If one firm **raises price** the response of competitors will be to keep their prices constant.

This **asymmetric response** on the part of competitors implies a kinked-demand curve facing the individual firm. By raising price many customers will be lost but by lowering price few customers will be gained. Above the **prevailing price** demand will be price-elastic whereas below the prevailing price demand will be price-inelastic as Figure 7.12 illustrates.

The prevailing price and quantity for a typical firm are p_0 and q_0. Above p_0 demand for the firms product is price-elastic, below p_0 demand is price-inelastic. The result is a kinked-demand curve for the firms product. If the firm were to raise price market share would fall significantly as other firms keep their prices fixed. If the firm lowers price others do likewise, in which case there will be some increase in sales (but not market share) due to rising market demand.

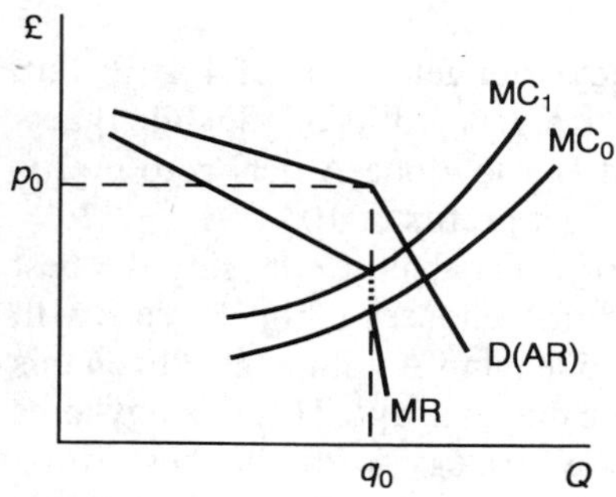

Figure 7.12: *Kinked-demand curve*

The kinked-demand curve implies a marginal revenue curve which has a discontinuity (vertical section) in line with the kink. This discontinuity may help to explain one of the features of these markets which is the relatively **stable prices**. Even if costs change, e.g. $MC_0 \rightarrow MC_1$, provided marginal cost continues to intersect MR along the vertical segment the profit-maximizing strategy (MC = MR) is to maintain the existing price and quantity.

The strength of the model is that it helps to explain the tendency for price stability in these markets. However a major weakness is that it fails to explain how the initial equilibrium price and quantity emerges in the first place or how equilibrium would be restored if there was some shock to the market.

7.6 *Game theory*

Game theory is a branch of mathematics which has been developed specifically to analyse decision-making in situations of uncertainty. Not surprisingly it has been applied to oligopolistic markets. In the following two-firm (duopoly) example the firms have to decide on a pricing strategy: quite simply whether to charge a **high price** or a **low price**.

The following **pay-off matrix** indicates the outcomes, measured in profits, for the different choices:

		B's choice of price Low	B's choice of price High
A's choice of price	Low	$\Pi_A = 4 \quad \Pi_B = 4$	$\Pi_A = 15 \quad \Pi_B = 0$
	High	$\Pi_A = 0 \quad \Pi_B = 15$	$\Pi_A = 10 \quad \Pi_B = 10$

Pay off matrix

If A charges a low price and B does likewise they both get profits of 4. If B were to charge a high price in response to A's low price A gets profits of 15 while B gets zero. By contrast if A charges a high price and B a low one A gets zero profits while B gets 15. If both charge a high price both get profits of 10.

The assumption is made that your competitor is capable of choosing the best option in response to your choice. For example if A chooses a high price B will respond with a low price thus getting profits of 15 leaving A with none. Given this assumption a ***minimax*** strategy is the appropriate one to adopt. This strategy aims to *minimize the maximum loss*, or, choose the strategy with the best worst outcome. The worst outcome for A if it chooses a low price is a profit of 4 whereas the worst outcome with a high price is a profit of zero. Firm A should therefore opt for a low price. The best response from B to A's choice of a low price is also to choose a low price resulting in a profit of 4 for both.

Choosing a low price is here an example of a ***dominant strategy***. A dominant strategy is one whereby you stick to your original choice irrespective of your competitors response. For example having chosen the low price it does not make sense for A to switch to a high price even if B also chooses a low price.

The equilibrium outcome in this ***game*** is for both competitors to charge a low price. However the temptation to collude is obvious. If both **agree** to charge a high price profits can be increased from 4 to 10.

Contestable markets

Barriers to entry may exist in oligopolistic markets. For example, the start-up costs for new entrants may be prohibitive. This would make it easier for existing firms to collude. However, there may be relative ease of entry into (and exit from) some markets with a high degree of concentration, in which case these markets are referred to as *contestable*. For example, in the air-transport industry companies may be able to switch aircraft into and out of particular routes. Existing firms in constestable markets are unlikely to be in a position to make supernormal profits in the long run. If existing firms were earning supernormal profits, this would attract new firms into the market. The entry of new firms into the market would raise the level of competition which in turn would lead to falling prices and the removal of supernormal profits.

REVISION FOCUS CHAPTER SEVEN

Key Areas

- Perfect competition
  → assumptions and implications → short- and long-run equilibrium of firm → loss-minimization and closure decision • supply curve of firm and industry
- Monopolistic competition
  → assumptions and implications → short- and long-run equilibrium of firm → excess capacity → choice versus efficiency
- Monopoly
  → assumptions and implications → barriers to entry → equilibrium of monopolist → criticisms of monopoly → in defence of monopoly
- Oligopoly
  → characteristics of market → kinked demand curve → game theory → contestable markets

Self Test

(1) If a perfectly competitive firm is in a short-run profit-maximizing equilibrium then both of the following conditions must hold: MC = MR, AC = AR — T/F

(2) A perfectly competitive firm might make supernormal profits in the short run but not in the long run — T/F

(3) Even if a firm is making losses, provided TR is greater than TVC the firm should remain in business, at least in the short term — T/F

(4) In long-run equilibrium, the firm in monopolistic competition is producing where AC is at a minimum — T/F

(5) When comparing perfect competition and monopoly the monopolist will always produce less and charge a higher price — T/F

(6) Freedom of entry into a market implies that supernormal profits will not be earned in the long run — T/F

(7) Oligopolistic markets are necessarily characterized by intense price-competition — T/F

(8) Whatever the market structure, all profit-maximizing firms will produce where MC = MR — T/F

Discussion Topics

- In the long-run equilibrium of perfect competition P = MC = AC = AR. Explain and illustrate.
- Only barriers to entry into a market will safeguard supernormal profits in the long run. Explain.
- With monopolistic competition there is a trade-off between efficiency and choice. Explain.

CHAPTER 8

MARKETS FOR FACTORS OF PRODUCTION

8.1 *Factor markets*

Firms supply goods or services to the product markets but they must also hire or purchase the required factors of production (labour, capital, etc.) in the factor markets.

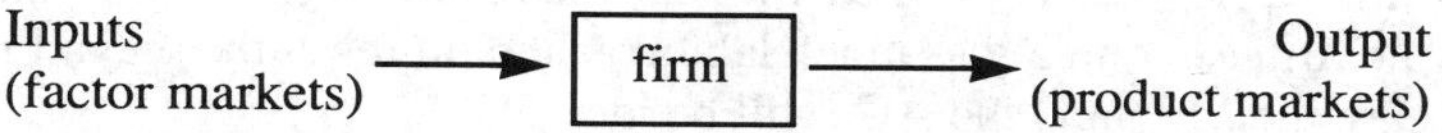

The firm's demand for factors of production is referred to as *a derived demand.* It derives from the demand for the firm's output in the product market. The strategy the firm is pursuing in the product market will determine the firm's behaviour in the factor markets. For example, if the firm is pursuing a profit-maximizing strategy in the product market (i.e. producing that level of output where MC = MR) then its behaviour in the factor markets must be consistent with profit maximization.

The standard analysis of factor markets is based on *marginal productivity theory.* The approach is to focus on the effect that employing an additional unit of the factor will have in both the product and the factor market. If employing an additional unit adds more to revenue received in the product market than to costs incurred in the factor market then profit maximization requires that it should be employed.

8.2 Labour markets

The issue for the firm is what level of labour to employ.

When deciding on the level of labour to employ the firm must compare the effect employing additional workers will have on costs and revenue.Three measures of cost are of interest.

- The total cost of labour (TC_L): simply the total cost of employing a particular type of labour. It is the wage (*W*) paid times the number of workers employed (*L*)

$$TC_L = WL.$$

Table 8.1

L	W (AC_L)	TC_L	MC_L
10	£5 ph	£50 ph	
11	£6 ph	£66 ph	16 ph
12	£7 ph	£84 ph	18 ph

- The average cost of labour (AC_L): the total cost of labour divided by the number of workers employed. The AC_L is the same as the wage being paid (it is assumed that workers of the same type receive the same pay).
- The marginal cost of labour (MC_L): the additional cost incurred by the firm as a result of employing an extra worker

The effect on these costs as the firm employs additional workers will depend on the level of competition in the labour market. Two possibilities exist.

- The firm is a price-taker – if the firm is a price-taker in the labour market this means the firm can employ as much labour as it requires at the prevailing wage. In this case the MC_L and the AC_L will be identical.
- The firm as monopsonist – monopsonists are in the unfortunate position of driving the price up against themselves as they purchase more. In the labour market the monposonist must offer a higher wage to attract additional workers. In this case the MC_L will be higher than AC_L.

The problem for the monopsonist is that not only must the additional worker be paid a higher wage than the existing ones but the existing ones must also get the higher wage. It follows that there can be a big difference between the MC_L and the AC_L in the case of monopsony as Table 8.1 above illustrates.

L stands for the number of workers being employed and *W* for the wage per hour that must be paid by the firm to attract them. When 10 workers are being employed the corresponding wage is £5 per hour implying a total wage bill (TC_L) of £50 ph. However if the firm wishes to employ 11 workers it must raise the wage to £6 ph if an 11th worker is to be attracted. As all workers are assumed to get the same wage the total wage bill will be £66 ph. The marginal cost of the 11th worker is therefore £16 despite being paid a wage of only £6.

Figure 8.1 illustrates the general shape of the AC_L and MC_L facing the firm in the labour market when the firm is a monopsonist. As the MC_L is rising by assumption the AC_L must also be rising but not as steeply. As the AC_L line indicates the wage that must be paid for different levels of employment it is a relationship between price (the wage) and quantity (of labour). In effect the AC_L represents the **supply curve of labour to the firm**.

Figure 8.2 illustrates the general shape of the AC_L and MC_L facing the firm in the labour market when the firm is a price taker. As by assumption the firm can employ additional workers at the prevailing market wage the AC_L and the MC_L are equivalent and equal to the prevailing wage (W). As the AC_L represents

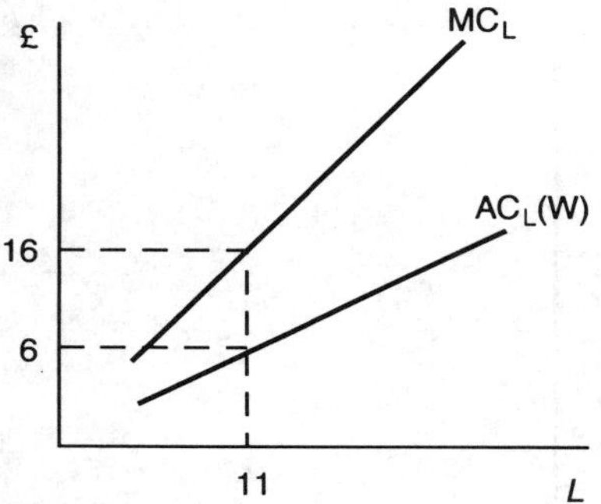

Figure 8.1: *Average and marginal costs of labour for monopsonist*

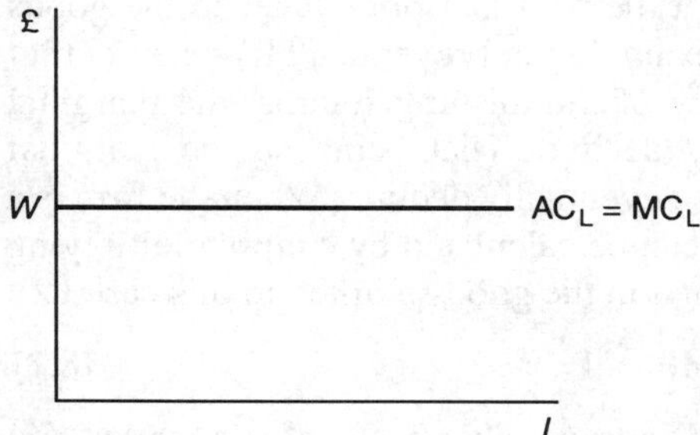

Figure 8.2: *Average and marginal costs of labour when the firm is a price-taker*

the supply curve of labour, the price-taker is faced with a perfectly elastic (horizontal) supply curve of labour.

Turning to the product market we wish to know what effect the additional worker will have on revenue earned for additional goods sold. The concept of interest is:

- The Marginal Revenue Product of labour (MRP_L).

The MRP_L is defined as the *change in total revenue resulting from the sale of the output of an additional worker*. The MRP_L depends on two things: the additional output resulting from the additional worker and the price that can be charged for this extra output. The additional output from the worker is the marginal product of labour (MP_L). We have seen (Section 5.4) that the MP_L is subject to the law of diminishing returns and must therefore eventually decline in the short run. The price that can be charged for the additional output depends on whether or not the firm is a price taker in the goods market (Section 6.1). If the firm is a price-taker it can sell additional output at the prevailing market price, if not it must reduce the selling price to sell the extra output.

Table 8.2: *MP_L and MRP_L*

L	*Q*	MP_L	TR (£)	MRP_L(£)
1	20	20	40	40
2	50	30	100	60
3	90	40	180	80
4	140	50	280	100
5	180	40	360	80
6	204	24	408	48
7	217	13	434	26
8	224	7	448	14

Table 8.2 illustrates the derivation of the MRP_L schedule using the production schedule from Table 5.1. It is assumed that the firm is a price taker in the goods market where the market price is £2. For example total revenue (TR) when output (*Q*) is 50 is 50 × £2 = £100. Given the law of diminishing returns, the marginal product of labour (MP_L) must eventually decline. That being so the marginal revenue product of labour (MRP_L) must also eventually decline. When the firm is a price-taker in the goods market the MRP_L can be calculated by simply multiplying the MP_L by the particular price being charged in the goods market, in this case £2.

$$MRP_L = MP_L \times P \qquad [8.1]$$

The above formula only works if the firm is a price-taker in the goods market and a unique price exists. Table 8.3 illustrates the derivation of the MRP_L schedule when the firm has monopoly power in the goods market and is faced with a downward-sloping demand curve.

The second and third columns of Table 8.3 represent the demand curve facing the firm in the goods market. For example if the firm wishes to raise sales from 90 to 140 it must reduce price from £1.90 to £1.85. The MRP_L is calculated by subtracting the total revenue generated at different levels of employment. For example, to calculate the MRP_L for the 5th worker (MRP_5) subtract TR_4 (£259) from TR_5

Table 8.3: *$MRPL_L$ and VMP_L*

L	*Q*	P (£)	TR (£)	MRP_L (£)	VMP_L (£)
1	20	2	40	40	40
2	50	1.95	97.50	57.50	58.50
3	90	1.90	171	73.50	76
4	140	1.85	259	88	92.50
5	180	1.80	324	65	72
6	204	1.75	357	33	42
7	217	1.70	368.70	11.90	22.10
8	224	1.65	369.60	0.70	11.55

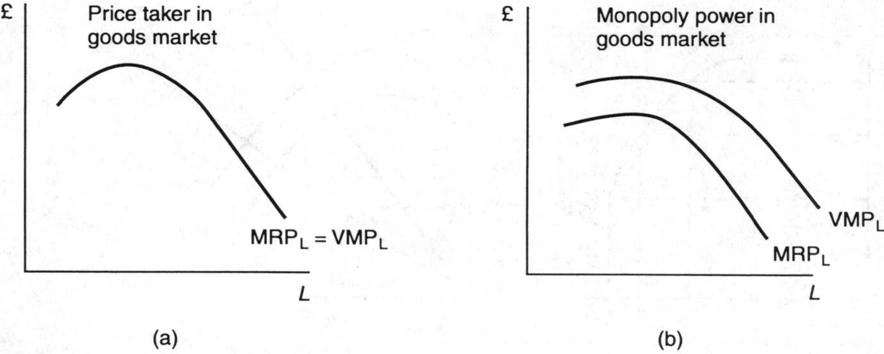

Figure 8.3: *Marginal revenue product of labour*

(£324) to get £65. Also calculated is the value of the marginal product of labour (VMP_L). This is simply what the additional output of each worker can be sold for and is arrived at by multiplying the MP_L by the corresponding price ($MP_L \times P$). When the firm is a price-taker the VMP_L and the MRP_L are equivalent. However where the firm has monopoly power in the goods market the VMP_L is greater than the MRP_L.

The general shape of the MRP_L and VMP_L curves are illustrated in Figure 8.3. For the price taker in the goods market the MRP_L and the VMP_L are identical [Figure 8.3(a)]. If the firm has monopoly power in the goods market the MRP_L will be less than the VMP_L [Figure 8.3(b)].

The profit maximizing level of employment

If by employing an additional worker more is added to revenue than is added to costs ($MRP_L > MC_L$) the profit maximizing firm should employ that worker. By adding more to total revenue than to total costs the effect must be to raise profits. By contrast if the additional worker adds more to costs than revenue ($MC_L > MRP_L$) the additional worker should not be employed.

The profit-maximizing level of employment for all firms is where:

$$MC_L = MRP_L \qquad [8.2]$$

If the firm is a price-taker in the labour market the average cost of labour, the wage and the marginal cost of labour are all identical (Figure 8.2). In this case Equation [8.2] can be rewritten as:

$$MC_L = W \qquad [8.3]$$

Equation [8.3] states that the profit-maximizing firm should employ labour up to the point where the marginal cost of employing one extra worker is equal to the wage that the worker must be paid.

Figure 8.4 illustrates the equilibrium level of employment for both the price-

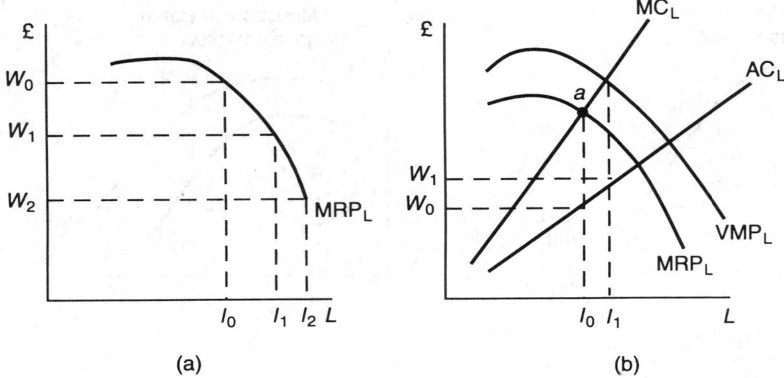

Figure 8.4: *The equilibrium level of employment for the firm*

taker in the labour market and the monopsonist. In Figure 8. (a) it is assumed that the firm is a price taker in both the product and labour market (perfect competition). Whatever the wage prevailing in the market this also represents the AC_L and the MC_L to the firm. To maximize profit the firm will employ that number of workers such that $W = MRP_L$. At a wage of w_0 the firm employs l_0 labour, at w_1 employment is l_1 at w_2 employment is l_2. The downward segment of the MRP_L curve is in fact *the firm's demand curve for labour*. It should be noted that at lower wages more employment is offered by the firm and vice versa.

In Figure 8.4(b) it is assumed that the firm is a monopsonist in the labour market ($MC_L > AC_L$) and has monopoly power in the goods market ($VMP_L > MRP_L$). To maximize profits the firm employs labour up to the point where $MC_L = MRP_L$ and thus offers l_0 workers employment at a wage of w_0. If the monopsonist was a price taker in the goods market the MRP_L curve would be the same as the VMP_L curve. In this case the level of employment offered would be l_1 at a wage of w_1. We have seen (Section 7.4) that monopolists tend to restrict output so not surprisingly they also tend to restrict employment.

In the perfectly competitive environment the worker receives a wage equal to the value of the marginal product of labour. Where monopsony and/or monopoly exists the worker receives a wage less than the value of the marginal product of labour.

Equilibrium in the labour market

The employment offered by the competitive firm at different wage levels was illustrated in Figure 8.4(a). The question arises: what determines the equilibrium wage in the competitive labour market? This equilibrium wage is determined by the total demand for labour by the industry and the total supply of labour to the industry.

As the competitive firm has a downward sloping demand curve for labour [Figure 8.4(a)] the competitive industry will likewise have a *downward sloping*

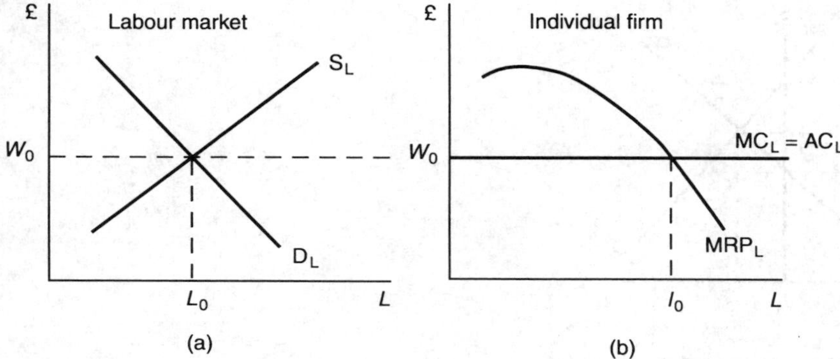

Figure 8.5: *Equilibrium in the competitive labour market*

demand curve for labour. Many workers have skills that are transferable between industries and workers newly entering the labour force will be attracted to industries offering higher wages. It is therefore reasonable to assume that one industry can attract additional workers by offering higher wages resulting in an *upward-sloping supply curve of labour to the industry* as Figure 8.5 illustrates.

The equilibrium wage in the perfectly competitive environment is determined at the intersection of the industry supply and demand curves for labour. W_0 is the equilibrium wage and L_0 is the equilibrium level of employment [Figure 8.5(a)]. The individual firm employs labour up to the point where the MRP_L is equal to this wage and offers l_0 employment [Figure 8.5 (b)]. It is assumed that l_0 is very small relative to L_0.

8.3 Relative Wages

The relative wage is concerned with the wage being received by one group of workers relative to another group. For example plumbers are likely to receive a high wage relative to roadsweepers but a low one relative to heart surgeons.

The relative wages will depend on three factors: the supply of labour to the particular labour market, the productivity of that labour and the price the product can be sold for in the goods market. The supply of labour will depend on such factors as the level of skill involved and how long it takes to acquire that skill and whether or not there are trade unions (Section 9.4) or professional associations restricting the supply of that labour.

If in Figure 8.6 the professional association can restrict the supply of labour to S_1 rather than the unrestricted supply of S_0, the equilibrium wage of members can be raised from w_0 to w_1. Whether total earnings for those employed ($w_1 l_1$) exceeds total earnings in the unrestricted case ($w_0 l_0$) depends on the price (or wage) *elasticity of demand for labour*.

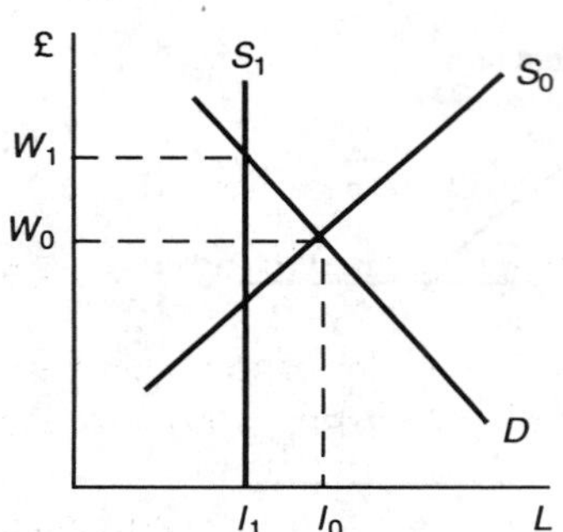

Figure 8.6: *Restricted supply of labour*

An increase in the demand for the good in the product market, by raising its price, will raised the MRP_L. This will cause the demand for labour to shift outward, as in Figure 8.7. Rising demand in the product market causes employment in the industry to rise ($l_0 \rightarrow l_1$) and the wage received by workers to rise ($w_0 \rightarrow w_1$). Obviously a fall in demand in the product market will have the opposite effect.

The effect of an increase in the physical productivity of labour is more ambiguous. All else being equal the MRP_L will rise causing the demand for labour to shift outwards. However if the industry is supplying more of the product the price can be expected to fall which will have the effect of reducing the MRP_L. Whether employment and incomes rise or fall will depend on the price elasticity of demand for the product. If demand is highly elastic there will be a big increase in demand for the product as price falls to the benefit of employment and income. For example rising productivity in the hi-tech sectors such as personal computers is leading to rising employment and output in these sectors, however rising productivity in, for example, the newspaper industry is more likely to lead to job loses in this sector.

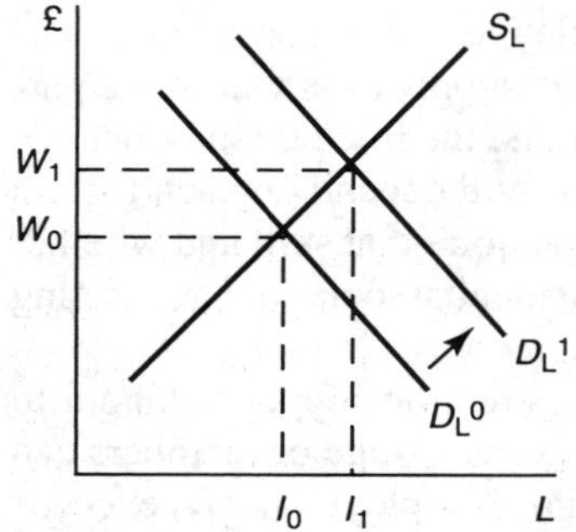

Figure 8.7: *The product market and the labour market*

8.4 The supply of labour

The total amount of labour available to an economy depends on a number of factors:

- the size of the population of working age – this determines the size of the potential labour force;
- the participation rate of the potential labour force – the participation rate represents the proportion either working or seeking employment and determines the actual size of the labour force;
- the individual's supply of labour – the number of working hours individual members of the labour force are willing to supply.

Except where migration of labour is a significant factor the size of the population of working age will not vary much in the short- term. Over the longer term, it will adjust to any changes in the size of the total population due to differences in birth and death rates.

The participation rate may be influenced by cultural factors. For example, changing perceptions of the role of women and men in society may lead to greater (or lesser) participation on the part of these groups. The availability of non-labour income and the expected real disposable income from employment are also factors. For example a relatively generous welfare system coupled with high taxes on low incomes may discourage participation thus causing ***voluntary unemployment*** (Section 15.4).

The individuals supply of labour may be determined by institutional factors. Terms and conditions of employment, including the length of the working week, may be the result of collective agreements negotiated by trades unions. Governments may impose legal upper limits on the number of hours (for example, the Irish government's implementation of the EU Social Chapter). Under these conditions the individual workers choice regarding the number of hours to work may be limited to the available legal overtime hours. But where institutional constraints do not exist (self-employed, contract work etc.), the worker will have greater freedom of choice regarding hours worked.

The individuals supply of labour

The analysis of the individual workers labour supply focuses on the ***trade off between leisure and income***. Time spent working represents a disutility to the worker in terms of leisure time forgone. Leisure time, however, has an opportunity cost in terms of the real disposable income forgone. It is assumed that there is a **diminishing marginal rate of substitution** (Section 4.1) between income and leisure – i.e. the fewer leisure hours the worker has, the greater the income per hour required if additional leisure hours are to be sacrificed and vice versa. Following the analysis in Chapter 4 the workers preferences can be represented by an indifference map.

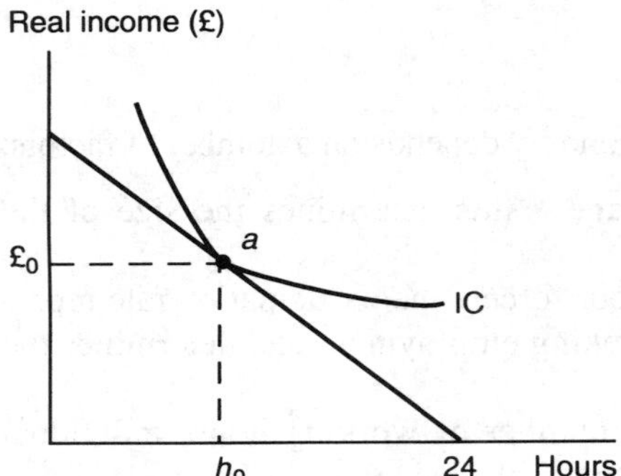

Figure 8.8: *The choice between leisure and income*

The workers *budget constraint* depends on the real hourly wage rate. The higher the hourly wage the steeper the budget line. For example, in Figure 8.8 an increase in the hourly wage would shift the budget line along the y-axis (more real income possible) while pivoting on the x-axis. The choice facing the worker concerns how much of the 24 hours available to spend working or at leisure. The worker maximizes utility from leisure and income at a point (a) where the indifference curve is tangent to the budget line. Leisure time is h_0 hours, while the remainder ($24 - h_0$ hours) is spent working for an income of $£_0$.

How will the worker respond to a rise in the hourly wage? The rise in the hourly wage shifts the budget constraint in Figure 8.8 outwards enabling the worker to establish a new equilibrium on a higher indifference curve. Whether the worker works more or less will depend on the income and substitution effects (Section 4.3) of the wage change. The higher wage makes leisure more expensive in terms of income forgone and work more rewarding in terms of income received. This will cause a ***substitution effect*** with the worker tending to substitute work for leisure. However if leisure is a ***normal good*** (Section 2.3) the worker will wish to have more leisure as income rises – a positive **income effect**. Whether the worker works more or less in response to the higher wage depends on the relative strengths of the income and substitution effects. Figure 8.9 illustrates the two possibilities.

In Figure 8.9(a) the substitution effect dominates causing the worker to work more (leisure hours fall from h_0 to h_1). In Figure 8.9 (b) the income effect dominates causing the worker to take more leisure ($h_0 \rightarrow h_1$) and therefore work less. The response of the worker illustrated in Figure 8.9(a) would imply a normal ***upward-sloping*** supply curve of labour; supplying more labour at a higher wage. The response illustrated in Figure 8.9(b) would imply a backward-bending supply curve of labour; as the wage rises the worker works less, preferring to have more leisure time. Figure 8.10 illustrates the two possibilities.

Up to a wage of w_0 in Figure 8.10 the substitution effect is greater than the income effect. Above w_0 the income effect dominates the substitution effect. With

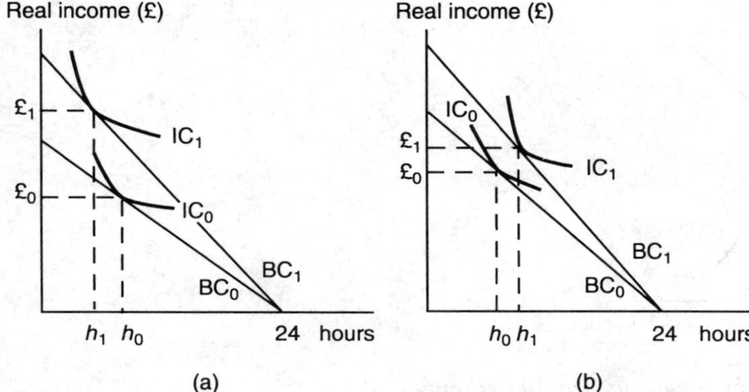

Figure 8.9: *Income and substitution effects in the labour market*

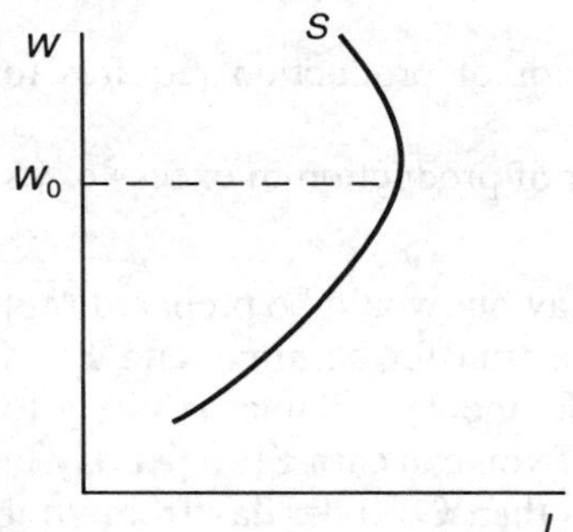

Figure 8.10: *Individual's supply of labour hours*

rising prosperity and relatively high levels of income it is not unreasonable that workers should opt for more leisure time. At high wages there may be a backward-bending supply curve of labour to the economy (ignoring migration). However this does not imply backward-bending supply curves of labour to particular firms or industries. Labour will always move between firms and industries in response to differences in pay. The firm or the industry can always attract more labour by paying more.

8.5 Transfer earnings and economic rent

Figure. 8.11 represents a competitive labour market with typical supply and demand curves for labour. The equilibrium wage and level of employment are w_0 and l_0 respectively. The total wage bill is $w_0 l_0$ which is identical to the total

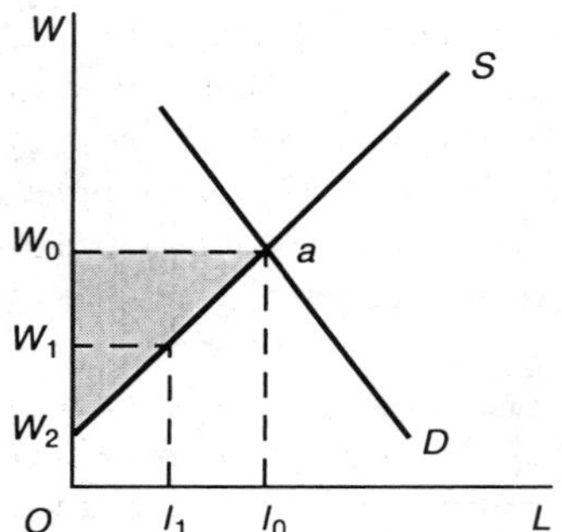

Figure 8.11: *Economic rent and transfer earnings*

earnings of labour. It is possible to divide these earnings into **transfer earnings and economic rent**.

- Transfer earnings: the minimum payment a factor of production requires to keep it in its present employment.
- Economic rent: any payment received by a factor of production in excess of its transfer earnings.

For example, if a worker receives £100 wages per day but would be prepared (not happily) to do the job for £95 per day, £95 is the transfer earnings and £5 is economic rent. The earnings in the next best employment available, is likely to determine the transfer earnings in the existing job. If you can earn £100 per day in some alternative job, you are unlikely to accept less than £100 per day from your present employer. Highly paid people in the world of sport and entertainment, etc. typically have a large element of economic rent in their earnings.

In a competitive labour market such as that illustrated in Figure 8.11 all workers receive the same wage of w_0. However the supply curve indicates that workers will be attracted to this labour market at a wage as low as w_2 and will enter in increasing numbers as the wage rises. For example l_1 quantity of labour would be prepared to work for a wage of w_1 even though they actually receive w_0. The total economic rent being earned is the shaded triangle above the supply curve ($w_2 w_0 a$). Only the marginal worker (the last one employed) receives no economic rent. The total transfer earnings is the unshaded area below the supply curve ($ow_2 al_0$).

Payments being received by factors of production in the form of economic rent serve no useful economic function. These payments (however welcome to those concerned) do not influence the allocation of resources in the economy. (As they influence income distribution they obviously have an indirect effect on resource allocation). If a perfect system of individual contracts could be arranged so that each worker only received their transfer earnings, the economic rent would disappear thus representing a saving to employers.

Lack of flexibility in contracts of employment can lead to misallocation of resources and inefficiencies. For example, in state systems of education all teachers are likely to be on similar contracts. It frequently occurs that there is a shortage of teachers in one subject area (e.g. maths) while there is an excess in another (e.g. history). The way to get more maths teachers is to offer them higher pay. However if all teachers get the higher pay this represents a costly increase in economic rent to be paid by the government. Not surprisingly, history teachers end up teaching maths as best they can.

The monopoly profits received by monopolists (Section 7.4) represents economic rent. A lump sum tax designed to reduce these profits would have the effect of reducing profits without altering the profit-maximizing level of output. Governments occasionally impose 'windfall' taxes on banks, etc.

8.6 Capital investment

A firm needs fixed capital (plant and equipment) to produce the goods or services it wishes to supply to product markets. The firm's expenditure on fixed capital is referred to as ***investment expenditure***. The quantity of capital the firm wishes to employ can be thought of as the desired level of investment expenditure by the firm. The level of investment expenditure determines the firm's ***capacity*** to produce.

There can be different reasons for investment expenditure:

- To replace existing capital equipment as it becomes obsolete, i.e. maintain existing capacity.
- To add to the existing capital stock, i.e. increase existing capacity.
- To create new capacity, i.e. research and development into new products followed by new capital stock.

Clearly the ***risk*** associated with investment expenditure will vary depending on the reason.

Investment projects will typically require ***initial expenditure*** with a view to generating ***future returns***. Investment projects are always (more or less) risky because the firm must try to anticipate future events. How can the firm be confident of the price it can change in the future; how can it know the future variable costs of production? Because investment projects have a time dimension (initial expenditure → future returns) it is necessary to consider the ***time value of money***.

Time value of money

If offered a choice between receiving £1000 now or in a years time the rational choice would be to have it now. Indeed if offered a choice between £999 now and £1000 in a years time the £1000 would still be an unlikely choice. The maximum amount you are willing to sacrifice now so that you may receive £1000 in a year's time is the present value of £1000 in a years time to you.

Finding the present value of future sums of money is referred to as ***discounting***. In the financial markets where money is constantly being borrowed and loaned the ***discount rate*** is the relevant market rate of interest.

For example the present value (PV) of £1000 receivable in one years time if the rate of discount (r) is 10% is:

$$\text{PV} = \frac{£1000}{(1+r)} = \frac{£1000}{(1.1)} = £909.09 \qquad [8.4]$$

Put another way, if you loan £909.09 for one year at 10% you will receive £1000 in a years time. £909.09 today or £1000 in a years time have equivalent value if the discount rate is 10%.

The present value of £1000 to be received in two years time is:

$$\text{PV} = \frac{£1000}{(1+r)^2} = \frac{£1000}{(1.1)^2} = £866.45 \qquad [8.5]$$

In general

$$\text{PV}(S_n) = \frac{S_n}{(1+r)^n} \qquad [8.6]$$

where S_n represents a sum of money receivable at the end of N year;r, the appropriate discount rate and n a given number of years.

An investment project will typically be expected to generate a cash flow over a number of years. The present value of the cash flow is simply the sum of the PVs of the annual figures:

$$\text{PV} = \frac{S_1}{(1+r)} + \frac{S_2}{(1+r)^2} + \cdots + \frac{S_n}{(1+r)^n} \qquad [8.7]$$

8.7 *The net present value*

The net present value (NPV) of an investment project can be arrived at by subtracting the initial cost (C_o) of the project from the PV of the future net cash flows:

$$\text{NPV} = \frac{S_1}{(1-r)} + \frac{S_2}{(1+r)^2} + \cdots + \frac{S_n}{(1+r)^n} - C_0 \qquad [8.8]$$

Assuming the appropriate rate of discount is used a positive NPV indicates an acceptable project while a negative NPV suggests the project should be rejected.

The appropriate rate of discount for the firm to use is the marginal cost of capital to the firm, i.e. the cost of raising additional finance. This in turn will be influenced by the level of business risk attached to the project and the source of the funds used to finance it. The riskier the project the higher the expected rate of return the investor requires to compensate for the risk. With regard to finance, a modern business will usually have two sources to choose from: shareholders funds (owners equity) or creditors (long-term borrowing).

Creditors are likely to receive fixed interest on their loan to the business and security against loss, whereas owners (or shareholders) will have an uncertain return and no security. Consequently shareholders will require a higher ***expected*** return than creditors to compensate for the extra risk. (Note there are two distinct types of investor here: suppliers of finance to the firm and the firm itself investing this finance in real capital equipment.) Therefore the cost of equity finance to the firm is likely to be higher than the cost of debt finance.

Whatever the source of finance (equity, debt or both combined) its cost will rise or fall as market rates of interest rise or fall. Clearly as interest rates fall the cost of borrowing falls but so also will the cost of equity as shareholders will typically require a fixed (%) amount above market rates of interest to compensate for additional risk.

It follows that the marginal cost of capital and interest rates will move in the same direction. As interest rates fall the appropriate discount rate also falls. For any given set of cash flow figures ($S_1 \ldots S_n$) in Equation [8.8] the lower the discount rate the higher the NPV. Therefore some projects that would be rejected at high rates of interest will be accepted at low rates and vice versa. We can conclude that the ***level of investment expenditure by firms will be inversely related to market rates of interest.***

Marginal efficiency of capital (MEC)

The NPV approach focuses on an amount of money – the amount by which the present value of future earnings exceeds the initial cost. An alternative approach is to focus on the rate of return from the project.

The **marginal efficiency of capital** (also known as the **internal rate of return**) is a rate of return found by setting the NPV equal to zero. In other words, the MEC is the rate of discount which equates the present value of the future net cash receipts with the initial cost (C_0).

$$C_0 = \frac{S_1}{(1+r)} + \frac{S_2}{(1+r)^2} + \cdots + \frac{S_n}{(1+r)^n} \qquad [8.9]$$

If the marginal efficiency of capital is greater than the marginal cost of capital the profit-maximizing firm should undertake the investment project.

It is reasonable to assume that the MEC declines as the firm undertakes more and more investment expenditure (if this were not the case firms would have exceedingly large capital requirements). As a firm chooses between investment projects these projects can be ***ranked*** in order of profitability. The profit-maximizing level of investment expenditure is where the marginal efficiency of capital (MEC) is equal to the marginal cost of capital (MC_k).

$$MEC = MC_k \qquad [8.10]$$

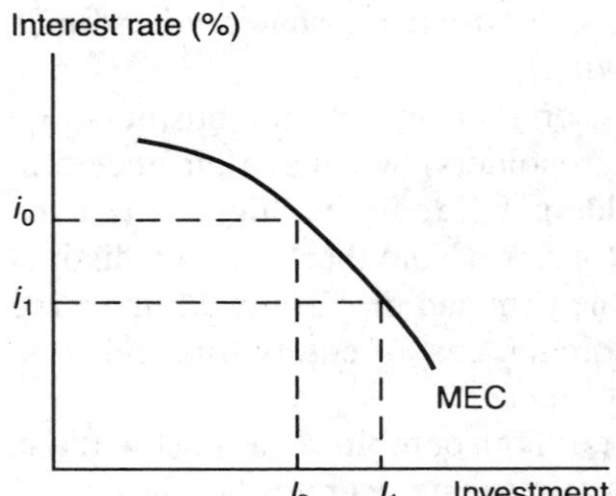

Figure 8.12: *The equilibrium level of investment expenditure*

This relationship represents the profit-maximizing condition for the level of investment expenditure by the firm. If we assume for simplicity that the firm can borrow as much finance as it requires at the prevailing market rate of interest (price-taker in the capital market) and that this rate represents the marginal cost of capital to the firm (equity finance is being ignored). Then the profit-maximizing level of investment expenditure is where the MEC equals the relevant market rate of interest as illustrated in Figure 8.12.

The MEC curve slopes downwards to reflect the declining rate of return as more and more investment is undertaken. If the firm wishes to maximise profit it should undertake investment up to the point where the MEC equals the prevailing market rate of interest. If the market rate of interest happens to be i_0 the appropriate level of investment expenditure is I_0 whereas at a rate of i_1 the appropriate level is I_1.

The MEC schedule can be thought of as the profit-maximising firm's demand for investment funds (or capital equipment). The inverse relationship between interest rates and investment expenditure is obvious, at higher rates there is less investment and vice versa.

Quasi rent

Economic rent (Section 8.5) is a payment to a factor of production over and above what is required to keep it in its existing employment. Economic rent is not a necessary payment in the sense that the factor of production will continue functioning without it. Profit is a payment to capital. Capital equipment is a fixed factor of production and once installed for its existing employment it is often not practicable to transfer it to alternative employment. It would appear, therefore, that profit income is equivalent to economic rent. However, if capital does not earn an acceptable level of profit in a given employment, *replacement investment* will not occur so that in the longer term capital will not continue in that employment. A payment to a factor of production which is immobile in the short run but mobile in the long run is referred to as **quasi rent**.

REVISION FOCUS CHAPTER EIGHT

Key Areas

- Marginal productivity theory
- Labour markets
  → total, average and marginal costs of labour → marginal revenue product of labour → profit-maximizing level of employment ($MC_L = MRP_L$) → supply curve of labour → firms demand for labour → relative wages → transfer earnings and economic rent
- Capital expenditure
  → time value of money/discounting → net present value → marginal efficiency of capital → marginal cost of capital → profit-maximizing level of investment ($MEC = MC_K$) → quasi rent.

Self Test

(1) The total supply curve of labour to an industry may be backward bending but not the individual's supply curve of labour T/F

(2) The marginal revenue product of labour will tend to decline as more workers are employed due to the law of diminishing returns T/F

(3) For the price-taker in the labour market the AC_L and the MC_L are equivalent but not so for the monopsonist T/F

(4) In profit-maximizing equilibrium the monopsonist pays a wage less then the MRP_L but for the price-taking firm they are equal T/F

(5) Transfer earnings represent income over and above what is required to keep the factor of production in its existing employment T/F

(6) If an investment project costs £1000 to set up and generates net receipts of £600 and £700 at the end of years 1 and 2, discounting at 10% the net present value is: (a) £124, (b) £300 and (c) −£240

(7) The profit-maximizing equilibrium level of investment is where $MEC = MC_k$ T/F

(8) Quasi rent represents transfer earnings in the long run T/F

Discussion Topics

- The relative wage received by different groups of workers depends on where the supply and demand curves for the different types of labour intersect. Explain.
- How might an improvement in technology in a particular industry impact on the demand for labour in that industry?
- Rising interest rates cause investment expenditure to fall. Explain.

CHAPTER 9

MARKET FAILURE

The fundamental economic problem is one of relative scarcity (Section 1.1) Choices must be made regarding *what*, *how* and *for whom* (Section 1.3). These choices all relate to the allocation of resources in society. A market economy is a complex system of interconnecting markets where the above choices are resolved, via the price mechanism, in a decentralized way. Economists talk about market failure when unregulated markets fail to allocate resources in an optimum fashion. Market failure is likely to lead to government intervention in an effort to improve the efficiency of the economic system.

9.1 *Externalities*

An **externality** occurs when the actions of some agent affects the welfare of others, but not through prices. The effect of externalities is for *private* and *social* costs (or benefits) to diverge. In an unregulated market economy there will be excessive production of products generating negative externalities and too little production of goods generating positive externalities. The result is a misallocation of resources in the economy.

The private costs of production are determined by the quantity of resources required to produce a given level of output. However the production process may generate costs for third parties. For example a chemical company may keep its private costs down by dumping effluent into a nearby river. Polluting the river is a profitable activity for the company but it imposes a cost on those who would otherwise benefit from a clean river. In this case the social costs (private plus external) exceed the private costs.

Negative externalities are commonplace: the motorist is unlikely to be over-concerned with the pollution being caused by driving nor is the smoker likely to quit the habit because of the negative effect on others, etc. Positive externalities result if third parties derive benefit from the economic transactions of others. The consumption of healthcare or education by individuals will usually generate wider social benefits; if your neighbours keep their houses and gardens attractive you will benefit from the pleasant environment, etc.

The problem with externalities is that in an unregulated market economy the agents generating them have no incentive to take account of their effects. Those suffering from negative externalities are likely to resort to political campaigns to seek redress in the absence of a market solution. Governments may ultimately ban certain activities (drug abuse, the use of asbestos, driving in the city) but more often activities giving rise to negative externalities will be discouraged through the imposition of a tax. Activities giving rise to positive externalities can be encouraged through subsidies (Sections 3.2 and 3.3).

Where a negative production externality exists social costs of production exceed private costs and in particular marginal social cost (MSC) is higher than marginal private cost (MPC). Figure 9.1 below illustrates how in an unregulated competitive environment there will be too much produced. In an unregulated, competitive environment the equilibrium will be where marginal (private) cost equals price. This is at point *a* in Figure 9.1 with q_0 being produced at a price of p_0. However output in excess of q_1 is having a negative effect on welfare as the cost to society of those extra units (MSC) is greater than the price consumers are willing to pay for them (indicated by the demand curve). The negative effect is illustrated by the shaded area. The socially optimum level of output is where **marginal social cost equals marginal social benefit**. Assuming no consumption externalities the demand curve indicates the marginal social benefit from additional output. The optimum output for society is at q_1 with a price of p_1 being charged. The way to achieve this is by imposing a per unit tax (Section 3.2) equal to *t*. At the new equilibrium point *b* tax revenue equal to $(p_1 - p_2)q_1$ is being raised which could be used to compensate those affected by the negative externality.

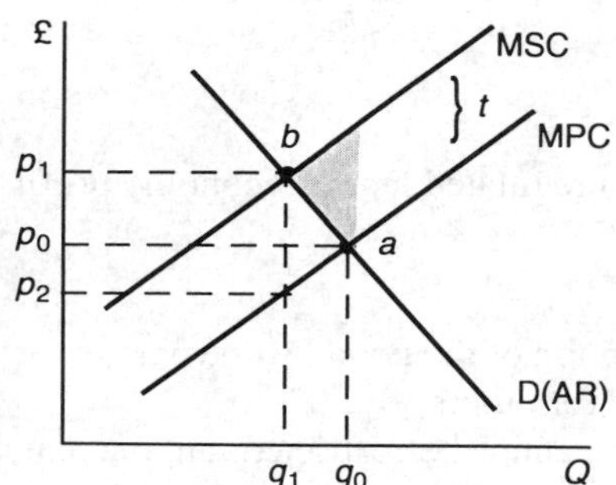

Figure 9.1: *Private and social costs*

With a positive consumption externality third parties benefit from the consumption of the product by others. Total benefit exceeds the benefit to the purchasers of the product. The market demand curve no longer indicates the true marginal benefit to society from the consumption of extra units. The marginal social benefit (MSB) will be higher than the price consumers are willing to pay for additional units. Figure 9.2 illustrates how in an unregulated competitive environment too little will be produced.

The unregulated competitive equilibrium is where MC = P, resulting in a level of output of q_0 at a price of p_0. However extra units produced beyond q_0 up to q_1 will generate greater benefit to society than cost. The optimum output is q_1. The

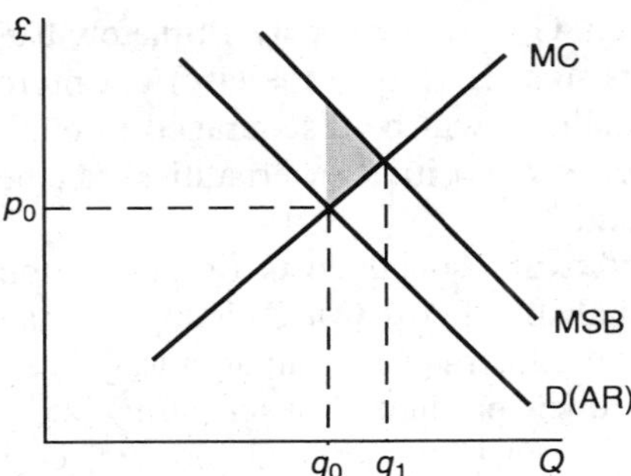

Figure 9.2: *Private and social benefits*

shaded area indicates the net loss to society resulting from the failure to produce the optimum level of output. An obvious policy, if the government wishes to encourage production, would be to subsidize production (Section 3.3). A per-unit subsidy would have the effect of lowering the MC curve. It is common for governments to subsidize activities where there would otherwise be a significant social loss from underproduction. Education and healthcare are obvious examples.

9.2 *Public goods*

Public goods are beneficial to society but in an unregulated market economy profit seeking firms are unlikely to provide them.

Public goods have two properties:

- non-diminishability – once provided consumption of the good by one person (or group) does not reduce the quantity available for others;
- non-exclusion – once provided consumption cannot be restricted, anyone can have free access to it.

Street lighting is a good example of a public good. It is of benefit to residents of an area to have street lighting but who is to pay for it? Public goods give rise to the *free-rider problem.* Each resident is aware that once the street lighting has been provided they cannot be excluded from its benefits. There will be an incentive to shift the cost on to others by failing to contribute to the cost. The only solution is for some public authority to levy a charge on the beneficiaries (national or local taxes) and finance provision of the public good through central funds.

Other examples of public goods are national defence, lighthouses, airwaves, etc. A private sector solution is sometimes available. For example firms may finance radio stations through advertising expenditure if they consider the advertising will increase sales. New technology can change the character of goods; for example TV signals would traditionally be regarded as public goods but fibre-optic cables now enable broadcasters to restrict access to programmes or whole channels.

9.3 *Natural monopoly (two-part tariff)*

A profit maximizing monopolist will restrict output and charge a higher price than the competitive firm, all else being equal (Section 7.4). Governments invariably have legal powers to regulate the emergence and performance of monopolies through *monopolies and mergers* legislation. A problem arises, however, in the case of natural monopoly (Section 5.7).

Natural monopoly is a situation whereby economies of scale exist to such an extent that the most efficient way to supply the market is with a sole supplier. Competition and efficiency are *mutually exclusive* in the case of natural monopoly. Typically there are very high fixed costs relative to variable costs in the production process. The result is declining unit costs over a wide range of output. The supply of water, gas, etc. to households tends to have this type of cost structure.

Figure 9.3 illustrates the key features of natural monopoly, in particular there is declining average cost over the relevant range of output. If this was a private sector profit-maximizing enterprise production would take place where MC = MR resulting in q_0 output and a price of p_0. Supernormal profits equal to $(p_0 - \mathrm{AC}_0)q_0$ can be earned. From the consumers point of view, however, the optimum level of output is where MC = P (Section 6.4) resulting in an output of q_1 at a price of p_1. The problem with this pricing policy is that it must lead to losses. Because AC is declining over the whole range of output MC must be lower than AC. In Figure 9.3 a loss equal to the distance *ab* per unit of output would be incurred with total losses equal to $(\mathrm{AC}_1 - p_1)q_1$.

If the natural monopolist is left in the private sector and pursues a profit-

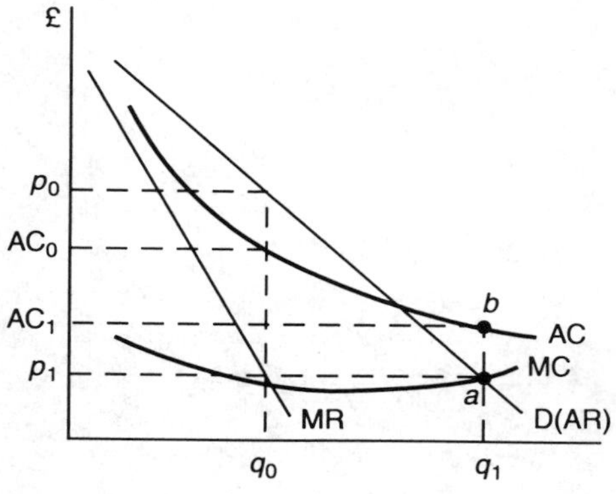

Figure 9.3: *Natural monopoly*

maximizing strategy it is subject to the standard criticism of monopoly – restricted output, and persistent supernormal profits. However, there is no free market solution in the case of natural monopoly because competition is precluded on efficiency grounds. In most societies the public utilities (water, gas, etc.) tend to be regulated by governments, often as semi-state or nationalized industries.

If the government is responsible for the pricing policy of the industry, one way of achieving MC-pricing without incurring losses is by means of a *two-part tariff*. This would entail a *fixed rental charge* plus a charge per unit consumed. For example, in Figure 9.3 a price of p_1 per unit of output plus a rental charge on consumers which would cover what would otherwise be a loss of $(AC_1 - p_1)q_1$. This would lead to an output level of q_1 which is the optimum use of resources from a consumer's perspective.

Two-part tariffs are commonly charged for gas, phones, water, etc.

9.4 Trade unions and labour markets

It is common for workers with similar skills to join together in trade unions or professional associations. Trade unions engage in *collective bargaining* on behalf of their members with employers. The aim of the union is to improve the conditions of employment for its members. Wage levels, overtime rates, length of working week, etc. are all issues for collective bargaining. When assessing the impact of trade unions in labour markets economists tend to focus on two issues: the impact of the union on the *level of wages* and the *level of employment*.

The effect a union will have in a labour market depends on the nature of that labour market in the absence of the union. In particular it depends on whether the labour market would have been perfectly competitive or not. In a perfectly competitive labour market (Section 8.2) the wage and the level of employment are determined at the point of intersection of the labour supply and labour demand curves. The competitive equilibrium is illustrated at point *a* in Figure 9.4.

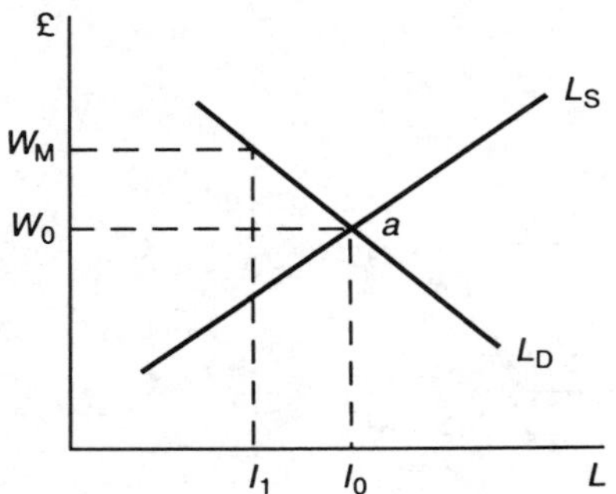

Figure 9.4: *Trade unions and a competitive labour market*

The wage paid is w_0, the level of employment is l_0 and total earnings are w_0l_0. Assume, under these free market conditions, that a union is formed and negotiates a minimum wage of w_m. An effective union is, in fact, a monopoly supplier of labour with an ability to ensure that no labour is supplied below the minimum wage. The level of employment that firms wish to offer at a wage of w_m is now l_1. If firms can, without cost, dismiss workers, employment will quickly fall to l_1. Either way, the longer term level of employment at a wage of w_m will be l_1. By raising wages the union has caused a loss of jobs. In a competitive labour market the union is faced with a *trade-off* between wages and employment. A higher wage can be achieved but at a cost of lost jobs.

Whether total earnings rise or fall (w_ml_1 compared to w_0l_0) depends on the price (wage) elasticity of demand for labour. If demand is inelastic there will be fewer job losses and higher earnings whereas if demand is elastic job losses will be greater with lower earnings. The wage-elasticity of demand for labour depends, among other things, on the price-elasticity of demand for the product being produced. The more inelastic the latter the more inelastic the former and vice versa.

If the labour market would not otherwise be perfectly competitive the trade union may be able to avoid this trade off between employment and the wage. If we assume a monopsonist employer of labour (Section 8.2) then the introduction of a union leads to a situation of *bilateral monopoly*. In the absence of a union the level of employment offered by the monopsonist and the wage paid will be determined where $MC_L = MRP_L$.

In Figure 9.5 (a) this results in an employment level of l_0 and a wage rate of w_0. If we introduce a trade union which negotiates a wage higher than w_0 the situation could result as illustrated in Figure 9.5(b).

If the union negotiates a wage of w_m in Figure 9.5(b) and workers refuse to work for less, then the supply curve of labour to the firm becomes $w_m a$ AC_L and the marginal cost of labour becomes $w_m ab$ MC_L. Quite simply the employer can

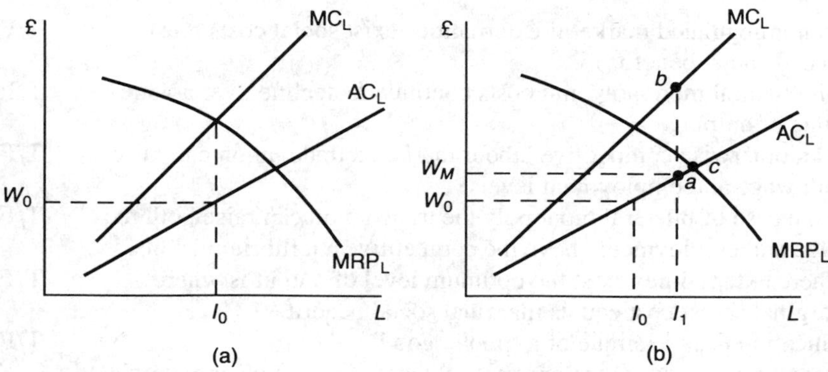

Figure 9.5: *Bilateral monopoly*

attract up to l_1 units of labour by paying each workers a wage of w_m but to attract in excess of l_1 it must pay higher than the union rate. Only beyond l_1 does the employer have to pay higher wages and therefore only beyond l_1 is the MC of labour higher than the wage that needs to be paid. The profit-maximizing strategy for the firm is still to employ where $MRP_L = MC_L$ but this is now at l_1 level of employment. The union has raised the wage from w_0 to w_m and the profit-maximizing strategy for the monopsonist is to *increase employment* from l_0 to l_1. The effect of the union, therefore has been to raise both wages and employment. If the union tries to negotiate a wage higher than point *c* it will be once again faced with a trade-off.

REVISION FOCUS CHAPTER NINE

Key Areas

- Externalities
  → nature of → private and social costs and benefits → optimum output (MSC = MSB)
- Public goods
  → nature of → free-rider problem
- Natural Monopoly
  → cost structure of → two-part tariff
- Trade unions
  → trade off between wages and employment → bilateral monopoly

Self Test

(1) If firms generate pollution the optimum solution would be to ban them T/F
(2) In an unregulated market if externalities exist social costs must exceed social benefits T/F
(3) With natural monopoly unit costs continue to decline over a wide range of output T/F
(4) In an otherwise competitive labour market, a trade union can raise both wage and employment levels T/F
(5) In the case of bilateral monopoly the trade union can raise both the wage and employment above the competitive equilibrium levels T/F
(6) Where externalities exist the optimum level of output is where marginal social cost equals marginal social benefit T/F
(7) Education is an example of a 'public good' T/F
(8) Producing luxuries at the expense of necessities is a clear example of market failure T/F

Discussion Topics

- Explain the causes of market failure and suggest appropriate government policies.
- Under what circumstances are trade unions faced with a trade-off between wages and employment?
- Using a diagram to illustrate, explain how a government might use an indirect tax when social costs of production exceed private costs of production.

CHAPTER 10

NATIONAL INCOME

10.1 *From micro-to macroeconomics*

The microeconomic analysis of previous chapters was concerned with particular markets and the strategies of economic agents in these markets. The focus was on the behaviour of the firm, the consumer, the worker, the determination of price in a competitive market, etc.

Macroeconomic analysis focuses on the performance of the economy as a whole, rather than the microeconomic features of it. The level of production in the whole economy; the level of employment/unemployment in the economy; the average price level of the whole economy; trade between the economy and the rest of the world; these are all macroeconomic issues. Because the focus is on the economy as a whole the variables of interest are often aggregates of microeconomic variable. For example, in microeconomics we might be concerned with consumers' expenditure on a particular product whereas in macroeconomics we might be concerned with total consumers expenditure in the economy.

Governments play a major role in modern economies. The policies adopted by governments are often guided by macroeconomic analysis. If for no other reason it is important that the analysis is reliable.

10.2 *Measuring economic activity*

There are three related measures of economic activity for an economy:

- Gross Domestic Product (GDP)
- Gross National Product (GNP)
- Net National Product (or National Income)

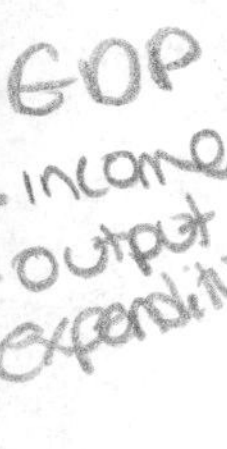

GDP is the value, in money terms, of the total output of final goods and services produced in an economy over a period of (usually) one year. Final goods include both consumer goods and capital gods. There are three alternative methods of calculating this value, the **income method**, the **output method** and the **expenditure method**. Table 10.1 gives a simplified illustration of how these measurements are calculated.

Table 10.1 illustrates hypothetical figures for stages of production, the final product being bread. The farms supply the mills with wheat; the mills supply the

Table 10.1: *Stages of production*

Producer	Farms	Mills	Bakeries	Retail
Output	Wheat	Flour	Bread	Bread
Value of output (Gross)	£100m	£140m	£180m	£200m
Value added (Factor incomes)	£100m	£40m	£40m	£20m

bakeries with flour, the bakeries supply the retailers with bread which is then sold to the final consumer.

To simplify the analysis it is assumed in Table 10.1 that there are no ***bought in*** inputs into the farms and therefore the £100m worth of wheat represents the net output of the farms. The only bought in input for the mills is the £100m of wheat, for the bakeries the £140m of flour and for the retail trade the £180m of bread.

The value of *final output* for the whole process is the £200m worth of bread sold by the retail trade, and it is this figure we wish to add to the GDP of the economy. The wheat, flour and wholesale bread are all **intermediate products** and care should be taken not to ***double count*** these items. The *value added* at each stage is the difference between the value of output and the value of bought in inputs. The value added can also be thought of as the gross earnings available to be paid as income (wages, profit, interest, rent) to the factors of production employed at that stage.

The three methods of measurement are all seeking to establish the contribution to GDP of £200m. The expenditure method focuses on the £200m that is spent purchasing the bread; the income method focuses on the sum of the gross factor incomes generated in all sectors (£200); the output method focuses on the sum of the value added of all sectors (£200m).

Because the three methods are merely different ways of measuring the same quantity the following identity must be true:

National Income ≡ National Output ≡ National Expenditure

In reality national income accounting is not as straightforward as the above example suggests. A modern economy is made up of many sectors with large, medium and small scale enterprises along with many self-employed traders. Monitoring all this economic activity is a difficult task. Furthermore, governments usually wish to measure economic activity so that the incomes earned can be taxed. The requirement to pay tax on income can operate as a disincentive to declare income resulting in a *black economy* (undeclared economic activity). Because of this there may be a tendency for the official figures to understate the true level of economic activity. The higher the rates of tax in a country the larger the black economy is likely to be.

Various problems need to be avoided if an accurate measure of GDP is to be achieved:

- When using the output method avoid *double counting*. For example if the gross output of the farms was added to the gross output of the mills the wheat would be included twice.
- When using the income method **exclude transfer payments. Transfer payments** are incomes unrelated to production. Welfare payments by government, student grants, etc. are examples of transfers. The aim is to include only those incomes that are earned in producing goods or services.
- When using the expenditure method it is necessary to adjust for the value of imports and exports. Domestic expenditure will include expenditure on imports, while foreigners will be buying domestically produced goods or services that are exported. The value of exports should be added to GDP while the value of imports should be subtracted.
- Another problem arises as a result of indirect taxes. If the bread in Table 10.1 was subject to 10% value added tax, consumers expenditure would be £220m but factor incomes would still be only £200m. The tax is a transfer payment to the government. To calculate *GDP at factor cost* from *GDP at market prices* it is necessary to subtract indirect taxes and add any government subsidies to producers.
- Finally goods produced in one period may be added to stocks (inventory investment) and sold in the next period. To calculate GDP in the first period any increase in stocks must be added to the expenditure figures for that period (reductions in stock levels are subtracted).

GDP and GNP

To get from GDP to GNP it is necessary to adjust for *net factor incomes from abroad* (NFIA). Economic activity in one country can be generating income for residents of another country due to repatriated profits from foreign investment. GDP measures the income generated in a particular country, no matter who has a claim to that income. GNP measures the income being earned by the residents of a country irrespective of where the income is generated.

$$GNP = GDP + NFIA \qquad [10.1]$$

Creditor countries (those accumulating net foreign assets) are net exporters of capital and consequently have positive NFIA. For creditor countries GNP exceeds GDP. **Debtor countries** (those accumulating net foreign liabilities) are net recipients of inward investment and consequently have negative NFIA with the result that GNP is less than GDP.

National income

To get from Gross National Product to Net National Product (NNP) it is necessary to adjust for the depreciation of the national stock of capital. Part of the capital

Table 10.2

Irish National Income (96)	Expenditure Method I£m
Personal consumption	23318
Public sector current expenditure	6244
Gross domestic fixed capital formation	7524
Change in stocks	389
Exports	33798
Imports	–29169
GDP at market price	42104
Expenditure taxes	–6503
Subsidies	2147
GDP at factor cost	37748
Net factor income from abroad	–5121
GNP at factor cost	32627
Depreciation	–4304
NNP at factor cost (national income)	28323

(Source: National Income and Expenditure 1996, CSO.)

stock will be **used-up** in the production of goods and services. NNP is calculated by subtracting an allowance for depreciation from GNP:

$$\text{NNP} = \text{GNP} - \text{Depreciation} \qquad [10.2]$$

When Net National Product is calculated on a *factor cost basis* this figure is accepted as the *National Income* figure.

Table 10.2 illustrates the calculation of Irish National Income for the year 1996.

If we denote personal consumption expenditure with a *C*; public sector current and capital expenditure with a *G*; private sector investment expenditure on capital and stocks with an *I*; exports with an *X* and imports with an *M* then

$$\text{GDP} \equiv \text{C+I+G+X}-M \qquad [10.3]$$

The above is a definition of GDP at market price.

10.3 *Interpreting the figures*

National income figures are designed to measure the extent of economic activity in an economy. The level of economic activity in turn determines the *material living standards* of the society. The figures give an indication of *how living standards in a particular country* (1) are changing over time and (2) compare on an international scale.

It must be remembered that the figures are exclusively concerned with material living standards and say nothing about the *quality of life* in a country. Living standards may be rising but some people may feel that the quality of life (however measured) is declining.

When measuring living standards the appropriate measure is per capita GNP which is arrived at by dividing GNP by the population:

$$\textbf{GNP per capita} = \frac{\textbf{Gross National Product}}{\textbf{Population}}$$

Living standards therefore depend not only on the income being earned by the members of a society (GNP) but also on the size of the population that the income must support. If a country has a growing population then GNP must be rising faster if living standards are to improve. The Irish National Income Accounts include a figure for Gross National Disposable Income (GNDI) which is GNP plus the net international transfers to Ireland arising mainly from Membership of the EU. Net transfers in 1996 were £1353m giving a GNDI of £38337m at market price.

Real and nominal income

When comparing living standards over time it is important to distinguish between *real income* and *nominal income*. The distinction is important when there is inflation in an economy as the change in nominal income will exaggerate the change in living standards. Table 10.3 gives hypothetical figures for an economy.

The figures indicate that GNP (in nominal terms) has been growing at 10% P.A. However the inflation index indicates that prices have risen by 5% from 1993 to 1994 and by 12% overall from 1993 to 1995. Nominal income is arrived at by multiplying output (quantities) by the prevailing prices but if prices are rising nominal GNP will tend to be rising whether or not real output is rising. To get a measure of the change in real output it is necessary to express the GNP figures at *constant prices* by removing the effects of inflation. The constant price figures are arrived at by *deflating* the market price figures with the appropriate *GNP deflator* which is 100/price index. For example the real GNP figure of 31,429 for 1994 is arrived at by multiplying 33,000 by 100/105. It can be seen that the economy has expanded in real terms (constant prices) by 4.76% (93/94) and 3.12% (94/95).

Even if real per capita income is growing over time it is important to be aware

Table 10.3: *Real income and nominal income*

Year	1993	1994	1995
GNP (£m) (current market prices)	30,000	33,000	36,300
Price index	100	105	112
GNP (£m) (constant prices)	30,000	31,429	32,411

of certain facts:

- It is only an average and therefore says nothing about the distribution of income or changes in the distribution of income over time. In other words growing per capita income is not incompatible with increasing poverty among some sections of society.
- It says nothing about the number of hours worked. Clearly it would be preferable if rising real income was achieved with a shorter working week rather than with a longer one.
- It fails to take account of any negative (or positive) externalities in production such as pollution (Section 9.1).
- It is a measure of output whether or not the output adds to welfare. If congestion on the roads means journeys are taking longer and more petrol is being consumed as a result, this will add to GNP while hardly improving welfare.
- It fails to include welfare increasing activities that do not involve market transactions. Unpaid domestic work and DIY activities are obvious examples.

International comparisons

Special problems arise when making international comparisons of living standards. Firstly a common standard of measurement is required which means that the national incomes of different countries must be expressed in a common currency. Secondly, if economies differ significantly in their structure comparing GNP figures may not be comparing like with like. Problems may arise if:

- exchange rates fail to reflect purchasing power parities and
- the scope of market transactions differ significantly between countries.

To illustrate the first problem we will use the following hypothetical figures for Ireland and France.

GNP per capita	I: Ir£10,000 Fr: ff140,000
Exchange rate	Ir£1 = ff10

On the basis of this (convenient) exchange rate per capita income in Ireland could be expressed as ff100,000 or the French figure could be expressed as Ir£14,000. Can we conclude that living standards are 40% higher in France? This conclusion is only valid if we assume that the purchasing power of Ir£1 in Ireland is equivalent to the purchasing power of ff10 in France. In other words we need to assume that similar products have the same real prices in both countries. In practice however exchange rates can be extremely volatile, particularly in the short term. We must conclude that prevailing exchange rates do not necessarily reflect **purchasing power parities** (Section 17.3).

The second problem stems from the fact that national income accounting focuses on marketable production rather than production in general. We have seen that unpaid domestic work and DIY activities are excluded from the figures. But for less developed economies much of their economic activity may be of this kind due to the fact that market relationships are less developed. Much of the economic activity, such as subsistence farming, takes place outside of market relationships. International comparisons based on GNP figures have greater validity when comparing countries at similar stages of economic development and with similar accounting standards.

Because of the problems involved in international comparisons via GNP figures comparisons are often made in alternative ways. The number of doctors per 1000 of population; pupil/teacher ratios in schools; the number of telephones or TVs per household, etc. can be used to make comparisons of living standards between countries.

REVISION FOCUS CHAPTER TEN

Key Areas

- Measuring economic activity
→ GDP, GNP, national income (NNP) → income, output, expenditure methods of measuring → problems arising → per capita income → interpreting the figures → real and nominal income → international comparisons

Self Test

(1)

Consumption expenditure (*C*)	6000
Investment expenditure (*I*)	2000
Government expenditure (*G*) on goods and services	2000
Value of imports (*M*)	2500
Value of exports (*X*)	3000
Indirect taxes (*T*)	850
Subsidies (*S*)	400
Net factor income	–750
Depreciation	1000

Calculate:
(a) GDP at market price
(b) NNP at factor cost
(c) GNP at factor cost
(d) GNP at market price

(2) The following should be included when measuring GDP:
(a) profits of second-hand car dealers T/F
(b) changes in the value of the housing stock T/F
(c) income of state pensioners T/F
(d) tips received by catering staff T/F

(3) GNP in nominal terms rises from £30bn to £33bn. If inflation was 5% over the period calculate the rise in real GNP

(4) Per capita GNP is a better measure of living standards than per capita GDP T/F

(5) Creditor countries are likely to have a GDP higher than GNP T/F

(6) An increase in the value of exports will cause net factor income from abroad to increase T/F

(7) Government expenditure on the salaries of the defence forces is a transfer payment and therefore not included in GDP T/F

(8) Rent paid to landlords is unearned income and therefore not included in GDP T/F

Discussion Topics

- Explain the three methods of measuring the level of economic activity.
- Give examples of problems to be avoided when measuring GDP.
- What problems might arise when making international comparisons of living standards?
- Changes in real national income rather than nominal national income determine changes in living standards. Explain.

CHAPTER 11

THE DETERMINATION OF NATIONAL INCOME

11.1 *Keynes and aggregate demand*

In the previous chapter we were concerned with the measurement of economic activity. In this and subsequent chapters we will be developing a system of macroeconomic analysis to help us investigate why the level of economic activity is what it is. It is often the case (in modern European economies for example), that GDP is significantly lower than it might be. High levels of unemployment imply that economies could be producing more. What are the causes of high levels of unemployment? What conditions are necessary for economies to be operating at their full-employment level of output?

The starting point for macroeconomic analysis is usually the work of John Maynard Keynes. Keynes wished to understand why economies tended to progress in a cycle of booms and slumps (***the business cycle***) and why they occasionally experienced prolonged recessions. The boom periods were characterized by high and rising levels of output and employment while the slumps were characterized by rising unemployment and falling output.

Keynes put forward a simple but persuasive explanation regarding the determination of output and employment in the economy. The level of output firms will be willing to produce, he argued, is determined by the aggregate demand (AD) for goods and services in the economy. The level of output firms are willing to produce will, in turn, determine the level of employment. The level of aggregate demand drives the economy:

AD → output → employment

If total demand in the economy were to rise firms would wish to produce more and therefore they would be offering more employment. If total demand were to fall firms would have accumulating unsold stocks leading them to cut production and employment. If we wish to know why the levels of output and employment tend to fluctuate, according to Keynes, the explanation is to be found in fluctuations in the level of aggregate demand.

Aggregate demand is concerned with the total level of *desired* (or planned) expenditure in the economy and has four components originating from four different sources.

- Households: consumption expenditure (C);
- Firms: capital and inventory investment expenditure (I);
- Government: current and capital expenditure (G)
- Foreign sector: The excess of exports over imports ($X - M$).

$$\text{AD} \equiv C + I + G + (X - M) \qquad [11.1]$$

Though similar to the accounting identity for GDP (see page 115), aggregate demand is not the same thing as GDP. The components of aggregate demand in the above identity relate to *desired levels of expenditure* whereas the components in the accounting identity for GDP relate to *realized outcomes*. Planned and realized outcomes may not necessarily coincide, only doing so when the economy is in equilibrium.

To understand why aggregate demand might fluctuate we need to understand why the components ($C, I, G, X - M$) might fluctuate. When we know this we can bring the components together to construct a theoretical *model* of the economy. It is important to realize that the model can take a simple form initially but be made more complex by relaxing or changing the *assumptions* underlying the model. The simplest model is that of a ***two-sector closed economy***. This focuses on the interaction between domestic households and firms while ignoring the impact of government and the foreign sector. By adding a government to the model we have a ***closed economy with government***. By adding the foreign sector we move to an ***open economy*** model. While simple models can be accused of lacking realism they are essential for developing the analysis by enabling us to isolate and focus on key macroeconomic relationships.

11.2 Two sector model

Consumption and savings functions

It is convenient to think of households and firms as being completely distinct. Households derive their incomes (wages, rent, interest, profit) from the factor services they provide to firms. If we assume that all the profit earned by firms is distributed then gross factor incomes is equal to GDP (Section 10.2).

Households have a simple choice with regard to the income they receive: they can either *spend it* or *save it*. If total income is denoted with a Y, total household spending with a C and total household savings with an S we have:

$$Y \equiv C + S \qquad [11.2]$$

The *consumption function* is concerned with all factors that may influence the level of consumption expenditure. The *savings function* is concerned with all factors that influence the level of savings. The single most important influence on the level of household consumption expenditure (C) is the level of household income (Y). It is assumed that as Y rises C will also rise, but not by the same amount. As Y rises household savings (S) will also rise, therefore:

$$\Delta Y = \Delta C + \Delta S \qquad [11.3]$$

where ΔC and ΔS are both positively related to ΔY.

The proportion of any change in income that is spent is known as the ***marginal propensity to consume*** (MPC) while the proportion that is saved is known as the ***marginal propensity to save*** (MPS).

Example:

Household income rises by £100m and as a result consumption expenditure rises by £80m and savings rise by £20m

$$\text{MPC} = \frac{\Delta C}{\Delta Y} = \frac{80}{100} = 0.8$$

$$\text{MPS} = \frac{\Delta S}{\Delta Y} = \frac{20}{100} = 0.2$$

It also follows that:

$$\text{MPC} + \text{MPS} = 1 \qquad [11.4]$$

The proportions of any *given* level of income that is spent is known as the average propensity to consume (APC) while the proportion that is saved is known as the average propensity to save (also known as the ***savings ratio***):

$$\text{APC} + \text{APS} = \frac{C}{Y} + \frac{S}{Y} = 1 \qquad [11.5]$$

The general shape of the *consumption function* and the *savings function* are as illustrated in Figure 11.1. The diagrams indicate that both consumption expenditure and savings rise as income rises. The slope of the consumption function at any point is the MPC while the slope of the savings function at any point is the MPS. By assumption the slopes are positive but less than one. The APC at any point on the consumption function is simply the level of consumption over the corresponding level of income (e.g. APC at point a is c_0/y_0). The APS at any point on the savings function is the level of savings over the corresponding level of income (e.g. APS at point b is s_0/y_0).

Other factors that are likely to influence the level of income spent or saved include:

- the market rate of interest (i);
- household wealth.

Rising interest rates will make saving more attractive and by implication consumption expenditure less attractive. If interest rates rise the proportion of income spent (APC) will fall while the proportion saved (APS) will rise and vice versa.

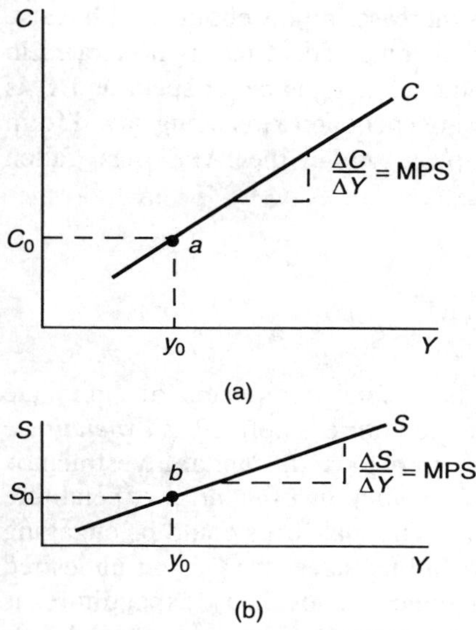

Figure 11.1: *Consumption and savings functions*

Increases in household wealth, e.g. an increase in the value of the housing stock, will mean that households will be less likely to save and more likely to spend and vice versa. Any changes, other than changes in household incomes, that cause C or S to change can be illustrated by a shift in the consumption and savings functions.

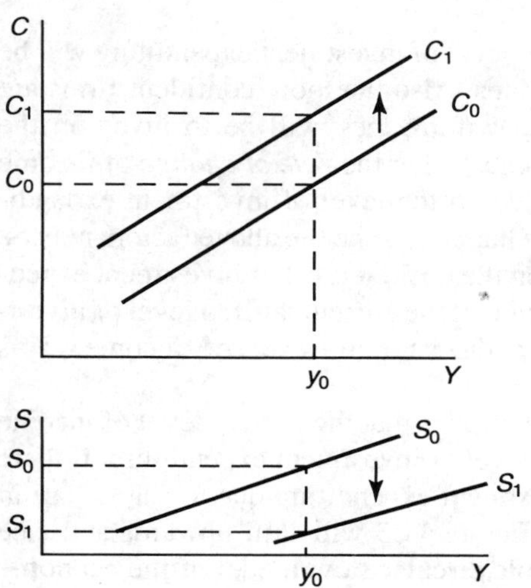

Figure 11.2: *Changes in the average propensities to consume and save*

Assume either a fall in interest rates or an increase in household wealth cause households to spend more (save less) of their income. The effect is illustrated in Figure 11.2 on the previous page. Prior to the change c_0 is being spent and s_0 is being saved from y_0. After the change c_1 is being spent and s_1 is being saved from y_0. Note the APC has risen $(c_0/y_0 \rightarrow c_1/y_0)$ while the APS has fallen $(s_0/y_0 \rightarrow s_1/y_0)$.

Investment function

The *investment expenditure* of firms (I) is the second component of aggregate demand in the two-sector model. Investment expenditure is defined as *expenditure on output that is not for consumption in the current period.* Capital investment is expenditure on plant and equipment while *inventory investment* is expenditure leading to increased stock levels. It is quite possible that firms could be engaging in *unplanned inventory investment* if, due to falling sales, there is an undesired accumulation of unsold stocks. This unplanned investment expenditure is included in GDP but is not included in aggregate demand. Changes in stock levels are the signal to firms to change their level of output and employment. If stock levels are falling due to rising demand firms will tend to expand production whereas if stock levels are rising due to falling demand production is likely to be reduced.

Factors likely to influence the desired level of investment expenditure are:

- interest rates;
- business confidence;
- the rate of change of income and expenditure.

We have seen (Section 8.7) that the desired level of investment expenditure will be negatively related to changes in interest rates. Also the more confident firms are about future market conditions, the more willing they will be to invest in the present period. The *accelerator theory* suggests that the *rate of change* of income and expenditure has an important influence on the level of investment expenditure. Whatever the present level of income happens to be the above factors may be exerting a positive or negative influence on the desired level of investment expenditure. It is assumed unless otherwise stated that the current desired level of investment expenditure is not influenced by the current level of income. This assumption is illustrated in Figure 11.3.

The horizontal investment function (I_0) implies that the current level of income (Y) is not a factor influencing the desired level of investment expenditure. If there is an increase in the desired level of investment expenditure due to, say, a fall in interest rates the investment schedule in Figure 11.3 will shift upwards and vice versa. From the point of view of the simple circular flow model of the economy investment expenditure is regarded as *exogenously determined*, i.e. it is not determined by variables which are themselves determined within the model.

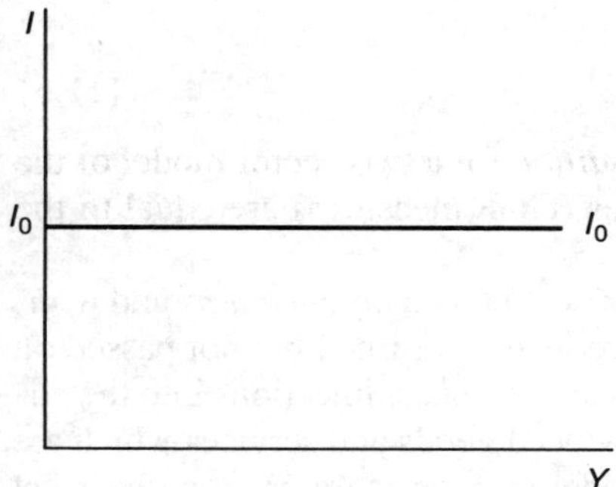

Figure 11.3: *Investment function*

Aggregate demand and equilibrium income

The aggregate demand schedule for the two sector economy can be arrived at simply by adding the desired level of investment expenditure (I) to the desired level of consumption expenditure (C). This is illustrated in Figure 11.4.

As income rises aggregate demand ($C + I$) rises due to the positive relationship between Y and C. The $C + I$ line will have the same slope (MPC) as the consumption function and it is arrived at by simply adding the investment function of Figure 11.3 to the consumption function of Figure 11.1(a).

The level of output in the Keynesian circular flow model is determined by firms simply adjusting their production levels to satisfy the level of aggregate demand in the economy. If the aggregate demand for goods and services exceeds the current output of goods and services ($C + I > Y$) then firms will expand production. If, on the other hand, aggregate demand is less than current output ($C + I < Y$) firms adjust by cutting production. The equilibrium level of output is where aggregate

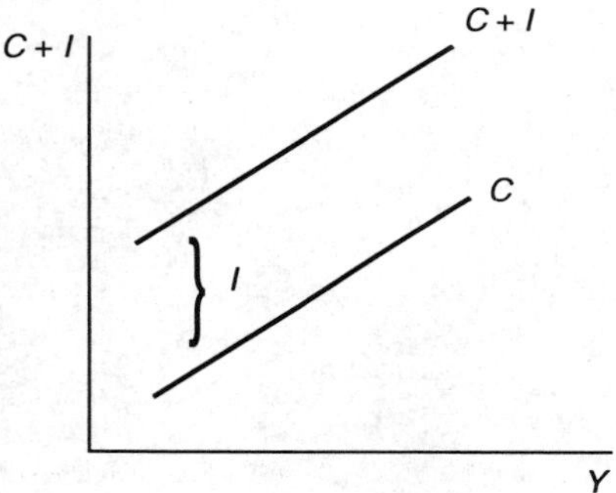

Figure 11.4: *Aggregate demand*

demand is equal to the current level of output:

$$Y = C + I \tag{11.6}$$

Equation (11.6) represents the *equilibrium condition* for a two-sector model of the economy. In equilibrium the realized outcomes (GDP measures) are equal to the planned measures (AD measures).

An alternative way of thinking of equilibrium is to focus on *injections* and *withdrawals*. Withdrawals from the circular flow are incomes earned but not passed on as expenditure on domestically produced goods and services. Injections into the circular flow are expenditures on domestically produced goods and services which are exogenously determined. In the two-sector model savings represent a withdrawal while investment expenditure represents an injection. The income expenditure equilibrium ($Y = C + I$) can be reformulated in terms of injections and withdrawals. We know that $Y \equiv C + S$. Substituting $C + S$ for Y in the equilibrium condition gives:

$$C + S = C + I \quad \text{or}$$

$$S = I \tag{11.7}$$

Equation [11.7] tells us that the economy is in equilibrium when the level of injections (investment expenditure) is equal to the level of withdrawals (savings). Both equilibrium conditions are illustrated in Figure 11.5.

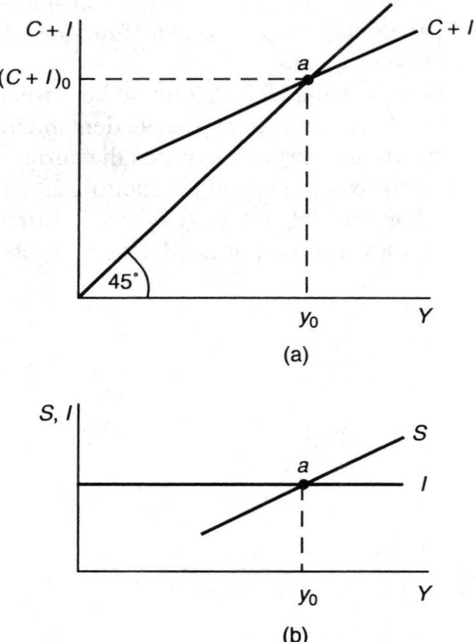

Figure 11.5: *Equilibrium in the two-sector model*

In Figure 11.5(a) the 45° line corresponds to the equation $C + I = Y$. Therefore *any point on the 45°* line satisfies the equilibrium condition for the economy. However the actual aggregate demand function for the economy $(C + I)$ has a slope less than one (= MPC) and therefore must intersect the 45° line. The point of intersection (a) represents the equilibrium for the economy with an equilibrium output of y_0 corresponding to the level of aggregate demand $(C + I)_0$. At output levels less than y_0 aggregate demand exceeds output so the economy will expand. At output levels greater than y_0 aggregate demand is less than output so the economy will contract.

Figure 11.5(a) is referred to as an 'income/expenditure' diagram, Figure 11.5(b) represents the corresponding 'injections/withdrawals diagram'. These diagrams represent alternative ways of illustrating the equilibrium output of the economy which in both cases is y_0. At output levels below y_0 in Figure 11.5(b) injections exceed withdrawals causing the economy to expand whereas at output levels above y_0 withdrawals exceed injections causing the economy to contract.

11.3 *Underemployment equilibrium*

The point that Keynes was concerned to emphasise was that the equilibrium level of income was not necessarily the **full employment** level of income. It was possible for the economy to be in equilibrium but with high levels of unemployment (an ***underemployment equilibrium***). This situation is illustrated in Figure 11.6.

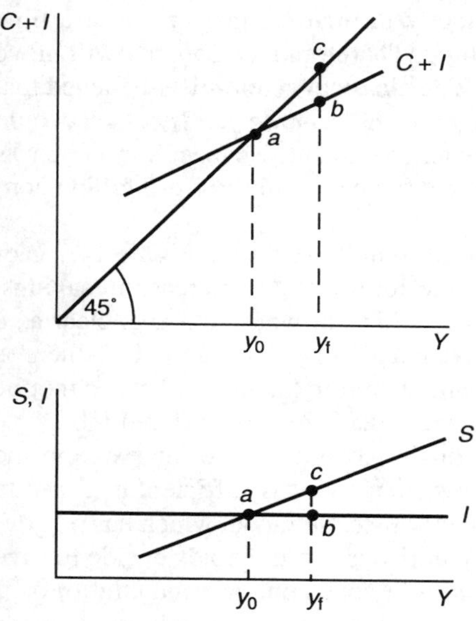

Figure 11.6: *Deflationary gap*

The equilibrium level of output is y_0 but y_f is the required level of output if full employment is to be achieved. This economy is experiencing a deflationary gap. i.e. too little expenditure. The *deflationary gap*, indicates the amount of new expenditure that needs to be injected into the economy and is equal to the distance *bc* in both diagrams.

The problem as Keynes saw it can be appreciated if we focus on the savings investment equilibrium ($S = I$). Decisions regarding the level of savings are being made by households while decisions regarding the level of investment are being made separately by firms. There was no reason to assume that these decisions would coincide at a full-employment equilibrium. The point is illustrated in Figure 11.7.

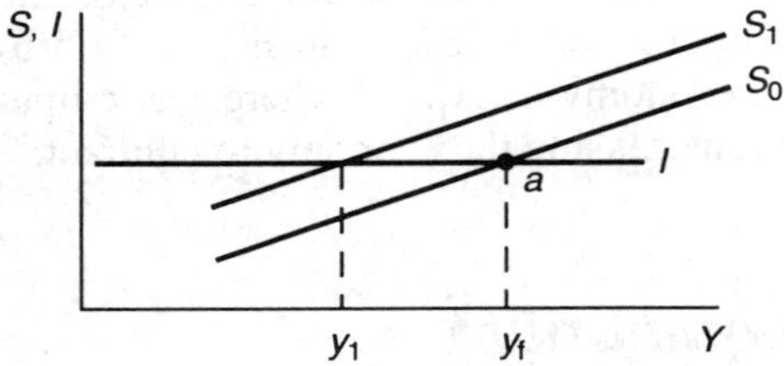

Figure 11.7: *Underemployment equilibrium*

Let's assume that, starting at a full employment equilibrium (*a*) households decide to save more (spend less), causing the savings function to shift from S_0 to S_1. Unless firms spend more on investment output will fall from y_f to y_1. But, according to Keynes, firms would be unlikely to increase investment at a time when demand and therefore sales were falling. Therefore the economy will move to an underemployment equilibrium at y_1. The **classical economists** believed that the increased savings represented an increase in *loanable funds* which would cause interest rates to fall and thus stimulate investment. Keynes, however, was more concerned with the blow to business confidence resulting from falling consumer demand.

The nature of the underemployment equilibrium illustrated in Figure 11.7 is of interest. y_1 is the equilibrium level of income following the increase in savings. However it is not like a micro-economics equilibrium where markets clear as a result of the equality between supply and demand. At y_1 in Figure 11.7 there is *involuntary unemployment* (Section 15.4) and therefore labour markets cannot be clearing. More workers are seeking employment than are being offered jobs.

Keynes argued that there was a need for the government to intervene in the economy to ensure that the level of aggregate demand was sufficient to generate full employment. However, sticking with our two-sector model which has no government, the only way aggregate demand can rise is if households decide to save less of their income (an autonomous increase in consumption expenditure) or if firms decide to raise investment expenditure. Either of these will result in an upward shift in the aggregate demand function.

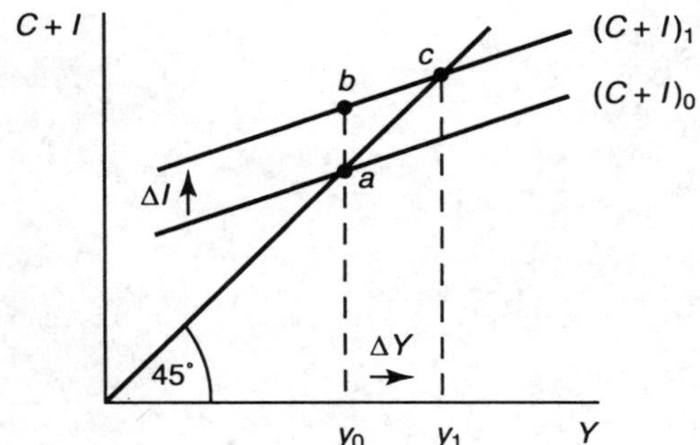

Figure 11.8: *Increasing aggregate demand*

Figure 11.8 illustrates with reference to an increase in investment expenditure. Assume the initial equilibrium y_0 is an underemployment equilibrium. An *exogenously determined* change in investment expenditure (i.e. we are not concerned to explain the cause of this change but merely to trace the effect of it) shifts the aggregate demand function from $(C+I)_0$ to $(C+I)_1$. The initial effect is for the economy to shift from point *a* to point *b*. However point *b* is not an equilibrium $(AD > y_0)$, the economy expands to the new equilibrium at point *c* with income equal to y_1. Certain features of this movement from y_0 to y_1 should be noted:

- In the simple circular flow model it is assumed that prices do not change. This *fix price* assumption means that the economy's GDP expands in **real terms** (Section 10.3) as a result of the increase in aggregate demand:
- There are exogenous and **induced** changes in expenditure occurring. The increase in investment expenditure (exogenous) causes income to rise but this rise in income causes further induced changes in consumption expenditure (the movement from *b* to *c*).
- Because of the exogenous and induced changes in expenditure the final change in income (ΔY) is greater than the initial change in investment expenditure (ΔI). This is known as the *multiplier effect.*

11.4 *The multiplier effect*

It can be shown that for Figure 11.8:

$$\Delta Y = \frac{1}{1 - \text{MPC}} \Delta I \qquad [11.8]$$

where $1/1 - \text{MPC}$ is the multiplier.

The multiplier effect is easily illustrated using the savings-investment diagram. In Figure 11.9 the initial equilibrium is y_0. The MPC is assumed to be 0.8

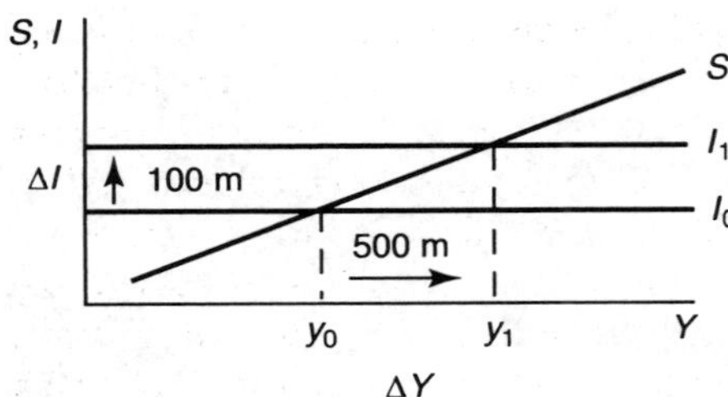

Figure 11.9: *Multiplier effect*

(i.e. MPS = 0.2). Investment expenditure rises by £100m. The value of the multiplier is 5 (i.e. 1/1 – 0.8). The final change in income is £500m.

$$\Delta Y = \frac{1}{1 - 0.8} \text{£100m} = \text{£500m}$$

Note as income rises from y_0 to y_1 there is an induced increase in savings. Income rises until the new level of savings is equal to the higher level of investment. The multiplier effect results from successive (but diminishing) rounds of expenditure following the initial increase in expenditure. Initially investment expenditure rises by £100m causing incomes to rise by the same amount. However because MPC = 0.8, £80m of this increased income will be spent causing incomes to rise by an additional £80m. £64m of this additional change will be spent ... and so on.

11.5 *The paradox of thrift*

The paradox of thrift relates to the possibility of households intending to save more (or less) but actually ending up saving less (or more). In Figure 11.10 it is assumed that the level of investment expenditure is positively related to the level of income (as illustrated by the upward slope).

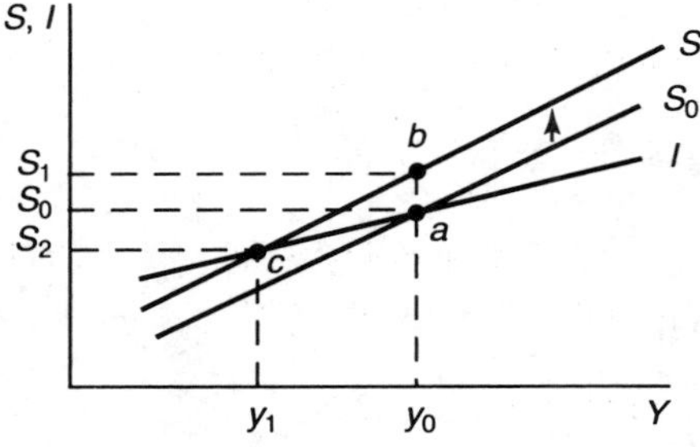

Figure 11.10: *Paradox of thrift*

The initial equilibrium is at point *a* with income level of y_0 and s_0 being saved. Households decide (for whatever reason) to save more and therefore spend less of their incomes. This is indicated by the upward shift in the savings function from S_0 to S_1. Because the increase in savings represents a fall in aggregate demand, the equilibrium level of income falls from y_0 to y_1 (point *c* represents the new equilibrium). Although the savings ratio has increased, the overall level of savings has fallen due to the fall in the level of income. Households had intended saving an amount s_1 from y_0 but end up saving an amount s_2 from y_1, i.e. the level of savings has fallen despite the original intention to increase savings.

REVISION FOCUS CHAPTER ELEVEN

Key Areas

- Aggregate demand ($C + I$)
- Consumption function
  →marginal propensity to consume→average propensity to consume
- Savings function
  →marginal propensity to save→average propensity to save
- Investment expenditure
- Equilibrium condition ($y = C + I$ or $S = I$)
  →underemployment equilibrium (deflationary gap)
- Multiplier effect ($k = 1/1 - \text{MPC}$)
- Paradox of thrift

Self Test (assume a two-sector model)

(1) If when income rises from £1000m to £1100m consumption expenditure rises by £80m, calculate the value of the multiplier (k) ___

(2) The MPC in an economy is 0.6. If investment expenditure (I) increases by £100m what will be the total change in income (ΔY). ___

(3) The value of output is currently £1000m but full employment output is £1200m. If the MPS = 0.2 calculate the required increase in investment expenditure (ΔI) for full employment to be achieved ___

(4) If investment expenditure is £100m and the MPC = 0.9 the equilibrium level of income is (a) £10,000m (b) £1,000m (c) £900m

(5) If households decide to save more (increase in the savings ratio) the equilibrium level of income will fall unless firms decide to invest more. T/F

(6) A deflationary gap can be removed by an increase in investment expenditure T/F

(7) An increase in the MPC will cause the value of the multiplier to fall T/F

(8) A deflationary gap measures the excess of savings over investment at the equilibrium level of income T/F

Discussion Topics

- The multiplier effect depends on the value of the MPC. Explain how the value changes as MPC changes.
- Distinguish between *autonomous* (or exogenous) and *induced* changes in expenditure.
- Explain and illustrate the paradox of thrift.
- Using a diagram to illustrate, explain how equilibrium is determined in the two-sector model.

CHAPTER 12

GOVERNMENT IN THE CIRCULAR FLOW

12.1 *Government policies and objectives*

Governments play a major role in all modern economies. *Public procurements* – government expenditure on defence, education, health, transport, etc. – represent a major claim on the economic resources of society. Government expenditure is therefore an important component of aggregate demand in the economy.

Governments also pursue broader policy objectives. Although the priorities can shift depending on circumstances, the following are the well established objectives of macroeconomic policy:

- Full employment;
- Low inflation;
- Economic growth;
- Satisfactory balance of payments;
- Redistribution of income in society.

The problem for governments is that these objectives are not always mutually consistent. Conflicts can emerge, for example, in trying to simultaneously achieve full employment and low inflation, or in trying to achieve economic growth while having generous policies for redistributing income from rich to poor. Priorities will have to be established and a trade-off between objectives may be necessary.

To achieve their macroeconomic objectives governments must formulate appropriate policies. Macroeconomic policies tend to be classified under two broad headings:

- Fiscal policy: using the powers of taxation and government expenditure to achieve objectives.
- Monetary policy: using interest rates and the money supply to achieve objectives.

In the context of the simple Keynesian circular flow model the focus is on the use of **fiscal policy** to achieve the **full employment** objective. Being a *fix price* model it is clearly inadequate for analysing issues concerning inflation.

12.2 Closed economy model

By including a government in the model we need to take account of an additional withdrawal from and injection into the circular flow of income and expenditure:

- **Taxation** (T) represents a withdrawal from the circular flow. It represents income earned which is passed to the government rather than passed on as expenditure on domestically produced goods and services.
- **Government Expenditure** (G) represents an injection of expenditure into the circular flow.

The fiscal policy being pursued by the government will be reflected in the annual budget. With regard to the impact of the budget on aggregate demand there are three possible scenarios:

- Balanced budget: ($G = T$)
  injections equal withdrawals implying a *neutral* effect on aggregate demand;
- Budget deficit: ($G > T$)
  injections exceed withdrawals causing aggregate demand to increase ('expansionary budget');
- Budget surplus: ($G < T$)
  withdrawals exceed injections causing aggregate demand to decrease ('contractionary budget').

A budget deficit will force the government to seek additional (besides taxation) sources of finance. Typically a budget deficit can be expected to result in a public sector borrowing requirement (PSBR). Annual borrowing in turn contributes to the *national debt*, which is simply all outstanding (unredeemed) public sector debt. A budget surplus may be used for public sector debt repayment (PSDR) which represents a reduction in the national debt.

In practice governments have additional sources of finance besides taxation and borrowing. These include the proceeds of privatization, the profits of state sector enterprises, or, in the Irish case transfers from the EU. However these sources are either one-off or relatively insignificant and will be ignored in the following analysis.

There are three components of aggregate demand in the closed economy:

$$\text{AD} \equiv C + I + G \qquad [12.1]$$

Government expenditure (G) is exogonously determined in that its level cannot be explained by reference to the economic variables of the model. The level of G depends on the ideological make-up of the government which may be sympathetic to relatively high or relatively low levels of public expenditure.

Because taxation exists it is necessary to distinguish between the *gross* factor incomes of households (Y) and the *disposable* income of households (Y_d). Disposable income is what remains after taxes have been deducted:

$$Y_d = Y - T \qquad [12.2]$$

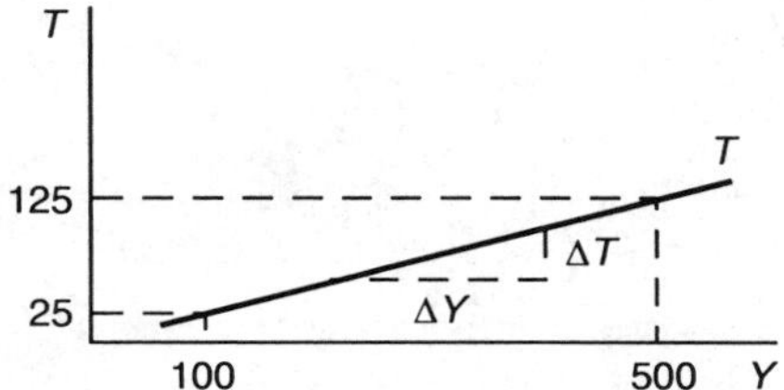

Figure 12.1: *Tax function*

If we assume for simplicity that all taxes are direct, then the level of taxation (T) depends on two things: *the rate of tax* and the *level of income* (Y). Taxation is therefore endogenously determined. Given the rate of tax the amount of tax is determined by the level of income. As income rises the level of tax rises and vice versa. Figure 12.1 illustrates a simple tax function.

As gross incomes rise tax revenue increases. The *marginal rate of tax* (MRT) which is the rate of tax on an additional £1 earned, is indicated by the slope of the line ($\Delta T/\Delta Y$). If we assume a simple tax function of the form $T = 0.25Y$ then for $Y = £100$, $T = £25$ and for $Y = £500$, $T = 125$, etc. The proportion of any change in income that is taken by the government in tax ($\Delta T/\Delta Y$) is sometimes referred to as the marginal propensity to tax (MPT).

Households must now decide how much of their disposable incomes (rather than gross incomes) to spend or save. A given marginal propensity to consume from disposable income (MPC) will mean a lower marginal propensity to consume from gross income (MPC_g).

Example

Assume:

- All income is taxed at a rate of 25% (MRT = 0.25)
- Households spend 80% of any additional disposable income (MPC = 0.8) and save 20% (MPS = 0.2). Then

$$T = 0.25Y$$

$$Y_d = Y - T = Y - 0.25Y = 0.75Y$$

$$\Delta C = 0.8\Delta Y_d$$

$$= 0.8(0.75)\Delta Y = 0.6\Delta Y$$

i.e. given a 25% marginal tax rate, a marginal propensity to consume from disposable income of 0.8 implies a marginal propensity to consume from gross income of 0.6.

The aggregate demand function for the closed economy can be illustrated as in Figure 12.2.

Aggregate demand at any given level of income is arrived at by simply adding the relevant levels of C, I and G. Both I and G are assumed to be independent of

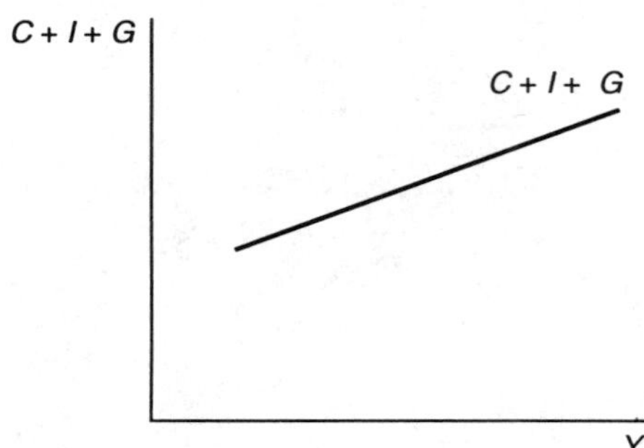

Figure 12.2: *Aggregate demand function for a closed economy*

the level of income whereas C is positively related to it. The slope of the aggregate demand function is $\Delta C/\Delta Y$ (i.e. MPC_g). The slope of the line in Figure 12.2 is flatter than that in Figure 11.1(a) due to the inclusion of taxation. It follows that the *multiplier effect is weakened* by the inclusion of taxation. The formula for the multiplier(k) is now:

$$k = \frac{1}{1 - \text{MPC}(1 - \text{MRT})} = \frac{1}{1 - \text{MPC}_g} \qquad [12.3]$$

Example

Using the figures from the previous example:

$$k = \frac{1}{1 - 0.8(1 - 0.25)} = \frac{1}{1 - 0.6} = 2.5$$

Quite simply the greater the scope for withdrawals from the circular flow the lower the proportion of any change in gross income that is passed on as expenditure thus reducing the multiplier effect.

Equilibrium in the closed economy

The equilibrium condition for the closed economy is:

$$Y = C + I + G \qquad [12.4]$$

When the sum of the desired levels of expenditure in the economy ($C + I + G$) is equal to the value of output (Y) being produced in the economy, there will be no tendency for economic expansion or contraction. The equilibrium can be illustrated using an income expenditure diagram as in Figure 12.3.

The equilibrium level of income is determined at the point where the aggregate demand function intersects the 45° line. This is at point a in Figure 12.3 with an equilibrium income of y_0.

An alternative formulation of the equilibrium condition is in terms of injections

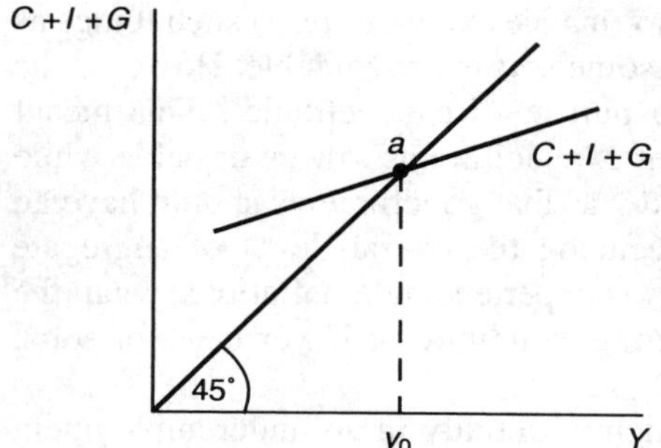

Figure 12.3: *Equilibrium in a closed economy (income/expenditure diagram)*

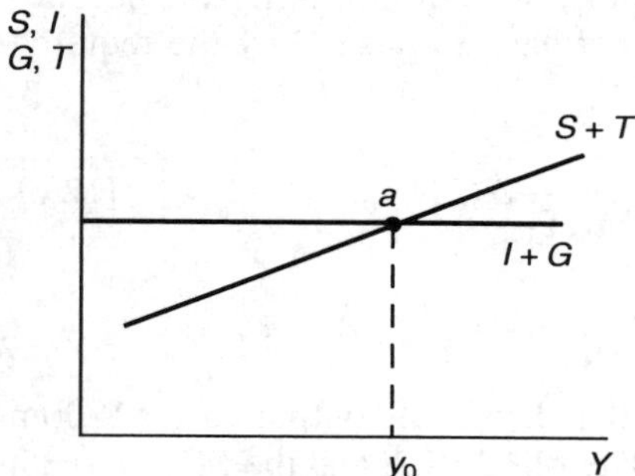

Figure 12.4: *Equilibrium in the injections/withdrawals diagram*

and withdrawals:

$$S + T = I + G$$

As both withdrawals (*S*,*T*) are positively related to the level of income and both injections (*I*,*G*) are independent of the level of income (exogenous) this equilibrium condition can be illustrated as in Figure 12.4.

The equilibrium level of income (y_0) is determined at the point of intersection of the injections and withdrawals functions (point *a*).

12.3 *Active fiscal policy*

As we have seen, Keynes was pessimistic about the capacity of an unregulated free market economy to generate a full employment equilibrium. The Keynesian analysis was developed in the inter-war period, a period of global economic and political instability. The depression of the early 1930s was characterized by mass unemployment. Not a time when one's confidence in the free market system was likely to be strengthened.

Because governments must raise taxes to finance expenditure on such things as defence, education, etc., a fiscal policy of some sort is unavoidable. However the traditional policy of governments was to pursue 'fiscal rectitude'. This meant keeping taxation and therefore government expenditure as low as possible while balancing the budget. What Keynes argued was that governments should have an **active fiscal policy** with a view to influencing the overall level of aggregate demand in the economy. If the economy was experiencing a deflationary gap the government should either raise government expenditure or lower taxes or some combination of both.

Figure 12.5 illustrates an economy which is initially in an underemployment equilibrium (point *a*).

By increasing expenditure by an amount equal to ΔG the government can shift the aggregate demand function from $(C+I+G)_0$ to $(C+I+G)_1$. A new equilibrium is achieved at point *b* which is a full employment equilibrium. Note because of the multiplier effect the government does not have to raise *G* by the required increase in *Y*

$$\Delta Y = \frac{1}{1 - \text{MPC}(1 - \text{MRT})} \Delta G \qquad [12.6]$$

Example

Assume the government needs to raise the level of output by £1000m ($\Delta Y = £1000\text{m}$) to achieve full employment. The MPC = 0.8 and the MRT = 0.25.

$$\Delta Y = \frac{1}{1 - \text{MPC}(1 - \text{MRT})} \Delta G$$

$$£1000\text{m} = \frac{1}{1 - 0.8(1 - 0.25)} \Delta G$$

$$\Delta G = \frac{£1000\text{m}}{2.5} = £400\text{m}$$

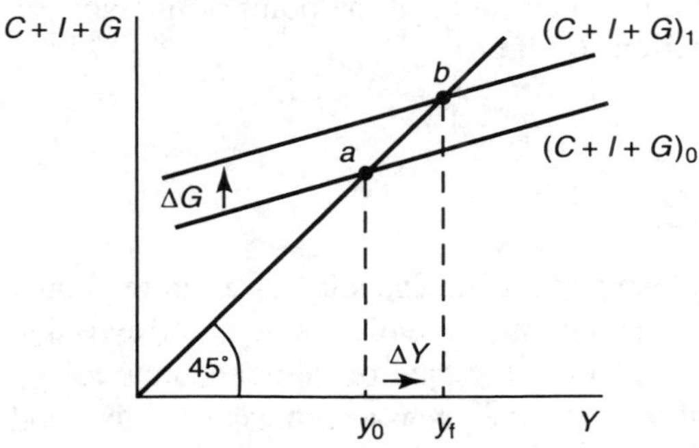

Figure 12.5: *Fiscal expansion: increased government expenditure*

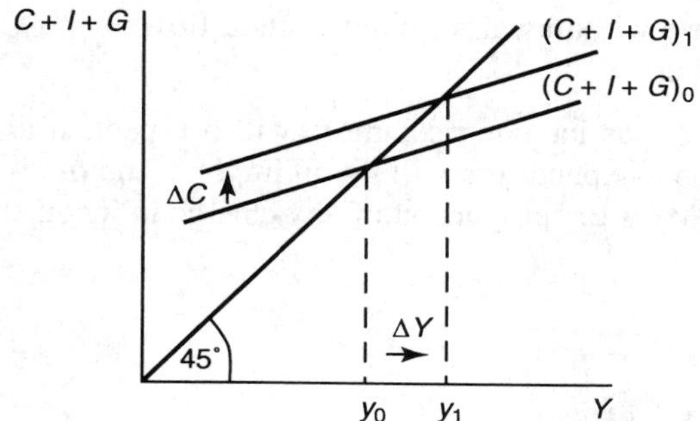

Figure 12.6: *Fiscal expansion: reduction in taxation*

Therefore if the government increases expenditure (ΔG) by £400m income will rise by £1000m.

If instead of increasing government expenditure the government **reduced taxes** it could stimulate household expenditure (C) by raising household disposable income (Y_d). However C will not initially increase by the full reduction in taxation as only some proportion (the MPC) will be spent while some proportion (the MPS) is saved. The initial increase in consumption will be equal to MPC times ΔT. Figure 12.6 illustrates fiscal expansion by way of a tax reduction.

In Figure 12.6 AC = MPC ΔT. The multiplier effect resulting from a reduction in taxation will be less than the multiplier effect for an increase in government expenditure:

$$\Delta Y = \frac{\text{MPC}}{1 - \text{MPC}(1 - \text{MRT})} \Delta T \qquad [12.7]$$

Equation [12.7] gives the multiplier effect of a lump sum change in taxes (ΔT).

Because the taxation multiplier [12.7] is less than the government expenditure multiplier (12.6) it is possible to achieve a **balanced budget multiplier effect**. If government raises taxation and expenditure by an equal amount, the increase in taxes will reduce income by a smaller amount than the increase in expenditure will raise it. The overall effect, therefore, will be positive. The net effect is the result of the government spending income that households had in fact been saving.

12.4 *Open economy model*

In an open economy we must take account of **international trade. Exports** are domestically produced goods the demand for which originates abroad. Foreign expenditure on the economy's exports (X) represents an injection of income and expenditure into the domestic economy. **Imports** are foreign produced goods the demand for which originates in the domestic economy. Domestic expenditure on imports (M) represents income earned which is not passed on as expenditure on domestic production and is therefore a withdrawal from the circular flow.

The value of imports will depend on:

- The level of domestic income (Y) – as income rises more will be spent. It is assumed that some of this additional expenditure will go on imports The **marginal propensity to import** (MPM) is the proportion of any change in income that is spent on imports

Example

$$\Delta Y = £100\text{m}$$
$$\Delta M = 20\text{m}$$
$$\text{MPM} = \frac{\Delta M}{\Delta Y} = 0.2$$

- The real exchange rate (Section 17.1) – the competitiveness of domestic goods and services relative to foreign ones will influence consumers' purchases. Competitiveness depends on the nominal exchange rate (Section 17.1) and domestic prices relative to foreign prices.

The value of exports will depend on:

- The level of world income – if income and expenditure is rising in the economies of trading partners this will lead to an increase in demand for exports (for example if the British economy is booming this will stimulate demand for Irish exports).
- The real exchange rate – if domestically produced goods and services lose competitiveness on world markets exports will be adversely affected and vice versa.

In the completed circular flow model there are three injections (G, I, X) and three withdrawals (S, T, M) as illustrated in Figure 12.7. All the injections are exogenously determined, i.e. their levels are determined by factors not included in the

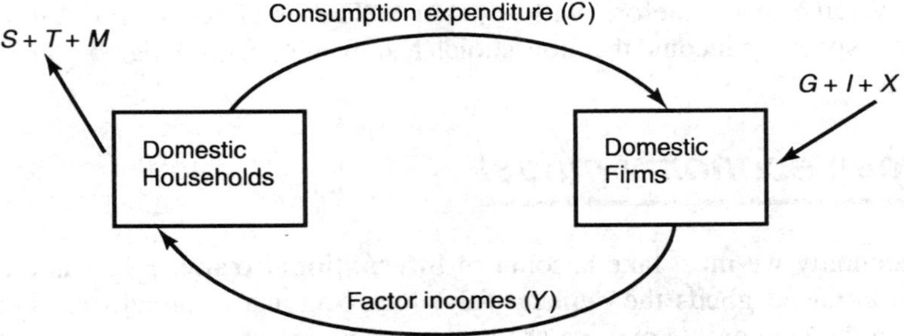

Figure 12.7: *The circular flow of income and expenditure*

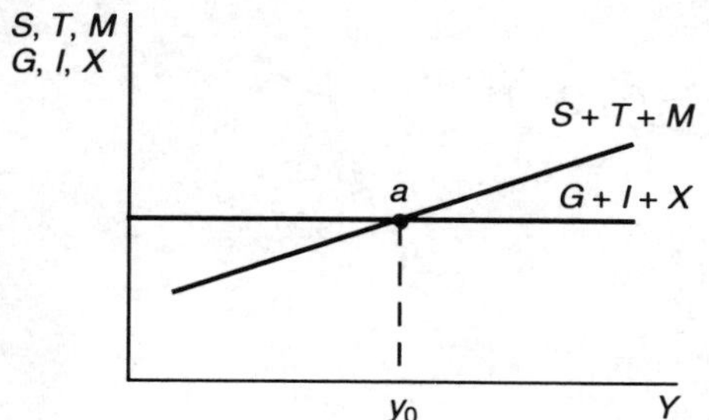

Figure 12.8: *Open economy equilibrium: (injections and withdrawals)*

model. The withdrawals are endogenously determined as the level of domestic income (y) has a positive influence on all of their levels.

The economy will be in equilibrium with no tendency for output to expand or contract when the sum of injections equals the sum of withdrawals:

$$S+T+M=G+I+X \qquad [12.8]$$

This equilibrium condition can be illustrated in an injections/withdrawals diagram as in Figure 12.8.

The economy is in equilibrium at point *a* where the injections line intersects the withdrawals line with income y_0.

Aggregate demand in an open economy

The aggregate demand for domestically produced goods and services in an open economy is:

$$\text{AD} \equiv C+I+G+(X-M) \qquad [12.9]$$

The **equilibrium condition** is that total desired expenditure be equal to the value of domestic output:

$$Y=C+I+G+(X-M) \qquad [12.10]$$

This equilibrium condition is an alternative formulation of Equation [12.8] and is illustrated in Figure 12.9.

Equilibrium is at point *a* with income at y_0. The aggregate demand function in Figure 12.9 has a slope which is flatter than that of Figure 12.2. This is because imports are positively related to the level of domestic income (i.e. endogenously determined) and are included in the function with a negative sign. It follows that the multiplier effect is weakened when we move from a closed to an open economy. The formula for the open economy multiplier is:

$$\text{k} = \frac{1}{1-\text{MPC}(1-\text{MRT})+\text{MPM}}$$

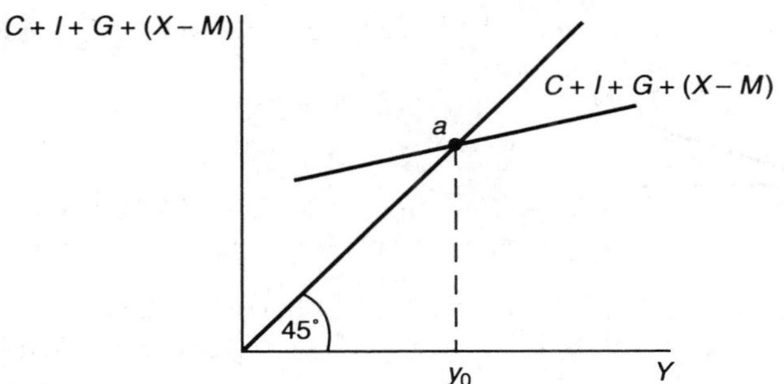

Figure 12.9: *Open economy equilibrium: income/expenditure diagram*

Example

$$MPC = 0.8$$
$$MRT = 0.25$$
$$MPM = 0.2$$

$$k = \frac{1}{1 - 0.8(0.75) + 0.2} = \frac{1}{0.6} = 1.67$$

Clearly the multiplier effect, resulting from any injection of demand into the economy, will be weaker the higher is the MPM. Figure 12.10 illustrates the multiplier effect with respect to a change in government expenditure (ΔG). Note, the relationship between ΔG and ΔY depends on the open economy multiplier.

$$\Delta Y = \frac{1}{1 - MPC(1 - MRT) + MPM} \Delta G$$

We can conclude that fiscal policy in an open economy will have less effect on

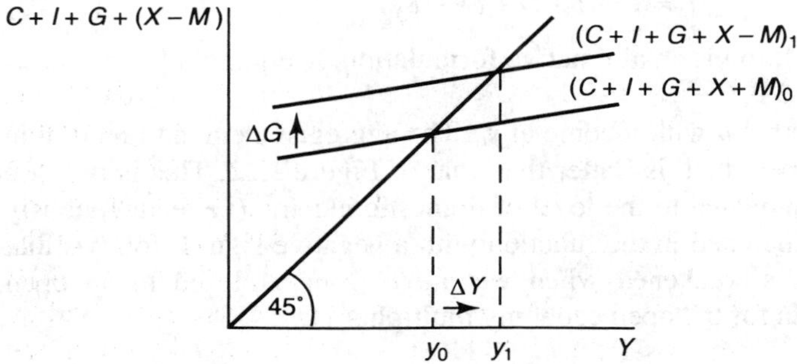

Figure 12.10: *Multiplier effect in an open economy*

economic activity than in a closed economy. The higher the MPM the smaller the multiplier effect and the less impact policy will have.

12.5 *Limitations of the simple Keynesian model*

The simple Keynesian model of income determination, developed in this and the previous chapter, explains the level of economic activity by reference to the level of aggregate demand. If there is unemployment in the economy government can remove it by raising aggregate demand by means of fiscal policy. All economic models simplify reality with a view to clarifying key relationships. All resort to the *ceteris paribus* assumption (Section 1.4) in order to make **conditional predictions**. For example, 'if aggregate demand is raised, *all else being equal*, the result will be increased economic activity' is the conditional prediction of the simple Keynesian model.

Models can be criticized if the assumptions are wrong or key economic relationships are being left out so that either way the predictions are unreliable. The main weakness of the simple circular flow model is the absence of a monetary system. It focuses on production to supply markets for goods and services but has nothing to say about money. Because monetary issues are outside the scope of the model it lacks the capacity to explain the following.

The Crowding Out Effect

An *increase* in government expenditure may lead to a fall in private sector expenditure ('crowding out'). For example, assume the government is pursuing an expansionary fiscal policy and is borrowing funds in the **capital markets** to finance a budget deficit. If this has the effect of raising **interest rates** then private sector investment expenditure and consumption expenditure are likely to fall. The crowding out effect calls into question the governments ability to control the level of aggregate demand (Section 14.4).

Stagflation

This is a situation where *unemployment* and *inflation* are simultaneously rising. The simple model has a 'fix price' assumption. We can interpret this to mean that if unemployment exists and aggregate demand rises real output rather than the price level will rise. If however the economy is fully employed and aggregate demand continues to rise, then as output cannot rise, inflation will occur. In the simple model, inflation can only be due to too much demand in the economy. It follows that simultaneously rising inflation and unemployment are precluded by the model. Stagflation was a widespread problem in the global economy in the 1970s and was a major factor leading to a loss of confidence in Keynesian economics.

Other problems include:

The Nature of Unemployment

The Keynesian model has a one-dimensional view of the cause of unemployment. The model explains unemployment by reference to the level of aggregate demand. If the latter is too low unemployment will be the result. However, unemployment may have a number of causes (Section 15.4). If so, simply increasing aggregate demand may not be an adequate policy.

Openness of Modern Economies

We have seen (Section 12.4) that fiscal policy may be relatively ineffective with regard to influencing economic activity if there is a high marginal propensity to import. Modern economies are much more open than was the case when Keynes was developing his analysis. The balance of payments figures for the Irish economy (Section 16.1) suggest a high MPM. Clearly small open economies (particularly with high marginal rates of tax) will have relatively weak multiplier effects and therefore fiscal policy as prescribed by Keynes will be correspondingly weakened.

REVISION FOCUS CHAPTER TWELVE

Key Areas

- Macro economic objectives and policies
- The budget and fiscal policy
- Aggregate demand in a closed economy $(C + I + G)$
  → effect of taxation and government expenditure on AD → marginal rate of tax (MRT) → gross income and disposable income → closed economy equilibrium condition ($Y = C + I + G$ or $S + T = G + I$) → closed economy multiplier (1/1 – MPC(1 – MRT)).
- Aggregate demand in an open economy$(C + I + G + X - M)$
  → impact of imports and exports → marginal propensity to import (MPM) → open economy equilibrium condition ($Y = C + I + G + X - M$ or $S + T + M = G + I + X$) → multiplier in an open economy (1/1 – MPC(1 – MRT) + MPM)
- Problems with the simple circular flow model

Self Test

(1) In a closed economy with MPC = 0.75 and MRT = 0.2 an increase in government expenditure of £1000m will raise equilibrium income by? ___

(2) A reduction in the MRT will increase the value of the multiplier T/F

(3) In a closed economy with G = £1000m, I = £1000m, MPC = 0.8 and MRT = 0.25, the equilibrium level of income is: (a) 5000m, (b) £6250m or (c) £2000m? ___

(4) The multiplier effect is smaller in an open economy the higher the MPM T/F

(5) A crowding-out effect occurs when an increase in government expenditure leads to a fall in private sector expenditure T/F

(6) An increase in the value of exports will lead to a reduction in the equilibrium level of income T/F

(7) A balanced budget multiplier effect can result if the government increases tax and reduces government expenditure by the same amount T/F

(8) If MPC = 0.8, MRT = 0.25 and MPM = 0.1 and the government wishes to raise equilibrium income by £1000m. Government expenditure needs to rise by: T/F
(a) £500m, (b) £400m or (c) £1000m? ___

Discussion Topics

- In the Keynesian analysis of the economy the level of aggregate demand is the crucial variable. Explain.
- Explain why the multiplier effect is likely to be weak in a small open economy.
- Using a diagram to illustrate, explain clearly the meaning of a deflationary gap.

CHAPTER 13

MONEY AND BANKING

13.1 *Money in modern economies*

Money plays a crucial role in modern economies. Without money trade would be based on *barter*. In a barter economy trade requires a *double-coincidence of wants* – if you have eggs but want cheese you must find somebody who has cheese but wants eggs. With barter the activities of selling and buying cannot be separated. The existence of money facilitates trade, division of labour and therefore economic development.

Money is usually defined by reference to the principal **functions** it performs:

- A medium of exchange (exchange function)
  Money is used as payment for goods and services. Its existence separates the activities of buying and selling and thereby removes the need for a double-coincidence of wants when trading.
- A store of value (asset function)
  To be acceptable as a medium of exchange money must act as a store of value. Money must be a means of storing *purchasing power*.
- A unit of account
  To act as a medium of exchange money must also act as a unit of account. It must be possible to measure the value of goods and services in terms of money. Without money national income accounting would be practically impossible.
- A standard of deferred payments
  By acting as a unit of account *over time* money facilitates the generalized use of *credit* in modern economies.

Anything that is generally acceptable as payment for goods and services can act as a medium of exchange. Traditionally money had an intrinsic value, e.g. gold. In modern economies, paper money has no intrinsic value and depends crucially on the confidence of the public (confidence in its purchasing power) for its effectiveness. Traditionally the confidence of the public was based on the *convertibility* of legal tender into gold at a *particular rate* (***gold standard***). It would be rare for a modern government to guarantee convertibility.

Payment for goods and services in the modern economy is typically by means of *legal tender* or *bank balances*. People will accept payment by cheque (claims on bank balances) but only if they are confident it is convertible into legal tender.

The two important components of money in a modern economy are therefore legal tender and bank balances.

Different **measures** of the amount of money in the economy can be got by drawing distinctions between cash in circulation and in bank tills, or between different types of bank deposit.

M0: cash in circulation + cash in bank tills + operational deposits of commercial banks held at Central bank
M1: cash in circulation + private sector current account deposits (*sight deposits*) in commercial banks
M3: M1 + private sector deposit accounts (*time deposits*) in commercial banks

M0 is known as the *monetary base*. M1 is a *narrow* definition of money whereas M3 is a *broad* definition of money. Alternative definitions can be got by including foreign currency deposits or building society deposits, etc.

It can be seen from Table 13.1 that cash is not the dominant form of money in modern economies. For the broad definition (M3) cash can be a very small proportion, bank deposits being by far the largest component (90% or more).

Table 13.1: *Source: Central Bank Bulletin Spring 1997*

Irish Money Supply Dec 31 1996	
Cash in bank tills	279m
Cash in circulation	2008m
M1	5899m
M3	27038m

13.2 *Credit creation and the money supply*

Commercial banks are profit-seeking institutions. To make profits banks must provide loans to creditworthy borrowers. Banks are **financial intermediaries**, receiving funds from some groups and advancing funds to other groups.

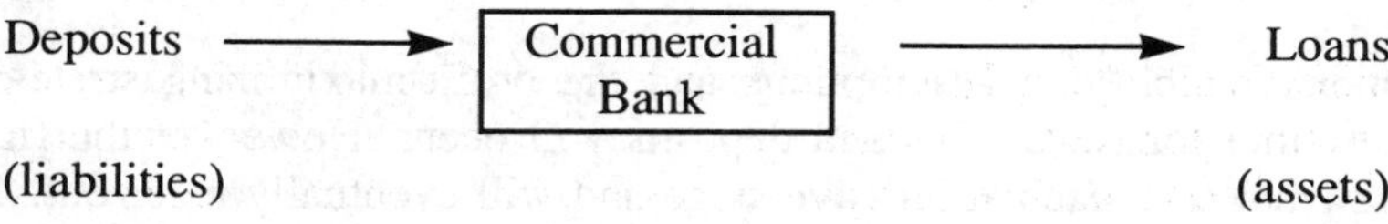

Modern commercial banking operates on the principle of *fractional reserve banking*. The bank only keeps a fraction of its deposit liabilities in liquid form the greater proportion being advanced as interest earning loans. The bank knows from experience that not all depositors are likely to seek to withdraw all their deposits at any given time. Therefore only a fraction of liabilities need be held in reserve to meet day-to-day obligations. The fraction of deposit liabilities held in reserve by the bank is known as the *reserve asset ratio* (RAR). Note: there is a conflict here between the pursuit of profit and the need to maintain adequate liquidity. Excessive reserves suggest that the bank should increase loans in pursuit of profit. However, if reserves are too low the bank faces the danger of being incapable of meeting its liabilities. Prudent management requires having sufficient liquidity (cash and liquid assets) to meet liabilities as they arise.

Fractional reserve banking leads to the *creation of money* by profit-seeking commercial banks.

Example

Assume a commercial bank, operating with a 10% RAR receives a cash deposit of £1000. The immediate effect is for the banks liabilities (£1000 deposit) and assets (£1000 in cash) to increase by the same amount. However the £1000 cash will not generate profit for the bank. Given the RAR of 10% the profit maximising strategy is to keep £100 in reserve and lend £900 resulting in the following assets and liabilities:

Liabilities	*Assets*	
Deposits: £1000	*Reserves:* £100	*Loans:* £900

Somebody has borrowed £900, presumably with a view to spending it. If we assume for simplicity that there is only one (multi-branch) bank in the economy and all receipts are deposited in this bank, then when the £900 is spent it will find its way back into the bank. This new deposit of £900 enables the bank to create further loans of £810 resulting in the following assets and liabilities:

Liabilities	*Assets*	
Deposits: £1900	Reserves: £190	Loans: £1710

When the £810 is spent and redeposited in the bank a further loan of £729 is possible

Liabilities	*Assets*	
Deposits: £2710	Reserves: £271	Loans: £2439

Given our simplifying assumptions and the profit-maximizing strategy of the bank, further loans, receipts and deposits will occur. Howegver the figures are getting smaller at each successive stage and will eventually peter out. The total effect on the bank's balance sheet will be as follows:

Liabilities	*Assets*	
Deposits: £10,000	Reserves: £1000	Loans: £9000

Ultimately, the initial increase in liquid reserves (£1000 cash deposit) has enabled the bank to advance loans of £9000.

It can be seen from the final figures that:

$$\text{Total assets} = \text{Total liabilities} = £10{,}000$$

$$\text{RAR} = \frac{\text{Reserve Assets}}{\text{Deposit Liabilities}} = \frac{£1000}{10{,}000} = 10\%$$

$$\text{Deposit Liabilities} = \text{Reserve Assets}\left[\frac{1}{\text{RAR}}\right] = £1000\,\frac{1}{0.1} = £10{,}000$$

The last relationship can be expressed in terms of *changes* to highlight the credit creation process. Letting D stand for deposit liabilities and RA for reserve assets:

$$\Delta D = \Delta \text{RA}\,\frac{1}{\text{RAR}} \qquad [13.1]$$

Equation [13.1] tells us that there will be a change in deposit liabilities (ΔD) equal to a multiple (1/RAR) of any change in reserve assets (ΔRA). The *credit multiplier* is simply the inverse of the RAR (i.e. 1/RAR). The credit multiplier effect will be larger the lower the RAR is and vice versa.

Example

A bank operates with an RAR of 20%. There is an increase in cash deposits of £1000. The total effect on the *money supply* is £1000 (1/0.2) = £5000. The initial cash deposit of £1000 has led to an expansion of bank loans of £4000. Here the credit multiplier is 5 (= 1/0.2).

It is important to realize that as bank deposits expand *all measures of money (except M0) are expanding*.

If we allow for a multibank system the previous analysis is still valid and equation 13.1 still holds, provided all banks operate with the same RAR.

In conclusion, bank deposits are the largest component of money in a modern economy. The pursuit of profit will lead banks to provide loans to the public. This process of credit creation leads to an expansion of the money supply in the economy.

13.3 *The central bank*

In modern economies central banks (indicated with a capital 'B') are invariably public sector institutions. The degree of autonomy enjoyed by the Bank may differ from country to country but ultimately they are all answerable in some measure to the government. Central Banks are primarily *regulators* rather than profit-maximizing institutions.

Typically the following functions are performed by a Central Bank:

- **sole issuer** of legal tender;
- **banker to the clearing banks** – the banks keep their operational deposits at the Bank. If one bank is writing a cheque payable to another it will be drawn on these deposits;
- **banker to the government** – the government keeps its accounts at the Bank;
- **supervision of financial system** – maintain public confidence in the system by ensuring that banks behave prudently;
- **lender of last resort** – if banks are incapable of meeting their liabilities due to a temporary shortage of liquidity, the Bank is usually willing to lend money to banks and thereby underwrite public confidence in the financial system (Note, this function gives rise to a *moral hazard* dilemma. If the Bank is always prepared to bail out the banks, then they will have less incentive to behave prudently.);
- **borrows money on behalf of government** – issues short term and longer term government securities. (This in turn gives rise to a need to manage the *national debt*. The Bank may or may not be responsible for managing the national debt. In Ireland, a specialist institution called The National Treasury Management Agency performs this task);
- **instrument of government monetary policy** – controls the amount of money in the economy, the level of interest rates and the exchange rate of the currency.

13.4 *Monetary policy*

Too much money in the economy can lead to inflation (Section 13.7) which undermines the value of the currency. The Bank may have a statutory obligation to protect the value of the currency irrespective of government policies (the *German Model*).

Controlling the amount of legal tender in the economy is a trivial task for any Bank given that they are the sole issuer. In practice the control of the money supply is concerned with the creation of bank deposits by commercial banks. We have seen (Section 13.2) that there is a definite relationship between bank deposits, bank liquidity (reserve assets) and the RAR of the form:

$$\Delta D = \Delta \text{RA} \ \frac{1}{\text{RAR}}$$

It is easy to see that if the Bank wishes to control ΔD then controlling the amount of reserve assets available to the banks and/or controlling the reserve asset ratio can be effective.

- **Controlling the RAR**

The Bank has the power to insist that banks keep a given proportion of their liabilities in the form of liquid reserves. On the other hand the Bank may leave it to the banks to decide their own 'prudential rate'. If the Bank wishes to restrict the capacity of the banks to create deposits it could insist on a *high minimum reserve asset ratio*. The higher the RAR the smaller is the credit multiplier. For example an RAR of 10% gives a credit multiplier of 10 whereas an RAR of 20% gives a credit multiplier of 5. A high RAR will mean that for any given level of reserve assets there will be less bank deposits and therefore less money in the economy.

- **Open market operations (OMO)**

OMO is the practice of buying or selling government securities by the Bank with a view to influencing commercial bank liquidity. For effectiveness these sales or purchases must be carefully targeted. If the Bank sells government securities to the *non-bank private sector*, these securities will be paid for by the public by the writing of cheques payable to the Bank to be drawn on accounts in the banks. The banks when honouring these cheques will be required to transfer funds to the Bank resulting in a loss of commercial bank liquidity. For a given RAR this will result over time in a multiple contraction of commercial bank deposits. An expansionary OMO would entail the Bank buying back securities from the non-bank private sector resulting in an increase in commercial bank liquidity.

An obvious problem with OMO is that it disregards the level of the *national debt*. If long-term securities are being sold by the Bank then the national debt is rising and vice versa. In practice governments tend to be concerned to control the level of the national debt in which case the casual issuing of government securities to control the money supply would be inappropriate.

- **Interest rates**

The process of credit creation, banks lending money, presupposes the existence of willing borrowers. The willingness to borrow will in turn depend on the rate of interest charged. The Bank has the power to influence interest rates and thereby the desired level of borrowing in the economy.

In a modern economy there is a structure of inter-related interest rates rather than a single rate. The rate charged to a borrower will depend on two factors: (i) the duration of the loan and (ii) the degree of risk attached to the borrower.

The length of the loan and the risk will both have a positive effect on the rate of interest charged.

Short-term interest rates (up to one year loans) are determined in the *money markets* whereas longer term rates are determined in the *capital markets*. The money markets are dominated by financial institutions (including the Bank) borrowing/lending among themselves. The Bank has a determining influence on rates charged in the money markets. The rate at which the Bank is willing to lend money to the money markets determines short term interest rates and ultimately the whole structure of interest rates in the economy. By raising this Bank rate the Bank raises the cost of borrowing funds for the commercial banks. This in turn will mean higher rates for those wishing to borrow from commercial banks. The overall effect will be to reduce the amount of borrowing and therefore the expansion of the money supply.

- **Alternative Instruments of Control**

The Bank may resort to alternative means of controlling credit creation. One way is by means of *special deposits*. This is where the Bank reduces the liquidity of the commercial banks by requiring them to deposit funds in special accounts at the Bank. These funds are not eligible to act as reserve assets. Another way is by means of *moral suasion*. The Bank indicates to the banks that it wishes them to curtail lending. Whether or not the banks comply will depend on how the banks expect the Bank to respond to non-compliance.

13.5 *The demand for money*

The demand for money is concerned with the willingness of people to hold non-interest earning cash. Besides being a medium of exchange money functions as a store of value – this is referred to as **the asset function** of money (Section 13.1). However money may be a relatively poor store of value. During periods of inflation money loses its value. Even without inflation if interest earning assets exist as an alternative why hold non-interest earning cash. There is an opportunity cost involved in holding money measured in terms of the interest forgone if interest earning assets were held instead of cash. Holding money is not costless and therefore needs to be justified.

To hold money is to express a preference for **liquidity** rather than less liquid interest-earning assets. The Keynesian approach to money demand is known as the *theory of liquidity preference*. The simplest approach is to assume a choice between holding non interest-earning cash or interest-earning assets such as government bonds. However the important point is the **trade-off** that exists between liquidity and the expected rate of return on less liquid interest-earning assets.

Keynes advanced three motive for holding cash:

- **the transactions motive;**
- **the precautionary motive;**
- **the speculative motive.**

The transactions motive stems from the fact that peoples' income and expenditures are not perfectly synchronized. For many people income is received periodically in a lump sum whereas expenditure is a continuous flow. People will tend to hold cash to meet ongoing expenditures. As the level of expenditure of an individual will be positively linked to the level of income it is reasonable to assume that *the desired level of cash balances for transactions purposes will be positively linked to the level of income*.

Other factors may also have an influence on the desired level of transactions balances. If *interest rates* are very high then people may wish to economize on cash holdings. Also the *pattern of payments* will be a factor: a person paid weekly will hold less cash on average than the same person paid monthly. For example a worker paid £100 per week will have average cash holdings of £50 whereas that worker paid £400 every four weeks will have average cash holdings of £200.

The precautionary motive for holding cash balances stems from the unpredictability of some transactions. People will hold cash balances *just in case* a need arises. As with transactions balances, the level of precautionary balances is likely to be primarily influenced by the level of income.

The speculative motive stems from the desire to avoid capital losses. Keynes suggested that there would be a tendency to switch out of interest-earning assets and into cash if there was a danger of incurring capital losses on these assets. The key to this analysis is the relationship between market rates of interest and the market value of fixed interest securities.

Governments borrow by issuing ('*gilt-edged*') securities. Assume a government bond with a 'coupon rate' of 10% and a *nominal value* of £1000. For simplicity we will assume that the bond has no redemption date (non-redeemable fixed interest securities are known as *perpetuities*):

Nominal value	: £1000
annual interest	: £ 100

The government has borrowed £1000 at 10% annual interest. The bond is effectively an IOU and ownership of this bond entitles the holder to *an annual income of £100* into an indefinite future. If market rates of interest fall to 5% then it would require £2000 to generate an annual income of £100. If market rates of interest were to rise to 20% it would require only £500 to generate an annual income of £100. It can be seen, therefore, that the *market value* of fixed interest securities will move inversely with market rates of interest.

If an investor *expects* market rates of interest to rise (i.e. bond prices to fall) it would make sense to sell bonds for cash rather than incur the expected capital losses. One obvious problem with this analysis is that any buyer of the bond must have different expectations to the seller regarding future interest rates, i.e. they wouldn't willingly buy the bond at a price that implied future losses. If everybody in the bond market has the same expectations then this will be reflected in *existing* market prices for bonds. In this case there will be nothing to be gained from selling bonds (unless the market underestimates the future rise in interest rates).

If we assume that different investors in the bond market have different expectations regarding future interest rates then speculative buying and selling of bonds will occur. Note if bonds are being sold, cash is being acquired because cash is regarded as less of a risk. These cash balances are the speculative balances. If we further assume that the higher interest rates are the more likely investors are to expect a fall and the lower they are the greater the expectation of a rise. Then at high rates (fall anticipated) bond prices will be expected to rise so that holding bonds rather than cash makes sense. At low rates (rise anticipated) bond prices will be expected to fall so that holding cash rather than bonds makes sense.

The speculative demand for money developed by Keynes implies an inverse relationship between the rate of interest and the desired level of speculative money

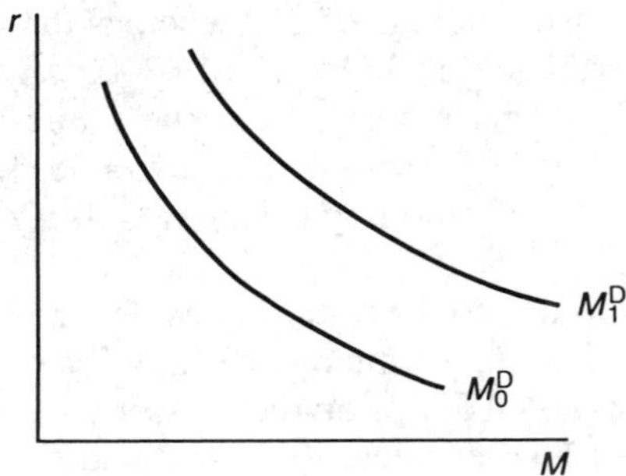

Figure 13.1: *The demand for money*

balances. It is likely that transactions and precautionary balances will also be economized on when interest rates are high. The overall result is a demand for money balances that is inversely related to the rate of interest but positively related to the level of income in the economy.

In Figure 13.1 each money demand curve is drawn for a different level of income. Both are downward sloping, reflecting the inverse relationship between the rate of interest and desired money balances. As income rises the demand for money rises, which is reflected in the outward shifting demand curve ($M_0^D \longrightarrow M_1^D$).

13.6 *Determination of the rate of interest*

It can be assumed that the money supply in the economy is determined by the Bank's monetary policy. This can be illustrated by a vertical supply of money at whatever quantity the Bank decides. Figure 13.2. brings the supply of and demand for money together.

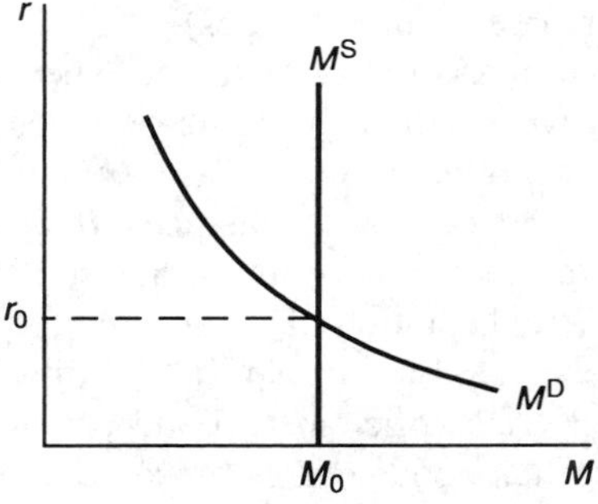

Figure 13.2: *The equilibrium rate of interest*

The equilibrium rate of interest will be determined at the point of intersection of the money supply and money demand curves. If the bank decides on a money supply of M_0 and if the demand for money in the economy is as represented by M^D, then the equilibrium rate of interest in the economy is r_0 (Figure 13.2).

If the Bank decides on expansionary or contractionary monetary policy then by implication it is choosing lower or higher interest rates.

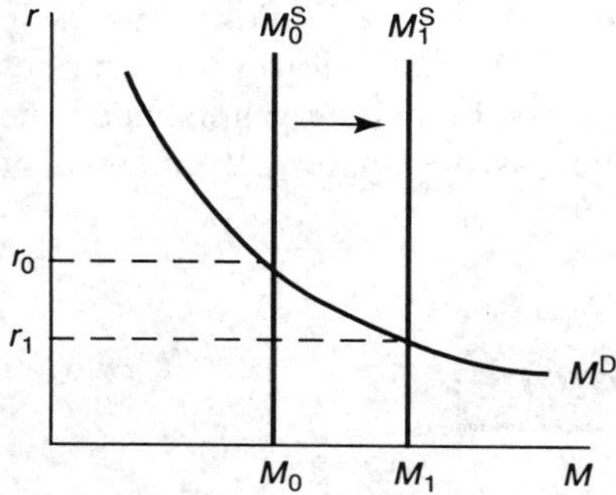

Figure 13.3: *Monetary policy and interest rates*

Figure 13.3 illustrates how an expansionary monetary policy (e.g. Bank buys government bonds) leads to a shift of the money supply from M_0 to M_1. As a result interest rates fall from r_0 to r_1 and bond prices rise. A contractionary monetary policy (e.g. selling government bonds) would lead to a leftward-shifting money supply a rise in interest rates and therefore a fall in bond prices. A tight monetary policy implies high interest rates whereas a loose monetary policy implies low interest rates.

Keynes suggested the possibility of a **liquidity trap**. At very low rates of interest the opportunity cost (interest forgone) of holding cash will be insignificant. If at a very low rate a change is more likely to mean an upward change then holding speculative cash balances rather than bonds would appear to make sense. At very low rates of interest therefore there may be a potentially limitless level of desired

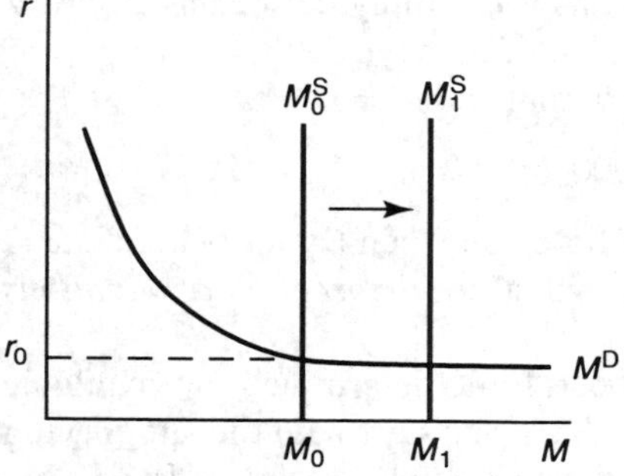

Figure 13.4: *Liquidity trap*

cash holdings. This can be illustrated by a perfectly elastic (horizontal) segment of the money demand curve at very low rates of interest as in Figure 13.4.

At r_0 there is a perfectly elastic demand for money. If the economy is in a liquidity trap then expanding the money supply ($M_0^s \rightarrow M_1^s$) will have no effect on the equilibrium rate of interest which remains at r_0. Governments might use an expansionary monetary policy to stimulate economic activity. An expansionary monetary policy means lower interest rates which should stimulate investment and consumption expenditure. However if the economy is in a liquidity trap as in Figure 13.4, an expansionary monetary policy will not lead to lower interest rates and therefore have no effect. Keynesians have traditionally recommended the use of fiscal policy rather than monetary policy as the appropriate method of influencing aggregate demand.

13.7 *The quantity theory of money*

The quantity theory of money (QTM) is concerned with the relationship between the quantity of money in the economy and the average price level. In particular it is concerned with the impact of a changing money supply on prices. The money value of expenditure in an economy depends on the price of goods and services and the quantity of goods and services purchased. If we let Y stand for the annual quantity of final goods and services purchased and P for the average price of these goods and services then PY is the money value of expenditure on final output.

The money value of expenditure can also be thought of as the amount of money in circulation multiplied by the number of times this money is spent. Letting M stand for the quantity of money and V for the number of times this money is spent annually then MV is also the money value of expenditure.

These four variables, M, V, P, and Y can be defined in such a way as to give us the *equation of exchange*:

$$MV = PY \qquad [13.2]$$

The equation of exchange is in fact an identity as V is simply defined as PY/M. V is referred to as the *income velocity of circulation* of money.

For example if $P = £2$; $Y = 10{,}000$ units of output and $M = £4000$

$$£4000(V) = £2 \times 10{,}000 \Rightarrow V = 5$$

As identities are true *by definition* they are of little use when trying to understand the cause of economic events. To do this we need *theoretical assumptions* regarding the relationship between variables.

The level of output Y clearly has an upper limit determined by available resources of land labour and capital (Section 1.2). If we start with the simplifying assumption that the economy is fully employed then Y can be treated as fixed at its upper limit, indicated by Y^*.

The velocity of circulation, V, depends on how effectively the existing stock of money is being used. This depends on the pattern of payments in the economy and to some extent on the level of interest rates. We saw (Section 13.5) that a worker being paid weekly would have lower average cash balances than a worker being paid monthly and that at higher rates of interest there is an incentive to hold less cash. The lower cash holdings are for any given level of nominal GDP the higher the velocity of circulation needs to be. For simplicity we will assume that these factors are all constant so that velocity can be treated as a fixed value. Given these assumptions and denoting the constant V with V^* we have:

$$MV^* = PY^* \quad [13.3]$$

Equation [13.3] gives us a simple quantity theory of money. As the LHS must equal the RHS a rise in M must result in a proportional increase in P. The QTM predicts that an increase in the money supply will cause inflation. As the quantity of money increases the value of money (its purchasing power) falls.

The simplicity of the QTM is part of its appeal. However in its simple form it is open to a number of criticisms:

- The assumption that Y is fixed at the full employment level may be inappropriate. If there is unemployment in the economy then an expansionary monetary policy may lead to an increase in real output.
- There is much evidence to suggest that V is subject to significant variability. That being so the simple link between M and P needs to be modified. If M rises but V falls then the link between M and P may be more complex than the simple QTM suggests.
- Logically it is possible to reverse causation. The QTM assumes that changes in M cause changes in P. What if changes in P cause changes in M? Cost–Push explanations of inflation (Section 15.5) would tend to argue that the money supply adapts to accommodate changes in prices.
- How is M to be measured? We saw (Section 13.1) that there are different **measures** of money depending on how it is defined. Which measure of M is appropriate for the QTM? Central Banks are sometimes unsure which measure of money to target.

The link between M and P is not as the simple QTM would imply. However few economists would deny that a rising money supply, particularly if it is rising faster than real output, must eventually cause inflation. The closer the economy is to full employment the more prone to inflation it is likely to be.

REVISION FOCUS CHAPTER THIRTEEN

Key Areas

- Functions of money
- Measuring the money supply

- Commercial banks
  → fractional reserve banking → reserve asset ratio → credit creation and the money supply → credit-multiplier (1/RAR)
- Functions of the Central Bank
- Monetary policy
  → alternative methods of controlling credit creation → money markets
- Demand for money balances
  → transactions, precautionary and speculative balances → interest rates and the value of fixed-interest securities
- Determination of the rate of interest
  → liquidity trap
- Quantity theory of money (QTM)
  → equation of exchange ($MV = PY$) → criticisms of QTM

Self Test

(1) If commercial bank liquidity increases by £100m, assuming a RAR of 12.5%, bank lending will ultimately increase by: (a) £700m, (b) £800m or (c) £1250m? ___

(2) The higher the RAR the greater the effect on the money supply of a given increase in bank liquidity T/F

(3) The effectiveness of open-market operations depends on how the sale/purchase of bonds is targeted T/F

(4) If the RAR falls from 10% to 5% the credit-multiplier falls from 10 to 5 T/F

(5) A reduction in the money supply will cause the equilibrium rate of interest to rise T/F

(6) An increase in interest rates will cause an increase in bond prices T/F

(7) If the RAR is 8% a £100m open market purchase of bonds by the Bank will cause the money supply to expand by: (a) £800m, (b) £1250m or (c) £1150? ___

(8) An increase in national income will cause the equilibrium rate of interest to rise unless the money supply expands T/F

Discussion Topics

- Outline alternative measures of monetary control.
- According to the QTM, inflation can be explained as 'too much money chasing too few goods'. Explain.
- Commercial banks must strike a balance between the *desire for profit* and the *need for liquidity*. Explain.

CHAPTER 14

IS/LM MODEL

14.1 *Derivation of the IS curve*

By bringing together the simple Keynesian analysis of output and employment (Chapters 11 and 12) with the analysis of the money market (Chapter 13), the IS/LM model can be constructed. *Simultaneous equilibrium* in both the goods markets and the money market is the focus of the model.

The equilibrium level of income is determined at the point of intersection of the aggregate demand function and the 45° line. Figure 12.3 illustrates with respect to a closed economy.

The level of interest rates (r) will influence the level of aggregate demand in the economy. The level of investment expenditure (I) is assumed to be inversely related to interest rates and the desired level of households savings (S) is assumed to be positively linked. If interest rates fall, therefore, aggregate demand will rise due to increases in I and C. This is illustrated in Figure 14.1.

As interest rates fall ($r_0 \rightarrow r_1 \rightarrow r_2$) aggregate demand rises causing equilibrium income to rise ($y_0 \rightarrow y_1 \rightarrow y_2$). The important point to note is the relationship between interest rates and the equilibrium level of income. As interest rates **fall** the equilibrium level of income **rises** and vice versa. This *inverse* relationship between r and y is the basis of the IS curve. Figure 14.2 illustrates.

The IS curve plots alternative rates of interest against the corresponding equilibrium levels of income In Figure 14.2 as interest rates fall ($r_0 \rightarrow r_1 \rightarrow r_2$).

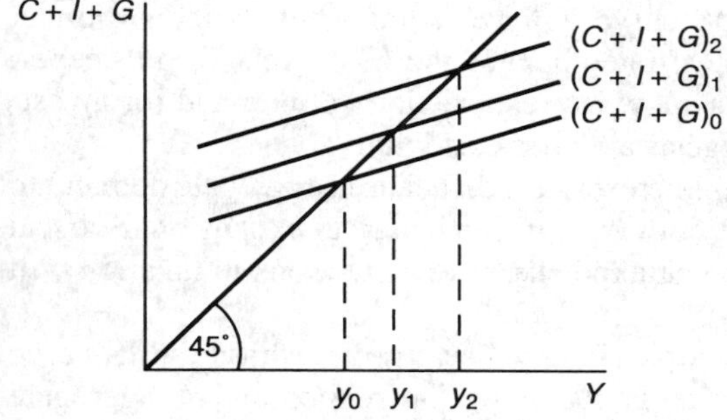

Figure 14.1: *Falling interest rates and rising equilibrium income*

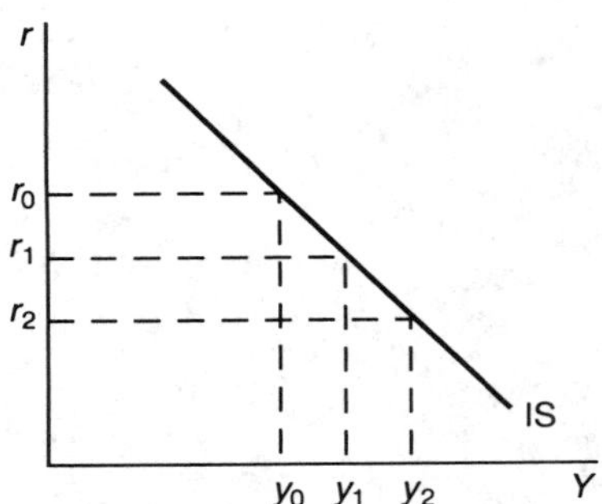

Figure 14.2: *IS curve*

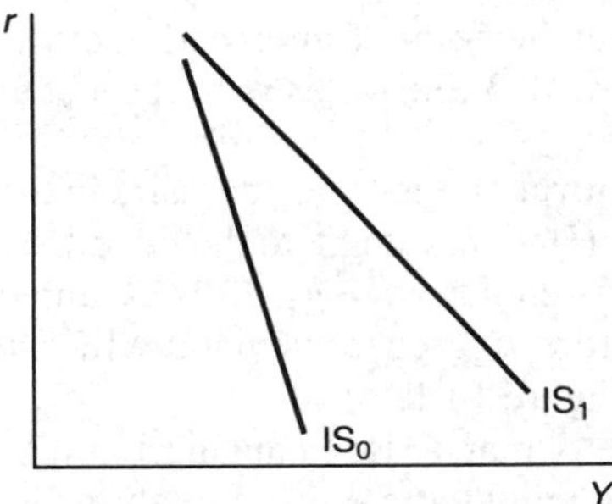

Figure 14.3: *The slope of the IS curve*

The equilibrium level of income rises ($y_0 \rightarrow y_1 \rightarrow y_2$). The slope of the IS curve depends on how responsive aggregate demand is to changes in interest rates.

If, for example, investment expenditure is highly sensitive to changes in interest rates all else being equal the IS curve will be flatter whereas if investment expenditure responds little to interest rate changes the IS curve will be steeper. Figure 14.3 illustrates. IS_0 suggests a low interest elasticity of demand for investment expenditure whereas IS_1, suggests a higher elasticity.

Anything, other than a change in interest rates, that causes aggregate demand to rise will cause the IS curve to shift outwards. In particular an expansionary fiscal policy due to either rising government expenditure or reductions in taxation will shift the IS curve outwards.

For example in Figure 14.4 an expansionary fiscal policy shifts the IS curve outwards ($IS_0 \rightarrow IS_2$). The opposite is the case for reductions in aggregate demand. If the Government raises taxes or reduces government expenditure the IS curve shifts inwards, ($IS_0 \rightarrow IS_1$).

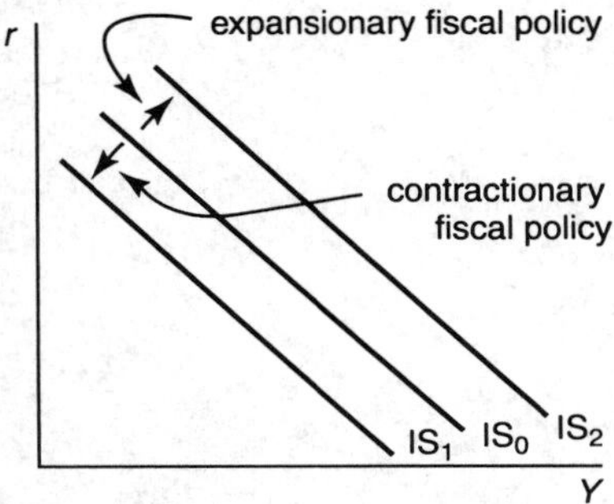

Figure 14.4: *Shifts in the IS curve*

14.2 *Derivation of the LM curve*

The IS curve is concerned with the relationship between different rates of interest and the equilibrium level of income. The LM curve, however, is concerned with the relationship between different levels of income and the equilibrium rate of interest in the money market.

The equilibrium rate of interest is determined at the point of intersection of the money supply and money demand curves (Figure 13.2).

The demand for money is assumed to be negatively related to the rate of interest but positively related to the level of income (Figure 13.1). If incomes are rising over time and if the Bank keeps the money supply constant, then the rise in income will cause interest rates to rise as illustrated in Figure 14.5.

As income rises ($y_0 \rightarrow y_1 \rightarrow y_2$) the demand for transactions and precautionary balances rise. This causes the money demand schedule to shift outward ($M_0^D \rightarrow M_1^D \rightarrow M_2^D$). If the money supply is held constant at M_0 then the equilibrium rate of interest will rise ($r_0 \rightarrow r_1 \rightarrow r_2$). The important point to note is that

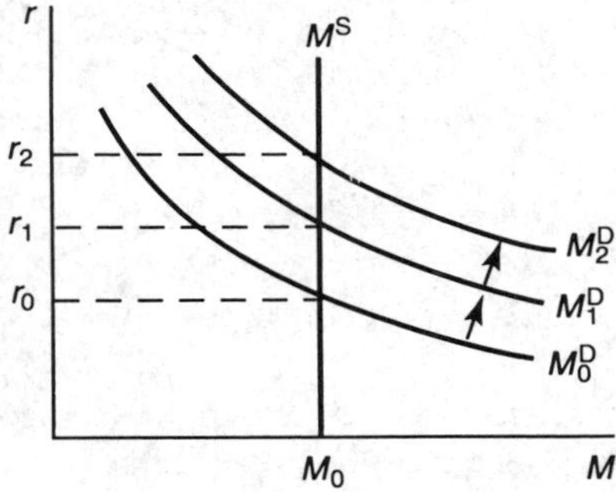

Figure 14.5: *Rising income and rising equilibrium rate of interest*

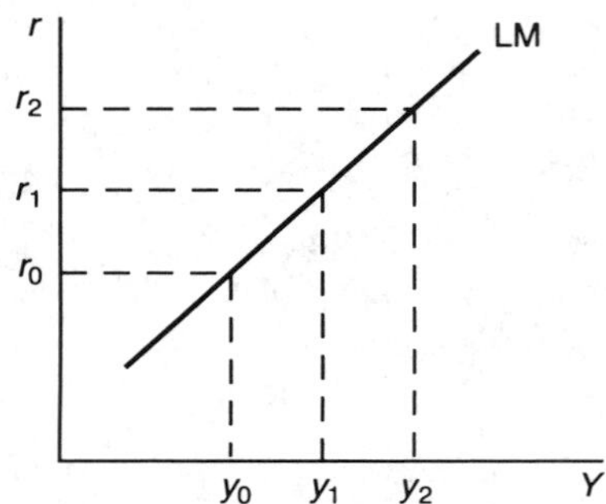

Figure 14.6: *LM curve*

there is a *positive* relationship between the *level of income* and the *equilibrium rate of interest* provided the money supply is held constant. This positive relationship is the basis for the LM curve (Figure 14.6).

The LM curve plots alternative levels of income against the corresponding equilibrium rates of interest holding the money supply constant. In Figure 14.6 as income rises ($y_0 \rightarrow y_1 \rightarrow y_2$) the equilibrium rate of interest rises ($r_0 \rightarrow r_1 \rightarrow r_2$).

The slope of the LM curve depends on how responsive the demand for money is to changes in interest rates and income. In particular, the higher the interest elasticity of demand for money the flatter the LM curve, the lower the elasticity the steeper the LM curve as Figure 14.7 illustrates.

The steep LM curve (LM_0) suggests that money demand does not respond significantly to interest rate changes. The flat LM curve (LM_1) of Figure 14.7 implies a demand for money balances that is highly responsive to interest rate changes.

If the demand for money is completely unaffected by interest rate changes then the LM curve would be vertical. The steeper the money demand schedules in Figure 14.5 the steeper the LM curve.

The LM curve will shift if either the money supply or the price level in the

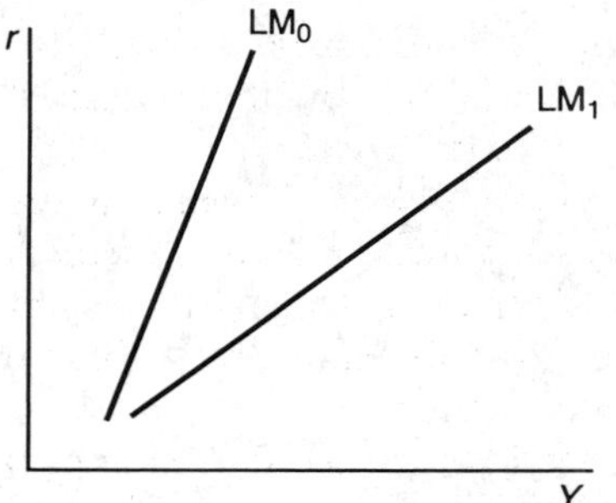

Figure 14.7: *The slope of the LM curve*

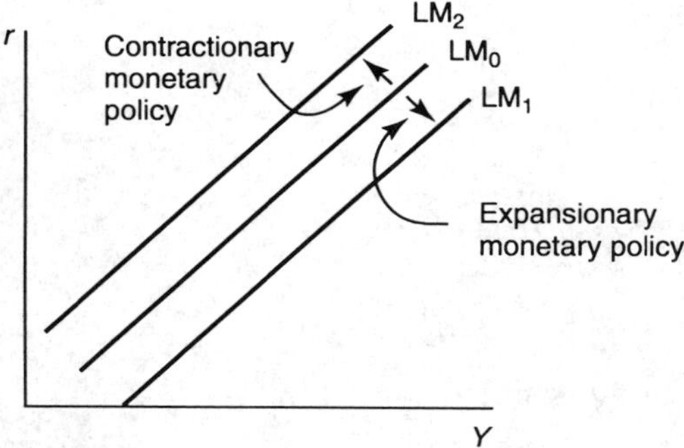

Figure 14.8: *Shifts in the LM curve*

economy changes. If the government increases the money supply lower rates of interest will be compatible with any given level of income. If the money supply increases therefore, the LM curve will shift to the right and vice versa. This is illustrated in Figure 14.8.

An expansionary monetary policy will shift the LM curve to the right. ($LM_0 \rightarrow LM_1$). A contractionary monetary policy would shift the LM curve to the left ($LM_0 \rightarrow LM_2$).

A change in the price level in the economy will affect the real value of any given money stock. If the price level falls a given money stock will have greater purchasing power and vice versa. A reduction in the price level will have the same affect on the LM curve as an expansionary monetary policy whereas an increase in the price level will have the effect of a contractionary policy.

14.3 *Monetary and fiscal policy*

By bringing the IS and LM curves together we can focus on simultaneous equilibrium in the money and goods markets (Figure 14.9).

At the point of intersection of the IS and LM curve (point *a*) there is simultaneous equilibrium in both the money and goods markets. The equilibrium rate of interest is r_0 and the corresponding equilibrium level of income is y_0.

As with the simple Keynesian model, the equilibrium level of income in the goods markets (y_0) does not necessarily imply full employment in the economy. The government may wish to influence the level of economic activity by way of monetary or fiscal policy. Monetary policy has the effect of shifting the LM curve whereas fiscal policy has the effect of shifting the IS curve.

If the aim of policy is to influence the level of employment and real output (y) then clearly the effectiveness of monetary policy depends on the slope of the IS curve whereas the effectiveness of fiscal policy depends on the slope of the LM curve. The diagrams of Figure 14.10 illustrate alternative possibilities.

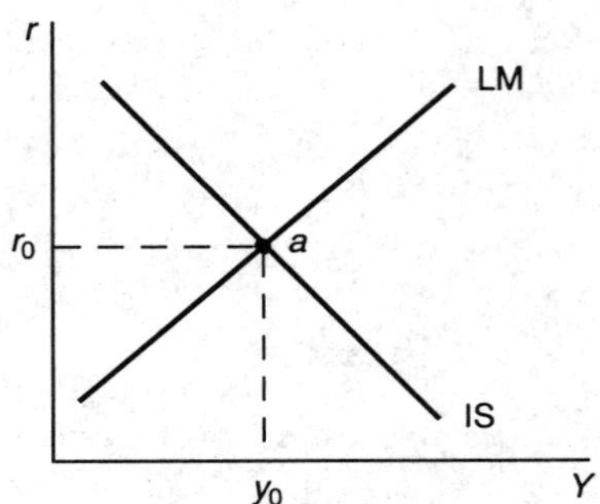

Figure 14.9: *Equilibrium in the IS/LM model*

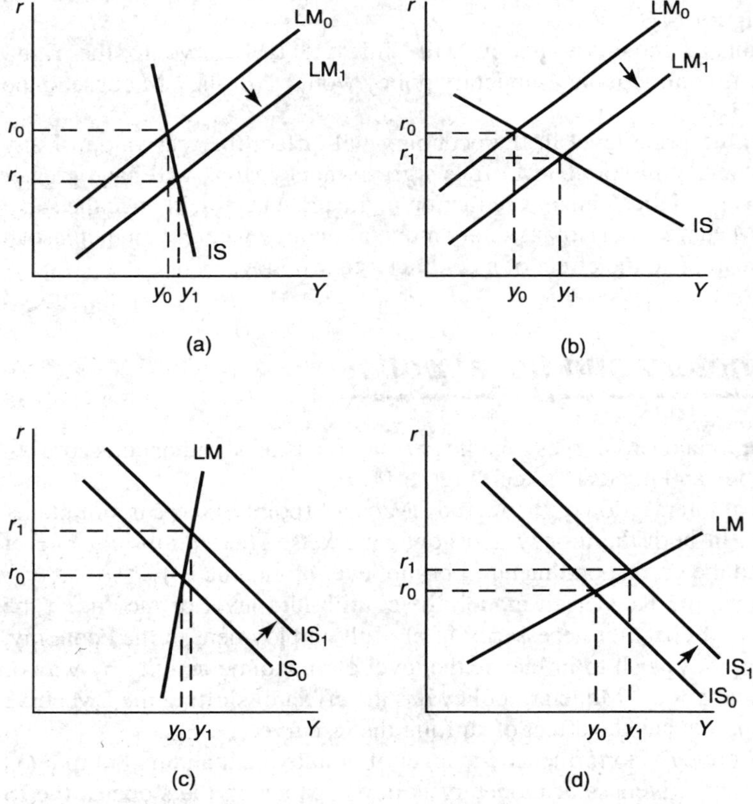

Figure 14.10: *Monetary and fiscal policy in the IS/LM model*

Diagram (a) illustrates a situation where monetary policy is relatively ineffective. The expansionary monetary policy leads to a fall in interest rates. However the steep IS curve implies that investment expenditure and consumption expenditure are both unresponsive to interest rate changes. The flat IS curve in diagram (b) implies that expenditure is responsive to interest rate changes. Monetary policy is effective here as a smaller fall in the rate of interest leads to a larger rise in income.

Diagram (c) illustrates a situation where fiscal policy is relatively ineffective. As the economy expands in response to the fiscal stimulus the effect in the money market is a significant rise in interest rates. The rise in interest rates has a negative effect on private sector expenditure which almost cancels the fiscal stimulus effect (Section 14.4). In diagram (d) fiscal policy is more effective as the impact on interest rates is not so great.

14.4 *The crowding out effect*

Keynes argued that governments should accept ultimate responsibility for the level of aggregate demand in the economy. If economic activity was slowing down and unemployment rising then the government should intervene to counteract these tendencies. Keynesians have traditionally believed that fiscal policy was the appropriate mode of intervention. The modern economy was assumed to be structured broadly in line with diagram (d) in Figure 14.10. The demand for money was assumed to be such that the LM curve was relatively flat and the response of private sector aggregate demand to interest rate changes was assumed to be such that the IS curve was relatively steep. Under these assumptions fiscal policy is highly effective in the context of a closed economy.

However, a significant crowding out effect would render fiscal policy less effective. If an increase in government expenditure *crowds out* private sector expenditure then the government's ability to regulate the overall level of aggregate demand is reduced. (The multiplier values of Chapter 12 would need to be significantly modified).

The crowding out effect results from the influence of changing government expenditure on interest rates. Assume an increase in expenditure is financed by borrowing on the capital markets through the issue of government securities. This increased borrowing will exert upward pressure on interest rates which in turn will depress private sector expenditure. The effect is illustrated in Figure. 14.11.

The economy is initially in equilibrium at point *a* with interest rates at r_0 and income at y_0. An expansionary fiscal policy shifts the IS curve from IS_0 to IS_1. If interest rates were unaffected by this fiscal expansion income would expand from y_0 to y_2. However increased borrowing in the capital markets and increased demand for money in the money markets (in response to rising income) both exert upward pressure on interest rates. As interest rates rise the effect is for private

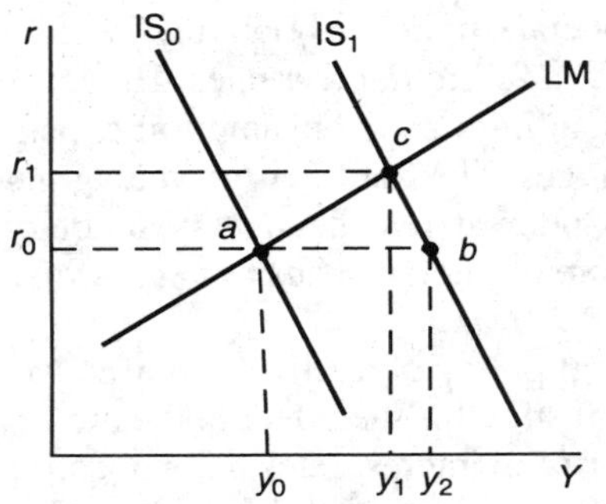

Figure 14.11: *The crowding out effect*

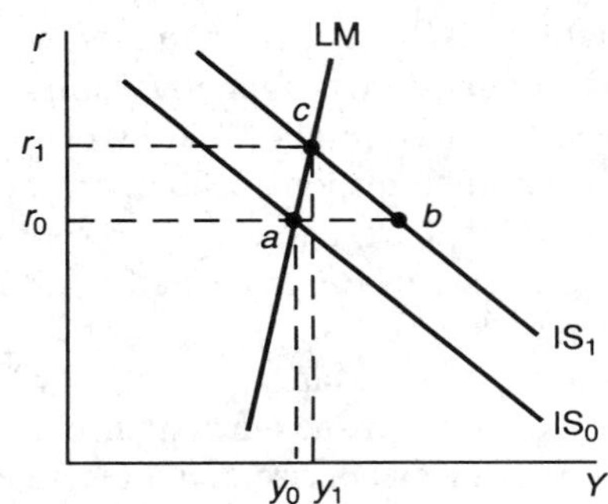

Figure 14.12: *Large crowding out effect*

sector investment expenditure and consumption expenditure to fall. The new equilibrium is at point *c*. The net effect of the fiscal expansion is for income to rise form y_0 to y_1 rather than y_2.

The steeper the LM curve and the flatter the IS curve the greater the crowding out effect will be. In Figure 14.12 the crowding out effect is almost total.

The relatively steep LM curve and the relatively flat IS curves means that even a large fiscal expansion will have little effect on real output and employment.

The 'monetarist' school of thought would tend to accept that a modern economy is structured broadly in line with Figure 14.12. Not surprisingly they would counsel against the use of active fiscal policy by government.

A combination of monetary and fiscal expansion could be implemented as a means of avoiding the crowding out effect. This is illustrated in Figure 14.13.

Starting at point *a* monetary policy alone would shift the economy to *b*; fiscal policy alone would shift the economy to *c*; a combination of monetary and fiscal policy shifts the economy to point *d*. By combining monetary and fiscal policy the government prevents interest rates rising in response to the fiscal expansion.

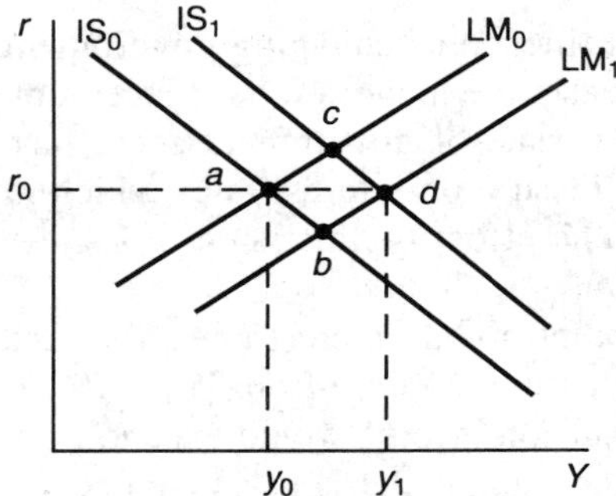

Figure 14.13: *Combined monetary and fiscal policy*

Students should note that the analysis in this chapter assumes a closed economy. The analysis becomes more complicated for an open economy. Changing levels of income and interest rates will have implications for international trade and capital flows. Chapter 17 deals with some aspects of these issues.

REVISION FOCUS CHAPTER FOURTEEN

Key Areas

- The IS curve
  →Slope and movement of
- The LM curve
  →Slope and movement of
- Monetary policy (shifting the LM curve)
- Fiscal policy (shifting the IS curve)
- The crowding out effect
  →Monetary and fiscal policy mix
- Keynesians and Monetarists

Self Test

(1) The IS curve slopes upward from left to right while the LM curve slopes downward from left to right — T/F

(2) An expansionary fiscal policy will cause the IS curve to shift outwards moving along the LM curve — T/F

(3) An expansionary monetary policy will cause the LM curve to shift inwards moving along the IS curve — T/F

(4) The more responsive the demand for money is to interest rate changes the flatter the LM curve — T/F

(5) The more responsive private sector expenditure (C + I) to interest rate changes the greater the crowding out effect — T/F

(6) There is always full employment at the equilibrium level of income in the IS/LM model — T/F

(7) An increase in the price level will cause the LM curve to shift inwards — T/F

(8) An expansionary fiscal policy causes interest rates to rise whereas an expansionary monetary policy causes interest rates to fall — T/F

Discussion Topics

- Using the slopes of the IS and LM curves to illustrate, explain the Keynesian and Monetarist attitude to fiscal and monetary policy.

- A policy mix can overcome the crowding out effect. Explain.
- If the demand for money is perfectly inelastic with respect to interest rate changes then active fiscal policy designed to influence the levels of output and employment becomes ineffective. Explain with reference to the slope of the LM curve.

CHAPTER 15

AS–AD MODEL

The macroeconomic analysis of previous chapters – the simple Keynesian model and the IS/LM model – assumed that the level of real output in the economy was determined by the level of aggregate demand. Given the fix-price assumption output rather than prices adjusted to the level of aggregate demand, at least up to the full employment level of output. The price level only entered the analysis in an indirect way.

The simple circular flow model focused exclusively on the determination of the level of output (y) in the economy. The IS/LM model focused on the simultaneous determination of the level of output and the rate of interest (r). The aggregate demand – aggregate supply (AS–AD) model focuses on the simultaneous determination of the level of output and the price level (P) in the economy.

15.1 *The aggregate supply curve (AS)*

The AS curve is concerned with the quantity of total output that firms in the economy would supply if different prices could be charged for this output. Clearly the capacity of all firms to supply will be limited by the available resources in the economy. The quantity and quality of the labour force, capital equipment, raw materials, etc. will set an *upper limit* to the economy's capacity to produce. Also the cost to firms of employing these resources will influence their willingness to supply goods and services whatever the price that can be charged. If we assume that the cost of inputs – the wage rate, interest rates, raw material prices, etc. – remain fixed in the short-run then we can reasonably conclude that firms would wish to supply extra output if higher prices can be charged. Higher prices with fixed input costs would make it profitable for many firms to produce more. Figure 15.1 illustrates the general shape of an AS curve given the above assumptions.

Up to a price level of p_2 firms would supply extra output as the price level rises, assuming the cost per unit of input remains constant. The upper limit to the real output that can be supplied given available resources is y_f.

The following points should be noted regarding Figure 15.1. The level of *real output* is being measured on the horizontal axis. The price level being measured on the vertical axis represents the average price of final goods and services but excludes the cost of factors of production. In particular as the wage rate is assumed to be fixed (at least in the short run) as the price level rises the *real wage*

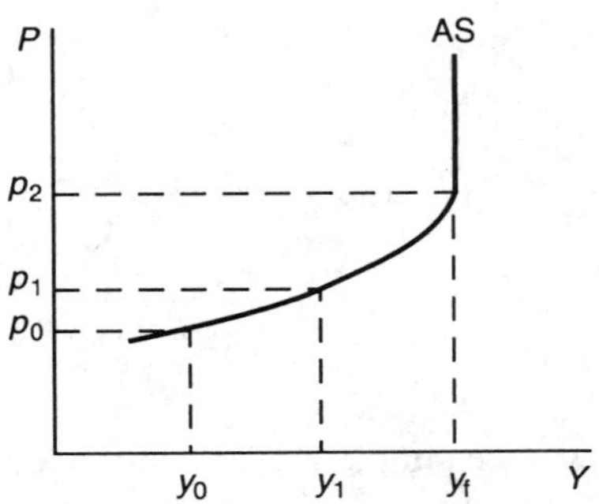

Figure 15.1: *Aggregate supply curve*

must be falling. It is the nominal wage that is assumed to be fixed but the purchasing power of this will fall if the price of final output is rising. The upward sloping segment of the AS curve will shift if the cost of factors of production change. The vertical section can only shift if there is a change in the quantity or quality of factors of productions available to the economy, (for example improvements in technology). The AS curve is drawn flatter the further from full employment output the economy is, i.e. flatter at y_0 (Figure 15.1) than at y_1. The common sense behind this is that the further from y_f the economy is the greater the spare capacity available. The more spare capacity the easier it is for firms to expand production.

Figure 15.2 illustrates the effect of an increase in the cost of an important input such as labour, oil, etc.

An increase in the cost of inputs would make it less profitable to produce at any given price level. Less will be supplied causing the AS curve to shift to the left ($AS_0 \rightarrow AS_1$) and vice versa. The full employment level of real output (y_f) is unaffected.

An improvement in the quality of the factors of production, (for example

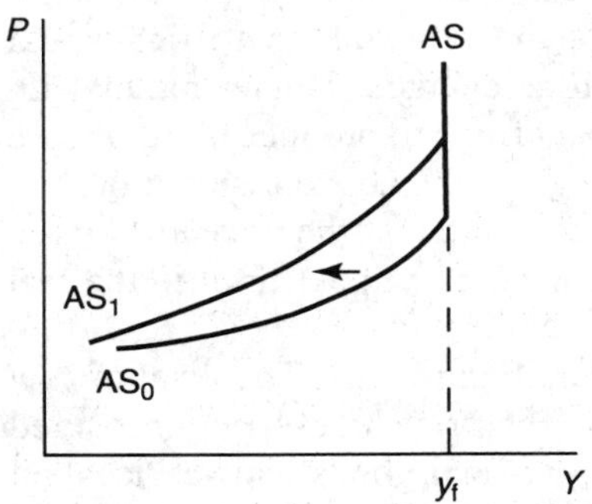

Figure 15.2: *An increase in input costs*

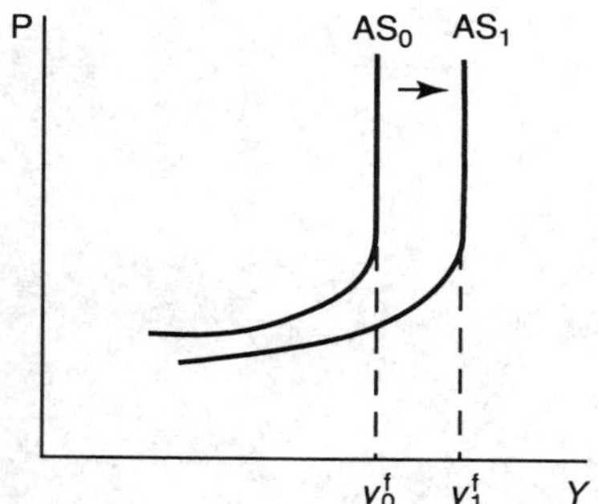

Figure 15.3: *Increase in productive capacity*

improvements in education or technology) by increasing the productive capacity of the economy shifts the AS curve to the right. This is illustrated in Figure 15.3.

Full employment output increases from y_0^f to y_1^f and this is reflected in the AS curve shifting form AS_0 to AS_1. The whole of the AS curve shifts to the right on the assumption that input costs remain constant. For example if there is rising labour productivity without a rise in the wage rate firms would find it profitable to produce more at any given price level. In this case the upward sloping segment would also shift to the right.

15.2 *The aggregate demand curve (AD)*

The AD schedule is concerned with the relationship between the desired levels of expenditure $(C + I + G + (X - M))$ in the economy and the average price level in the economy. When deriving the AD curve it is assumed that all prices are flexible.

If all prices (including wages, etc.) in the economy were to double real incomes would not change as the purchasing power of incomes would be unaffected. Does it follow that the average price level will have no affect on the level of aggregate demand? Not necessarily:

- The real balance effect – the real value of financial assets with a fixed nominal value will be affected. For example the value of a given sum of savings will be less the higher the price level is. This *wealth effect* may cause households to spend less as the price level rises and vice versa.
- Monetary effect – as with the effect on savings so also on the real value of the stock of money in the economy. At a higher price level there would be less real money (purchasing power) in the economy and vice versa. Interest rates will tend to rise if the real money supply falls causing aggregate demand to fall and vice versa.

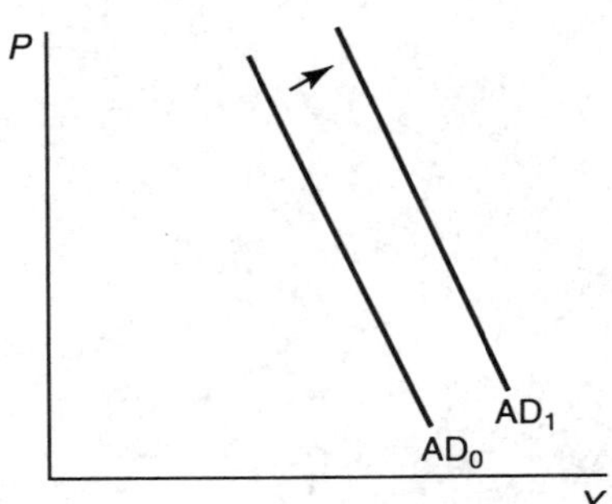

Figure 15.4: *The aggregate demand curve*

- Foreign trade – In an open economy a lower domestic price level will tend to stimulate foreign demand for the country's exports and vice versa.

For the above reasons it can be assumed that all else being equal the level of aggregated demand will be lower the higher the price level and vice versa as illustrated in Figure 15.4.

The AD curve slopes downward from left to right due to the real balance effect, the monetary effect and, in an open economy, the foreign trade effect. At a lower price level there will be greater demand for real output. Anything, other than a change in the domestic price level, that causes aggregate demand to rise or fall will lead to an outward or inward shift in the AD curve. For example, an expansionary fiscal or monetary policy will cause the AD curve to shift outwards as in Figure 15.4 ($AD_0 \rightarrow AD_1$) whereas a contractionary policy would cause an inward shift.

15.3 *Aggregate demand and aggregate supply*

The equilibrium level of output and the corresponding equilibrium price level will be determined at the point of intersection of the AD and AS curves. The important issue for policy makers is whether or not this equilibrium will be a full employment one. Figure 15.5 illustrates the alternatives.

In Figure 15.5 (a) the equilibrium output (y_0) is too low to generate full employment. The analysis suggests that the problem concerns the relationship between the price level (p_0) and input costs. In particular it can be assumed that the prevailing wages are too high. Figure 15.5(b) illustrates a full employment equilibrium.

The great issue in macroeconomic theory is, whether a modern economy, without government intervention to assist it, will achieve an equilibrium such as that depicted in Figure 15.5(b). Furthermore even if the economy unaided can achieve a full employment equilibrium how long will it take and can the government speed up the process? The '*new classical*' school believes that a modern

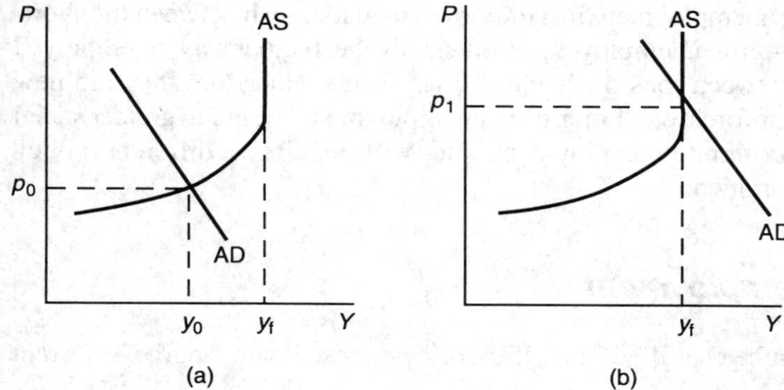

Figure 15.5: *Equilibrium in the AS/AD model*

economy characterized by *flexible markets throughout* can be relied upon to achieve a full employment equilibrium as in Figure 15.5(b). The Keynesian school has less confidence in an unregulated economy, believing that full employment will not be achieved or that the process will take too long. If the speed of price and wage adjustments is too slow the economy may remain in an underemployment equilibrium as in Figure 15.5(a) for a long period.

15.4 *Unemployment*

A person is unemployed if they would wish to have a job at the wage levels that exist but is unable to find a job offer. Unemployment is therefore a constraint which prevents the individual realizing their economic goals.

A person may be **'voluntarily unemployed'** if for example, their unearned income gives them the freedom to choose not to work. This person is not unemployed from an economics point of view but is simply putting leisure before income. The person who is voluntarily drawing the dole is no more unemployed than for example a person living off inherited wealth. Unemployment is, therefore, an involuntary state. It is not unusual for labour force surveys of unemployment to indicate lower levels of unemployment than live register measures. The latter is based on all those signing on whereas the former is based on those seeking employment. The labour force, quite simply, is *all those either working or actively seeking employment.*

The economic cost of unemployment to society at large is the *forgone output* (opportunity cost) that could have been achieved if the unemployed were working. This cost is spread across the society in terms of the higher taxes required to finance transfer payments (Section 10.2) to assist the unemployed. Wider social costs deriving from relative poverty such as loss of self esteem, pressure on family life, etc. add greatly to the problems associated with unemployment.

When analysing unemployment it is important to distinguish between the short-term and the long-term unemployed. People may be temporarily unemployed because they are between jobs or, having just finished education, they are new entrants to the labour force, etc. Long-term unemployment is a much greater social problem than short-term unemployment and will require a different policy response from government.

Causes of unemployment

Unemployment can be classified into different *types* based on a range of different causes.

Frictional unemployment: unemployment experienced by those who are between jobs or have recently entered the labour force. A modern economy is subject to continuous change, some firms expanding others closing or contracting. It follows that some proportion of the labour force is constantly between jobs. Frictional unemployment is therefore inevitable but is short term in character. As the problem is not a shortage of jobs the appropriate policy is to keep those out of work informed about employment opportunities through for example a network of employment offices. By this means frictional unemployment can be kept to a minimum.

Structural unemployment: unemployment due to a significant change in the structure of an economy. The cause may be the closure of a major employer in a region ('regional unemployment') due either to domestic or international competition or the introduction of new technology in industries ('technological unemployment') causing a fall in demand for certain skills. Structural unemployment often results in a *mis-match* between the skills of the unemployed and the skills required in expanding industries. Furthermore it can result in long-term unemployment requiring a policy response from government. Schemes aimed at improving the *occupational mobility of labour* (i.e. retraining); *the geographical mobility of labour* or *the location of new industries* may be appropriate.

Demand deficient unemployment: sometimes referred to as 'Keynesian unemployment' as it is due to the level of aggregate demand in the economy being too low. It could be argued that this type of unemployment is in fact due to wages and prices being too high for the existing level of aggregate monetary demand. However, as Keynes regarded wages and therefore prices as 'sticky-downwards' (i.e. not sufficiently flexible in a downward direction) he recommended the use of fiscal policy to increase aggregate demand as the appropriate remedy (Section 12.3). Otherwise, he argued, this type of involuntary unemployment could persist into the longer term.

Classical unemployment: so called because it is the cause of unemployment suggested by the classical or pre-Keynesian economists. This type of unemployment is due to wage rates in labour markets being above the market-clearing wage (Section 8.2). If labour markets were sufficiently flexible there would be no involuntary unemployment according to the classical school. Wages are deliberately kept above the market-clearing level through the abuse of union power, minimum wage legislation, etc. Although unemployment is involuntary it is voluntarily created by *insiders* excluding *outsiders* from employment. According to adherents of the new classical school the remedy for unemployment is to deregulate labour markets with a view to making them more flexible.

There are a range of impediments that may face those who are seeking new employment including lack of information, lack of requisite skills and geographical immobility. At any given point in time some proportion of the workforce will be involuntarily unemployed through an inability to find a suitable job offer. There is, therefore, a **natural rate of unemployment** in any economy. The natural rate of unemployment is the rate of unemployment remaining when labour markets are clearing.

'Full employment' is defined in such a way as to allow for the natural rate of unemployment. The full employment level of output represents the potential output of the economy when there is equilibrium in the economy's labour markets.

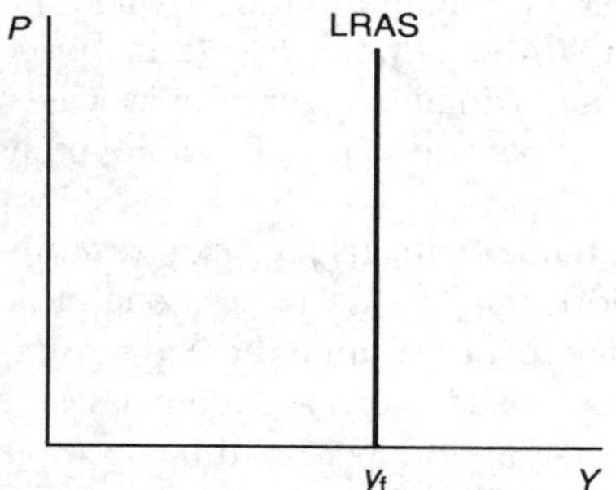

Figure 15.6: *Long-run aggregate supply curve*

The long-run aggregate supply curve (LRAS) for the economy is determined by the full employment level of output. It represents the potential output of the economy and is indicated by a vertical line through the full-employment level of output. In Figure 15.6 the LRAS is drawn for a given level of technology. Improvements in technology will raise the potential output for the economy and shift the LRAS to the right. If the natural rate of unemployment can be reduced (better information, training schemes, etc.) this will also shift the LRAS to the right and raise the potential output of the economy. If 'voluntary unemployment' can be reduced (for example by reducing taxes on relatively low paid jobs and thereby increasing take-home pay) this can also raise the potential output of the economy and shift the LRAS to the right.

Figure 15.7 represents an economy initially in a full employment equilibrium at point *a* and subjected to a *demand side shock*.

The short-run aggregate supply curve (SRAS) indicates how the economy may adjust in the short-term if there is not full wage and price flexibility. Assume

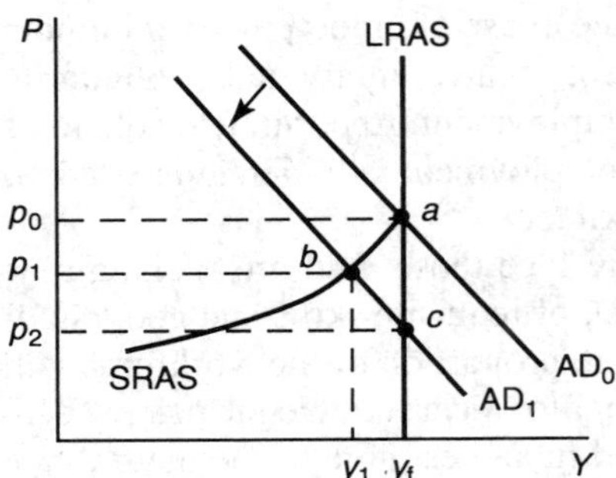

Figure 15.7: *Short-run and long-run adjustments*

aggregate demand falls from AD_0 to AD_1. The fall in demand will exert downward pressure on the price level. Unless wages fall in line with prices there will be an increase in the real wage causing the demand for labour to fall. If wages do not adjust to falling prices the new equilibrium will be at point *b* with the price level at p_1 and real output at y_1 which is lower than y_f. In the longer term as wages adjust there will be a new long run equilibrium at point *c* with full employment restored.

Figure 15.8 illustrates the simple Keynesian model with its *fix price* assumption, – i.e. wages and prices are fixed in the short run. The fix price assumption implies a horizontal SRAS at the prevailing price level. Assume the economy is initially at full employment equilibrium at point *a* and there is a demand side shock shifting AD_0 to AD_1. Given the fix price assumption there will be no wage or price adjustments and the economy will move to point *b* resulting in significant unemployment. In the long run wages and prices will adjust taking the economy to point *c*. However Keynes was less concerned with the long run observing that 'in the long run we are all dead'. He advocated the short-term use of fiscal policy by the government to shift the AD schedule back out to AD_0.

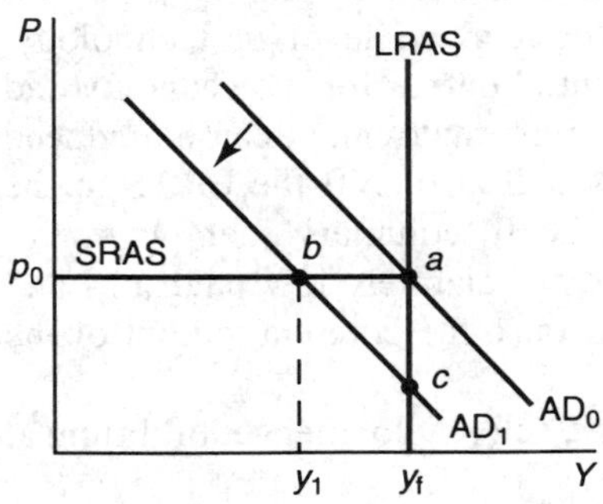

Figure 15.8: *The fix price model*

15.5 *Inflation*

In its simplest form the QTM (Section 13.7) implies that an increase in the stock of money in circulation will lead to an equal proportional increase in the price level. However, there are alternative views as to how inflation is caused. *Cost push* explanations of inflation emphasize the importance of rising costs of production. For example if costs are rising due to rising wages or rising import prices, etc. then, assuming firms attempt to recoup these costs they will pass them on in higher prices. The difference between cost push explanations of inflation and the QTM has to do with the role of money. For the QTM a rising money supply *initiates* the inflationary process whereas for the cost–push explanations the money supply adapts to *accommodate* the process. The mechanism may well be the monetary authorities allowing the nominal stock of money to expand so as to prevent the real money supply falling.

$$MV = PY$$

For the QTM: $\Delta M \longrightarrow \Delta P$. With cost–push explanations $\Delta P \longrightarrow \Delta M$.

Despite possible differences of opinion among economists regarding the 'cause' of inflation, most would agree that controlling the money supply is a sufficient condition for the control of inflation. An inflationary process could not continue without the money supply expanding.

Inflation can lead to a range of problems for an economy, particularly when the rate is high and the future rate is uncertain. Problems include:

- those on fixed money incomes, e.g. pensioners, will experience a fall in real income;
- borrowers may gain at the expense of lenders due to a divergence between nominal and real interest rates (Section 15.6);
- governments may gain at the expense of taxpayers unless tax allowances are adjusted in line with inflation – *fiscal drag*;
- those with savings will see the real value of savings fall whereas those in debt (e.g. mortgage holders) will see the burden of their debt declining;
- industrial relations may be adversely affected as workers negotiate nominal wage increases with at least the anticipated rate of inflation in mind.

All of the above may lead to *an arbitrary redistribution of income* in society. Furthermore for open economies:

- international competitiveness will be adversely affected, particularly if the country is a member of a fixed exchange rate system (Section 17.4).

It is increasingly common for western governments or their central banks to set *monetary targets* as part of their anti-inflationary policies. Ideally the money supply is allowed to expand in line with the expected growth of real output. Taking the equation of exchange:

$$MV = PY$$

If V is assumed to be constant and Y is expected to grow at, say 3% p.a. then allowing M to expand at 3% p.a. is consistent with zero inflation.

In some countries monetary policy is complemented by centralised systems of wage bargaining with a view to preventing wage negotiators generating cost–push inflationary pressure through high wage demands. For example in Ireland the partnership 2000 agreement negotiated in 1997 established the annual wage increases for many sectors for the subsequent three years.

15.6 *Real and nominal interest rates*

Nominal interest rates can be thought of as the return to the lender (or cost to the borrower) measured in money terms, whereas the real rate of interest is the return to the lender measured in terms of *purchasing power*. During periods of inflation prices are rising. It follows that money loses its purchasing power, as a unit of currency will buy fewer goods at the end of an inflationary period. The problem for the lender is that the money being repaid after a period of inflation is not as valuable as the money that was originally loaned.

The real rate of interest can be calculated as:

$$r_r = \left[\frac{1 + r_n}{1 + P}\right] - 1$$

where r_r represents the real rate, r_n the nominal rate and P the rate of inflation.

Example

The nominal rate of interest is 10% and the rate of inflation is 5%.

$$r_r = \left[\frac{1.1}{1.05}\right] - 1 \cong 4.8\%$$

The formula can be rearranged as:

$$r_r = \left[\frac{r_n - p}{1 + p}\right]$$

which indicates that when P is low $r_n - P$ gives a good approximation to r_r. When inflation is high it is not unusual to get negative real interest rates resulting in lenders compensating borrowers.

15.7 *The Phillips curve*

The Phillips curve is not based on any theory but is simply a statistical relationship. An inverse relationship between nominal wage rates and unemployment rates was found (1958) to exist for UK data. Given the high correlation between money wages and prices. The evidence suggested that during periods of high inflation unemployment tended to be low, whereas when inflation was low unemployment tended to be relatively high, as figure 15.9 illustrates.

The Phillips curve indicated a stable inverse relationship between the unemployment rate and the inflation rate
A *trade-off* seemed to exist whereby governments could achieve lower unemployment but at a cost in terms of higher inflation. For example, a government determined to keep unemployment low could locate the economy at point *a* (Figure 15.9) with low unemployment (1%) but relatively high inflation (4%). The assumed existence of the stable relationship encouraged governments to intervene in the economy with a view to *fine-tuning* its performance. Given the slope of the curve each additional reduction in unemployment could only be achieved by accepting increasingly higher additions to the inflation rate. Nonetheless appropriately designed policies could locate the economy on the Phillips curve at a point to suit the preferences of the government.

In the 1970s, many western economies were beset with a phenomenon referred to as *stagflation*. This was a situation of simultaneously rising unemployment and inflation rates. In terms of Figure 15.9 economies were moving in a north-easterly direction (i.e. away from the Phillips curve). This development undermined the empirical validity of the Phillips curve relationship.

Even before these events the Phillips curve was challenged from a theoretical standpoint by Milton Friedman. Friedman pointed out that employers and workers were concerned with the *real wage*, not the nominal wage, when they were offering and accepting jobs in labour markets. If employers were offering and workers accepting a greater number of jobs simply because nominal wages rather than real wages were rising then they must be suffering from **money illusion**. Friedman introduced the distinction between a *short-run* Phillips curve (SRPC) which was negatively sloped and a *long-run* Phillips curve (LRPC) which was vertical (Figure 15.10).

Assume the economy is located at point *a* in Figure 15.10 with zero inflation ($\dot{p}$) and 3% unemployment (*U*). To shift the economy to point *b* the government

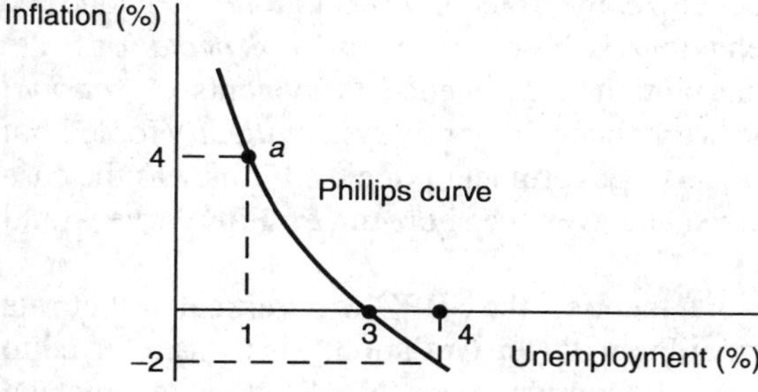

Figure 15.9: *The Phillips curve*

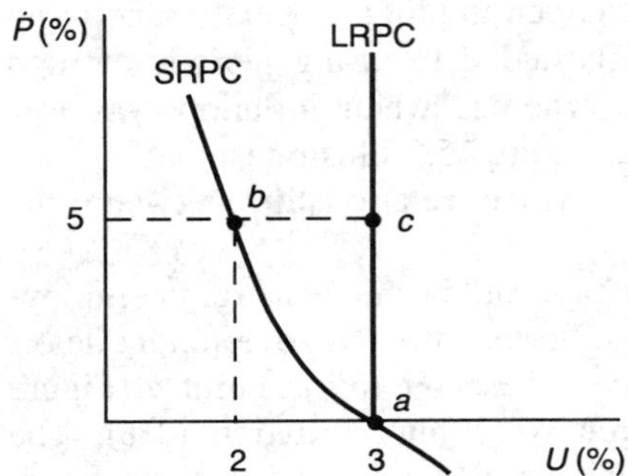

Figure 15.10: *Short-run and long-run Phillips curve*

must increase aggregate demand. This increase in money expenditure will, according to Freidman, cause wages and price to rise. However the change in the average price level will be interpreted as a change in *relative prices*. When firms realize their selling prices are rising they will think it profitable to produce more not realizing that other prices are rising in line. Voluntarily unemployed people will be attracted into the labour force thinking real wages rather than purely nominal wages are rising. The economy will move to point *b* with lower unemployment and increased output. However when firms and workers realize what is really happening they will revert to their original strategies shifting the economy to point *c*. Governments might be able to reduce unemployment below its natural rate in the short-run but not in the long-run. The long-run Phillips curve was vertical implying that expansionary aggregate demand policies could not have a long-term effect on unemployment but would merely lead to inflation.

Friedman argued that *expectations* regarding the future rate of inflation were based on past experience and that these expectations would be adapted in the light of future experience. Friedman's analysis suggested that workers and firms could be continuously fooled into changing their behaviour provided they did not correctly anticipate the future rate of inflation.

Friedman's insight was to recognize the role of *expectations* in economic behaviour. However for him, behaviour is based on *adaptive expectations*, i.e. always catching up on rather than anticipating events. Proponents of *rational expectations* argued that firms and workers could not be *systematically* fooled but would be able to anticipate the effects of government policies. If this was the case then money illusion would not persist and even the short-run Phillips curve would be vertical as in Figure. 5.11.

According to rational expectations theorists the SRPC was vertical at that rate of unemployment which was compatible with zero inflation. This was referred to as the non-accelerating-inflation rate of unemployment (NAIRU) and is indicated by u^* in Figure. 15.11.

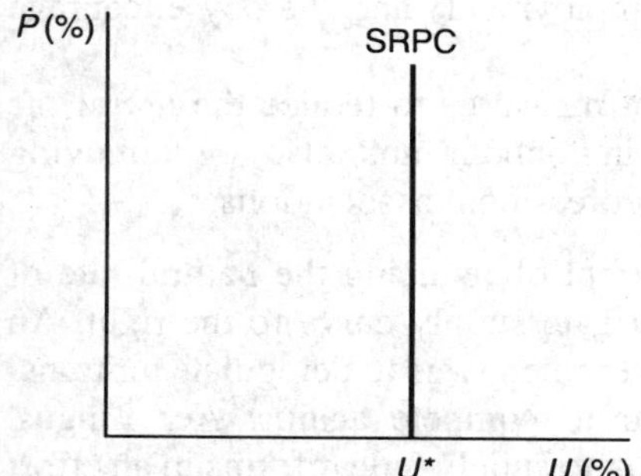

Figure 15.11: *The short-run Phillips curve with rational expectations*

Given this analysis demand-management policies will influence the price level but not the level of output. If the aggregate demand curve shifts form AD_0 to AD_1 (Figure 15.12). The sole effect is for prices to rise from p_0 to p_1. Output remains at the full employment output (y_f).

Only unsystematic (i.e. unpredictable) behaviour by governments could reduce unemployment. Otherwise, adjusting aggregate demand to influence the level of employment in the economy would simply lead to inflation with no effect on employment even in the short-run. An implication of the rational expectations analysis is a vertical aggregate supply curve for the economy even in the short run as illustrated in Figure 15.12.

The only appropriate policies for government given this analysis are **supply-side policies**. These are designed to make markets more flexible and competitive. For example:

- removing barriers to entry (Section 7.4) where they exist and thereby opening up existing markets to greater competition;

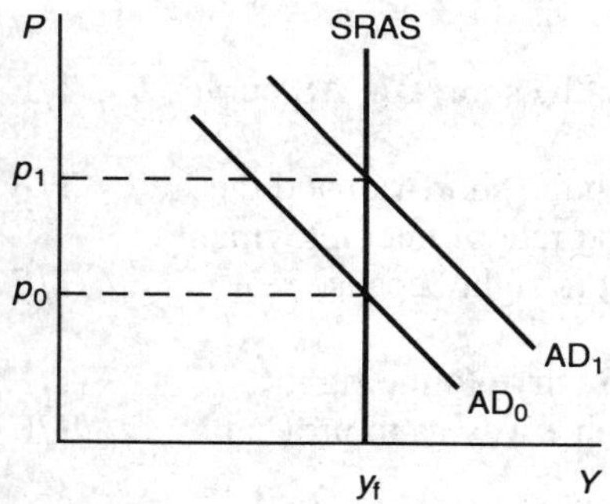

Figure 15.12: *The aggregate supply curve with rational expectations*

- tax reforms to discourage 'voluntary unemployment' and thereby encourage greater participation in the labour force;
- more flexible labour markets as a result of measures to reduce the *non-wage costs* (social insurance, etc.) of employing labour and also by removing restrictive practices of trades unions and professional associations.

Successful supply-side measures have the effect of reducing the natural rate of unemployment and thereby shifting the aggregate supply curve to the right. An important supply-side reform by the Irish government was to deregulate air transport in the mid-1980s by allowing Ryanair to compete against Aer Lingus. European governments are increasingly turning to supply-side reforms in an effort to make the economy of the EU more competitive (Section 18.3).

REVISION FOCUS CHAPTER FIFTEEN

Key Areas

- The AS curve
  →shape and movements of
- The AD curve
  →shape and movements of
- Equilibrium in the AS/AD model
  →full employment and under-employment equilibrium
- Unemployment
  →an involuntary state→causes(or types) of→natural rate of→NAIRU
- Inflation
  →cost-push and monetarist views→problems caused by→real and nominal interest rates
- The Phillips curve
  →money illusion→rational expectations
- Supply-side policies

Self Test

(1) Given the Keynesian fix-price assumption, the short-run AS curve is horizontal T/F
(2) According to the new classical school, both the short-run and the long-run AS curve are vertical at the natural rate of unemployment T/F
(3) The AD curve slopes downwards from left to right because real incomes are higher at lower prices T/F
(4) Supply side policies aim to shift the LRAS curve to the right T/F
(5) Monetary policy should be designed in such a way as to prevent any increase in the money supply T/F
(6) Active fiscal policy designed to raise aggregate demand is an appropriate policy to reduce frictional unemployment T/F

(7) During periods of inflation real interest rates exceed nominal interest rates T/F

(8) The natural rate of unemployment cannot be influenced by government policies T/F

Discussion topics

- Using AS and AD curves to illustrate, under what circumstances will an outward shift in the AD curve: (a) raise real output but nor the price level, (b) raise real output and the price level and (c) raise prices but not real output.
- Explain alternative causes of unemployment and indicate appropriate government policies in each case.
- Explain what is meant by 'supply-side' economic reforms.

CHAPTER 16

International Trade

16.1 *Balance of payments*

The ***balance of payments*** accounts represent a record of all transactions between residents and firms located in one country and the rest of the world. Depending on the nature of the transaction the details will be recorded in either of two accounts: the current account or the capital account.

The current account

The current account records ***current income*** from and **current payments** to the rest of the world. The transactions concerned may be related to visible trade; invisible trade; profit, interest and dividend flows; or international transfers. Transactions leading to income received by the host country are entered with a plus sign whereas transactions requiring payments abroad are entered with a minus sign.

Visible trade – or merchandise trade – is concerned with trade in tangible items such as food, manufactures, etc. Exports are entered with a plus sign while imports are entered with a minus sign. Invisible trade relates to trade in services such as transport, financial and other services and also includes income and expenditure relating to tourism. Profit, interest and dividend flows result from the foreign ownership of assets. Domestic owners of foreign assets receive property income from abroad whereas foreign owners of domestic assets receive property income from the host country. International transfers relate to transactions such as foreign aid; government contributions to and current receipts from the EU budget; private transfers such as remittances from emigrant workers, etc. It is not uncommon for all items, other than visible trade, to be collectively referred to as *invisibles*.

Table 16.1 summarises the 1996 current account for the Irish economy. The impact on the economy of the foreign multinationals located in Ireland can be seen in the figures. The surplus on visible trade, £8416m, is to a large extent due to the export activities of the multinationals. This is reflected in the £5310m outflow of profits, interest and dividends which is largely the result of the multinationals repatriating profits, (this figure also includes interest payments to foreign holders of the Irish national debt equal to £905m). The impact of multinationals can have a distorting effect on international trade figures due to the large number of ***intra-***

Table 16.1: *A summary of the current account figures for the Irish economy for 1996* (The figures given represent the net figures for each section)

Current Account, Irish Economy 1996	*(Ir£m)*
Merchandise	+ 8416
Invisible trade	– 3597
Profits, interest, dividends	– 5310
Current transfers	+ 1353
Balance on current account	+ 862

Source: National Income and Expenditure 1996 CSO

company transactions. For example the invisible trade deficit of £3597m includes head office charges on Irish subsidiaries for services such as R&D, marketing, etc. Due to these *within-company* overseas transactions, multinationals can engage in ***transfer pricing***, which enables them to attribute their profits to operations in a particular country though the actual productive activity may be occurring elsewhere. The motive for transfer-pricing is to minimize their tax liability on profits.

The sum of current incomes and payments, both visible and invisible, gives the **current account balance**, which was a surplus of £862m for the Irish economy in 1996. A surplus on current account, representing an excess of foreign earnings over foreign expenses, suggests that a country is 'paying its way in the world'. A deficit would indicate that the country concerned was either incurring net foreign liabilities or using up foreign assets to finance the deficit.

The capital account

The capital account records changes in overseas **assets** and **liabilities**. When a foreign multinational invests in the domestic economy, the multinational acquires an asset however the economy acquires a liability in the sense that there will be a subsequent outflow of repatriated profits to provide a return on this inward investment. The reason why the inward investment is desirable, of course, is the fact that typically the investment will generate enough earnings not only to finance repatriated profits, but also to provide incomes for domestic employees. When an Irish multinational invests overseas foreign assets are being acquired which should lead to an inflow of property income on the current account at a later date.

Inward capital flows – i.e. those generating liabilities for the home economy – are entered with a plus sign whereas outward flows – i.e. those generating overseas assets – are entered with a minus sign. These capital flows are referred to as **foreign direct investments** (FDI) if they finance the acquisition of real assets (such as factories) or as **portfolio investments** if they finance the purchase of financial assets (such as government bonds, bank deposits, etc). Also included is foreign borrowing (+ sign) or lending (– sign) by domestic private sector financial institutions. **Official** capital flows refer to government borrowing (+ sign) or lending (– sign) and to changes in **official reserves** at the Central Bank (increases

Table 16.2: *A summary of the capital account figures for the Irish Economy for 1996*

Capital Account Irish Economy 1996	Ir£m
Capital flows	–594
Financial institutions	–1229
Capital transfers*	+489
Official borrowing/lending	+38
Official reserves	+55
Balance on capital account	–1241
Balancing Item (net residual)	379

Source: National Income and Expenditure 1996 CSO
* Represents capital receipts (mainly) from EU budget

with a – sign, reductions with a + sign). Table 16.2 summarises the capital account for the Irish company for 1996.

All capital inflows are recorded with a plus sign whereas capital outflows are recorded with a minus sign. However it is the minus entries that represent an increase in the economies overseas assets or a reduction in overseas liabilities. For example the change in official reserves of +£55m represents a **decrease** in reserves whereas the –£594 figure for capital flows represents a **net increase** in overseas assets.

It is important to note that the Balance of Payments, taken in total, must exactly balance. All transactions should lead to a **double-entry** of equivalent values but with opposite signs. For example, if an Irish exporter of merchandise to the UK invoices in punts to the value of Ir£10m then the UK importer must spend the sterling equivalent to purchase 10m punts to settle the account. That means somebody else must be selling 10m punts to buy sterling. The exporter's transaction leads to a + Ir£10m entry on the current account whereas the seller of the 10m punts is causing an entry of -Ir£10m on either the current or capital account (depending on why sterling is being purchased). Therefore the surplus of Ir£862m on the 1996 current account should be exactly matched by a deficit on capital account of an equal amount. As the figures are never 100% accurate a **balancing item** is typically required to balance the accounts. In 1996 the balancing item was Ir£379m.

Disequilibrium

The balance of payments, taken overall, must balance. However subsections of the accounts may not be in balance. For example, a deficit on current account typically represents an excess of current expenditures over current earnings. This deficit must be financed somehow, and the financing of it will be reflected in a surplus on the capital account. This in turn means an increase in foreign liabilities or a decline in foreign assets. The excess is being financed whether by using up official foreign reserves or foreign borrowing or some other capital inflow.

A *balance of payments deficit* is generally interpreted to mean a reduction in the official reserves held at the Central Bank. This reduction may be caused by a current account deficit which is not being financed by private sector capital inflows, or alternatively despite a surplus on current account a larger outlfow of private sector capital is occurring. A *balance of payments surplus* is indicated by an increase in official reserves, and on this definition the Irish economy had a modest deficit (£55m) in 1996 despite a sizeable surplus on current account (see also Section 17.5).

16.2 Comparative advantage

While the balance of payments accounts merely record international trade and capital flows the theory of comparative advantage attempts to **explain** the pattern of international trade. International trade is based on an international division of labour. Countries specialise in producing and exporting a particular product mix while importing a different product mix. The theory of comparative advantage specifies the conditions whereby countries can benefit from specialisation and trade.

The basic principles can be established by way of a ***2-country-2 good*** model. Figure 16.1 illustrates the (simplified) production possibilities available to two countries.

Given the resources available to country *A* it can produce a maximum of 10,000 units of *Y* per time period if no *X* is produced or a maximum of 5000 units of *X* if no *Y* is produced. If country *A* pursues a policy of **autarky** (i.e. self-sufficiency) it must divide its resources between both sectors. An equal split of resources, will be assumed leading to a production of 5000*Y* + 2500*X* (point *a*). If country *A* wishes to produce additional units of *Y* then 0.5 unit of *X* must be sacrificed per unit

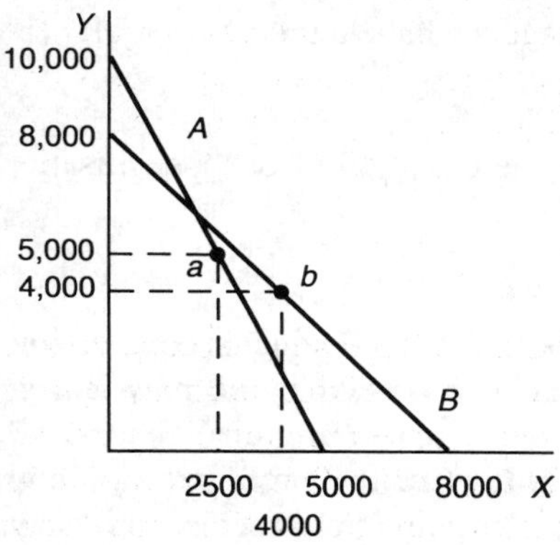

Figure 16.1: *Production possibilities and comparative advantage*

increase in Y. Alternatively if extra units of X are required then 2 units of Y must be sacrificed per unit increase in X.

Country A
Opportunity cost of unit of $Y = 0.5X$
Opportunity cost of unit of $X = 2Y$

Similarly for country B, the maximum output of Y if no X is produced is 8000 units, whereas the maximum output of X if no Y is produced is 8000 units. If autarky is pursued as a policy the country must split its resources between both sectors and point b is a feasible point with $4000\ Y + 4000\ X$ being produced. For country B the opportunity cost of a unit of X is $1Y$ and the opportunity cost of a unit of Y is $1X$.

Country B
Opportunity cost of unit of $Y = 1X$
Opportunity cost of unit of $X = 1Y$

Without international trade, and with an equal division of resources between both sectors, total production is:

$$9000Y + 6500X$$

In the absence of specialization and trade it is not possible to increase production of Y above 9000 units without reducing the output of X below 6500 units and vice versa. To increase output in either sector resources must be shifted from the other sector. However it can be easily shown that if both countries **specialize according to comparative advantage** there can be increased output of both goods.
When comparing two countries, **a country has a comparative advantage in producing that good for which it has a lower opportunity cost**. Therefore country A has a comparative advantage in the production of good Y while country B has a comparative advantage in the production of good X. If we now assume total specialisation according to comparative advantage we have a total output of:

$$10{,}000Y + 8000X$$

Comparing these figures to those under autarky there is a **gain** from specialisation and trade of:

$$1000Y + 1500X$$

What could not be achieved under autarky has been achieved under specialization: an increase in the output of both sectors. In practice specialization may lead to greater gains if opportunities to exploit economies of scale (Section 5.5) exist.

Even if one country has an **absolute advantage** in the production of both goods, provided opportunity costs differ there can be gains from specialisation and trade. (Figure 16.2).

Country B has an absolute advantage in the production of both goods as it can

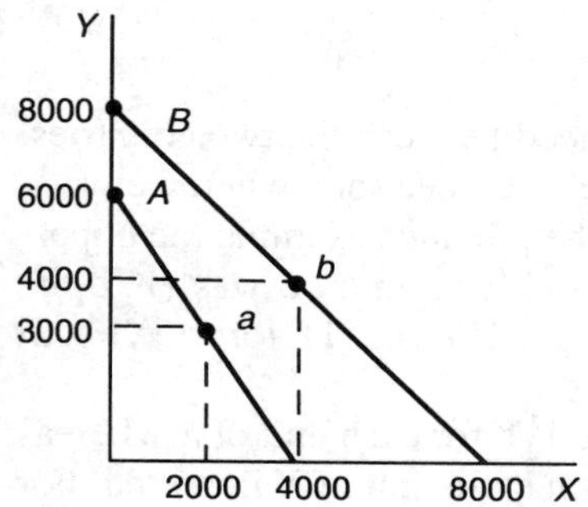

Figure 16.2: *Absolute advantage and comparative advantage*

produce more of both when compared to country *A*. However country *A* has a comparative advantage in the production of good *Y*.

Country *A*
Opportunity cost of a unit of $Y = 2/3X$
Opportunity cost of a unit of $X = 1\frac{1}{2}Y$

Country *B*
Opportunity cost: $1Y = 1X$

It can be seen that each extra unit of *Y* produced by country *A* has an opportunity cost of $2/3$ *X* whereas for *B* it is higher at $1X$. As country *A* has a lower opportunity cost it has a comparative advantage in the production of *Y*

Without specialization points *a* and *b* (Figure 16.2) represent feasible combinations of output giving a total output of:

$$7000Y + 6000X$$

As before, it is not possible to increase output in one sector without reducing output in the other if both countries pursue a policy of autarky. If however country A completely specialized in good Y it can produce 6000 units and if country B splits its resources, for example, 25 : 75 in favour of good *X* it can produce $2000Y + 6000X$ giving a total output of:

$$8000Y + 6000X$$

This represents a gain of $1000Y$.

The gain from specialization represents an *increase in real output*. Therefore living standards will be improved as a result of using international resources more efficiently.

Distribution of the gain

The question arises as to how the gain will be divided between the two countries. Will both countries gain? Provided the rate of exchange lies somewhere between the opportunity costs both countries will gain. In the previous example the opportunity cost of one unit of X for country A was $1\frac{1}{2}Y$ and for country B was $1Y$. If the countries specialize and trade at a rate of, say, $1X$ for $1\frac{1}{4}Y$ (i.e. $1Y$ for $4/5X$) both countries will gain.

Prior to specialization country A had to sacrifice $1\frac{1}{2}Y$ for each unit of X whereas with trade only $1\frac{1}{4}Y$ is sacrificed (exported) for each extra unit of X imported. For country B a full unit of X was sacrificed for each unit of Y before specialization. After specialization only $4/5X$ is exported for each additional unit of Y imported.

Some qualifications

The following factors need to be borne in mind when considering comparative advantage:

- Transport costs – despite countries being able to produce goods at lower relative cost high transport costs may negate the gains from specialization. Innovations in transport, leading to lower costs have a major impact on global trading.
- Unemployment – the gains from specialization and trade are clear cut once resource reallocation has taken place and a new equilibrium has been established. However, in practice resources do not move smoothly and costlessly from one industry to another. The operation of comparative advantage can lead to the decline of important industries in countries resulting in structural unemployment (Section 15.4) at least in the short to medium term.
- Relative costs and relative prices – if free international trade is to lead to specialization according to comparative advantage then the relative prices of internationally traded goods need to reflect relative costs. Quite simply, relatively low cost producers should have relatively low international prices. However fluctuations in exchange rates and the failure of prices to reflect costs (e.g. subsidized exports) can have a distorting effect.

16.3 The terms of trade

The terms of trade is concerned with the rate at which one country's goods exchange for those of other countries. Changes in the terms of trade indicate whether a country must export more or less in order to purchase a given volume of imports. A terms of trade index (TOT) can be calculated as:

$$\text{TOT} = \frac{\text{weighted average of export prices}}{\text{weighted average of import prices}} \times 100$$

The index is a *trade-weighted* one, i.e. the various prices are weighted according to the relative importance of that product regarding the total value of imports or exports. The prices are denominated in a single currency and the index is typically set equal to 100 in a base year (the year in which the weights are established).

An improvement in the terms of trade is indicated by an increase in the index an adverse change by a reduction. An 'improvement' means less needs to be exported to purchase a given volume of imports (or more imports for a given volume of exports). An improvement can result from:

- An increase in export prices;
- A reduction in import prices;
- An increase in the nominal exchange rate (Section 17.1).

An 'improvement' in the terms of trade does not necessarily benefit the balance of payments or employment. For example, an increase in domestic prices means fewer goods need be exported to purchase a given volume of imports. However, it may now be more difficult to sell these goods with the result that the value of exports may fall. A fall in the price of an important import (such as oil) typically represents an unambiguous improvement in the terms of trade.

16.4 *Inter-industry and intra-industry trade*

What is the source of comparative advantage? Why do countries differ in their abilities to produce goods and services? David Ricardo (1772–1823), who first formulated the theory of comparative advantage, suggested that differences in **labour productivity** between countries was the reason for differences in relative costs between countries. Access to different levels of technology could explain differences in labour productivity.

Two Swedish economists (Heckscher and Ohlin) developed this analysis further and argued that even countries with access to similar technologies could have different relative costs due to differences in their overall endowment of factors of production. Countries would tend to specialize in producing those products requiring the factors in which they were favourably endowed. For example, countries with a relative abundance of labour would tend to specialize in labour intensive products whereas countries with a relative abundance of capital would tend to specialise in capital intensive products. Differences in natural resources would also play their part in determining relative costs between countries.

The important point about the above analysis is the focus on the **differences** between countries. Given the differences in factor endowments different countries would tend to specialize in different products. This type of specialisation is the basis for **inter-industry trade**. This is where countries export different products to the ones they import. For example the Irish economy traditionally tended to export food but import manufactured goods.

The ability of the theory of comparative advantage to explain the pattern of international trade has been diminished by the growth of **intra-industry trade**. This is where countries import and export *similar* products. For example many economies both import and export motorcars; Ireland imports and exports whiskey, etc. By emphasizing the differences between countries the theory of comparative advantage fails to explain intra-industry trade which has much to do with *similarities* between countries.

Intra-industry trade is based on product differentiation. Countries will import and export variations, usually branded versions, of a basic product. Thus Germany exports BMWs while importing Citroens, etc. The growth of intra-industry trade is linked to an increasing demand for greater consumer choice and the existence of economies of scale in production. With rising prosperity in a country consumers tend to want greater choice regarding the goods they purchase. If this greater choice was to be catered for exclusively by home producers there would be a tendency for a larger number of relatively small producers to emerge. However where there is relatively free international trade producers can cater for similar market segments in different countries and exploit any economies of scale that might exist. We would therefore expect intra-industry trade to be more important the more integrated economies are and the more similar they are in terms of living standards. Not surprisingly intra-industry trade is the dominant feature of the growing trade in consumer goods between the member-states of the EU.

16.5 *Free trade and protection*

There are gains from international specialization and trade. International specialization can be expected to result in a more efficient use of global resources. This in turn implies improved living standards for consumers in the countries concerned. However, it is commonplace for governments to have **commercial policies** which include a range of barriers to free international trade. For example:

- Tariffs – a tax on imports having the effect of raising the price of the imports on the domestic market.
- Quotas – an upper limit on the quantity of a product that it is permissible to import.
- Non-tariff barriers – (see Section 18.2).
- Export subsidies – enables exporters to sell in foreign markets at prices that do not reflect the true relative cost.

Trade barriers are designed primarily to protect **domestic producers** from foreign competition. A range of arguments are put forward in support of protectionist measures:

- Unemployment – there can be major adjustment costs if domestic industries are forced to adjust to foreign competition. This can be particularly so when there is a significant shift in comparative advantage from one country or region to another. For example, the growing competitiveness of many SE Asian economies in manufactured goods poses major problems for European economies.

- Infant industries – some industries may require protection from superior foreign competitors if they are to develop and prosper. Particularly where efficiency is based on economies of scale, protectionist measures may enable an industry to develop on the home market and become internationally competitive in the longer term.
- Strategic industries – the government, for political reasons, may consider it undesirable to be over-dependent on foreign suppliers of certain products such as food or armaments. Self-sufficiency in food production was at least part of the reason for the introduction of CAP (Section 3.5).
- To improve the balance of payments (see Section 17.5).

Free international trade can result in gainers and losers and therefore have important implications for the distribution of income in society. Despite long-term benefits there may be significant short-term costs. Governments must decide, usually under pressure from local interests, where the balance of advantage lies. However, there is no economic case for the **permanent** protection of inefficient domestic industries. Inefficiencies in one sector inevitably translate into higher costs in other sectors either by way of higher input prices or less demand or both. The result is living standards lower than they might otherwise be.

16.6 *Impact of a tariff*

The effect of the imposition of a tariff can be illustrated as in Figure 16.3.

The *S* and *D* curves represent domestic supply and demand conditions. If we assume that the country can import as much as it wishes at the prevailing world price (known as the 'small country assumption'), this can be illustrated with a

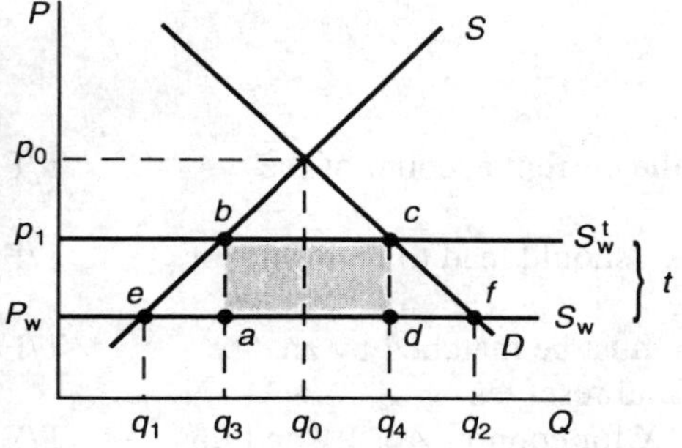

Figure 16.3: *Impact of a tariff*

perfectly elastic supply curve (S_w) drawn at the world price (p_w). If the country's commercial policy is to keep out imports completely the domestic price will be p_0 with domestic production at q_0. If the country adopts a policy of free trade the domestic price will fall to the world price p_w, domestic production falls to q_1, consumption expands to q_2, with $q_2 - q_1$ being imported.

Assume, starting from a position of free trade, the country imposes a per unit tariff (t) on imports. This can be illustrated by an upward shift of the world supply curve by an amount equal to the tariff ($S_w \rightarrow S^t{}_w$). The effect of the tariff is to benefit domestic producers at the expense of domestic consumers and foreign producers. The domestic price rises to p_1 which is the world price plus the tariff ($p_w + t$). Domestic production expands from q_1 to q_3 but domestic consumption falls from q_2 to q_4. Imports, which were $q_2 - q_1$, fall to $q_4 - q_3$. The government's tariff revenue from these imports is $q_4 - q_3$ times t (indicated by the shaded area abcd).

Consumers' surplus (Section 3.1) has fallen by $p_w p_1$cf as a result of the tariff. This has been converted into increased profits for domestic producers ($p_w p_1$be), tariff revenue for the government (*abcd*) and payment for the higher costs of domestic producers (*eba*). The triangle dcf represents a deadweight loss (i.e. a loss with no corresponding gain).

REVISION FOCUS CHAPTER SIXTEEN

Key Areas

- Balance of payments
  → current account → capital account → official financing → surpluses and deficits
- Comparative advantage
  → gains from specialization and trade → terms of trade → inter-and intra-industry trade → barriers to trade and reasons for
- Impact of a tariff
  → on producers and consumers

Self Test

(1) Repatriated profits are recorded in the current account of the balance of payments T/F

(2) An increase in domestic interest rates should lead to an inflow of funds on the capital account. T/F

(3) A current account surplus or deficit must be matched by an equivalent deficit or surplus on official reserves T/F

(4) The opportunity cost of producing 1*X* for country *A* is 2*Y* and for Country *B* is 1.5*Y*. Country *A* has a comparative advantage in producing good *Y* T/F

(5) An improvement in the terms of trade must improve the current account of the balance of payments T/F

(6) Given the gains from specialization and trade there can be no economic justification for restricting free trade T/F

(7) Comparative advantage explains inter-industry but not intra-industry trade T/F

(8) Autarky is good for employment and therefore must benefit living standards T/F

Discussion Topics

- Using a diagram to illustrate, explain the impact of a tariff on domestic and foreign producers and domestic consumers.
- Despite trading with countries having an absolute advantage in producing all goods, a country can still benefit from specialisation and trade. Explain.
- The balance of payments must balance. Explain.

CHAPTER 17

EXCHANGE RATES

17.1 *Nominal, effective and real exchange rates*

An exchange rate is simply the price of one currency in terms of another. For example, £1 = $1.50, or £1 = DM 2.50 etc. These are examples of the **nominal exchange rate** (NER) and clearly there are as many NERs as there are currencies. The NERs of significance for the economy are those with the country's important trading partners.

It is possible that one currency is gaining value against some currencies but losing value against others. The **effective exchange rate** (EER) is an index which attempts to measure the overall change in the value of one currency against a range of other currencies.

Example

Assume the £/$ rate changes from £1 = $1.50 to £1 = $1.35, (a –10% *depreciation* of £) while the £/DM rate changes from £1 = DM 2.50 to £1 = DM 2.75; (a +10% *appreciation* of £). For simplicity assume that 75% of the country's trade is with Germany and 25% with the USA. The change against the DM will have a greater impact on the economy than the change against the $ and will therefore receives a correspondingly greater weighting:

$$(+10\% \times 0.75) - (10\% \times 0.25) = +5\%$$

The EER has a base year value equal to 100 and is adjusted in the light of **trade weighted** changes in relevant NERs. For the above example the EER would increase, say from 100 to 105, indicating an overall appreciation of 5%.

The **real exchange rate** (RER) is an index which measures changes in the *international competitiveness* of a country's goods and services.

Example

Price of bottle of Irish whiskey	= Ir£10
Price of bottle of Scotch whisky	= £10
Irish punt/sterling rate:	Ir£1 = £1

The competitiveness of the Irish whiskey will be affected if either the NER changes or the domestic price of either whiskey changes. For example if the price of Irish whiskey increases then it will lose competitiveness unless the value of the punt falls against sterling. The RER incorporates changes in both relative prices and NERs and can be calculated as the ratio of domestic prices (P_d) to foreign prices (P_f) the latter converted to domestic currency terms:

$$\text{RER} = \frac{p_d}{p_f \times \text{EER}}$$

An appreciation of RER, due to domestic prices rising faster relative to foreign prices or an appreciation of the EER (resulting in cheaper foreign goods) implies a loss of competitiveness.

17.2 *Determination of the nominal exchange rate*

The NER is a price and like any price the value will be determined by buyers and sellers in a market, in this case the **foreign exchange markets**. These are highly competitive markets, resembling perfectly competitive ones in some respects. For example, homogeneous products; a large number of financial institutions dealing; well informed dealers using advanced communications systems.

Only money is being traded and therefore the seller of one currency is of necessity the buyer of another. By focusing on just two currencies a particular NER can be isolated and the analysis simplified. If we take just the Irish pound (Ir£) and the Deutchmark (DM) then sellers of Ir£ by definition are buyers of DM and vice versa. Anything causing increased demand for DM (i.e. increased sales of Ir£) will cause the Ir£ to **depreciate** against the DM (i.e. the DM to **appreciate** against the Ir£). For example if the exchange rate changes from Ir£1 = DM 2.50 to Ir£1 = DM 2.60 the Ir£ has appreciated while the DM has depreciated.

By isolating the motives for buying a foreign currency we can better understand the forces of supply and demand at work. Germans wish to buy Ir£ for a number of reasons including the following:

- to finance the purchase of Irish goods and services (imports, tourism, etc.);
- to invest in Ireland: (a) in real assets (FDI) and (b) in financial assets (portfolio investments);
- the German Central Bank may wish to influence the Ir£/DM exchange rate.

The first above represents a current account transaction while the other two are capital account transactions (Section 16.1). The willingness of foreigners to buy a countries exports will depend on how competitive they are in terms of price and quality. All else being equal, a successful trading nation can expect to have a strong currency. Inward investment in real assets will depend on the *long-term* prospects for the economy to generate an acceptable rate of return to prospective foreign investors. Investments in financial assets on the other hand will be influenced by **relative interest rates** and the *shorter term* prospect of capital *gains or* *losses*. If interest rates rise in Ireland relative to Germany, all else being equal, this will attract funds into the Irish financial system and vice versa. If the pound is expected to lose value in the future this will result in increased selling (note the self-fulfilling expectation) and vice versa.

Portfolio investments are highly liquid and can have a destabilising effect on money markets. Sudden or short-term fluctuations in the value of a currency are not caused by current account transactions or by long term capital flows (FDI). Sudden (and sometimes dramatic) changes are caused by changes in interest rates or changing confidence in the future value of the currency. With the removal of *exchange controls* as part of the Single Market Programme (Section 18.3) speculative flows of funds became much more important in EU foreign exchange markets.

The traditional analysis of exchange rate determination focuses initially on current account transactions, in particular, the supply and demand for currencies to finance international trade. When the Ir£ is strong relative to the DM Irish goods will be more expensive in Germany for any given Irish price level. By implication the Germans will want fewer pounds to buy Irish exports when the Ir£ has a high rate against the DM. This can be illustrated (Figure 17.1) by a downward-sloping demand curve for Ir£. At higher exchange rates fewer pounds are bought by Germans with a view to buying Irish goods and services.

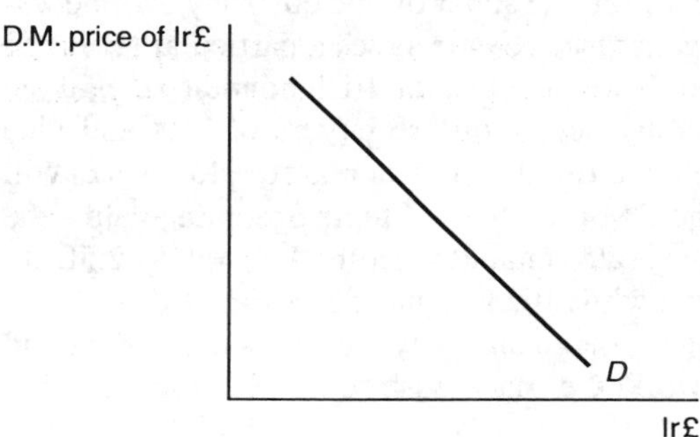

Figure 17.1: *Demand for Ir£*

The demand curve in Figure 17.1 will shift if there are changes in such things as the popularity of Irish goods, Irish interest rates relative to foreign rates, expectations regarding the future exchange rate, the Irish price level, etc.

The supply of Ir£ for current account transactions is equivalent to the demand for DM to import German goods and services into Ireland. As the exchange rate of the Ir£ rises, German goods are cheaper in Ireland for any given price level in Germany. So, more German goods will be bought in Ireland if Ir£ has a high exchange rate. However it does not follow that more pounds are necessarily being spent on these extra imports which require fewer pounds to buy them. Only if the

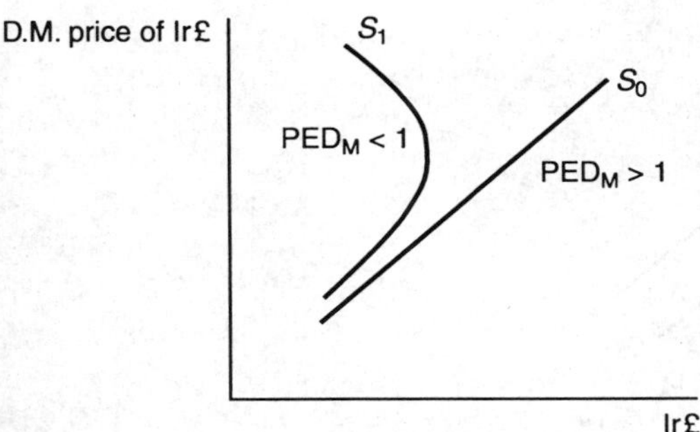

Figure 17.2: *Supply of Ir£*

price-elasticity of demand (Section 2.5) for German imports (PED_m) is elastic will more pounds be actually spent buying the extra German goods.

Assuming this is the case ($PED_m > 1$), we can represent the supply of pounds to buy German goods with an upward-sloping supply curve. If demand were price-inelastic there would be a backward-bending supply curve as illustrated in Figure 17.2.

If the demand for German imports remains price elastic in Ireland the supply curve of Ir£ will remain upward sloping (S_0), if demand becomes price-inelastic the supply curve bends backwards (S_1).

By bringing the supply and the demand curves together the analysis of the determination of the NER can be based on straight forward supply and demand analysis. Figure 17.3 illustrates this (assuming $PED_m > 1$).

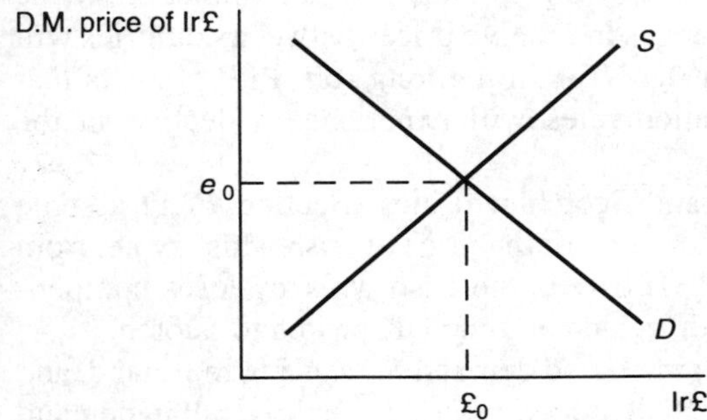

Figure 17.3: *The equilibrium exchange rate*

The equilibrium Ir£/DM exchange rate (e_0) is determined at the intersection of the supply and demand for pounds. $£_0$ represents the equilibrium quantity c pounds traded for the given period.

If the demand curve in Figure 17.3 shifts outward (rising Irish interest r attracting an inflow of funds for example) the equilibrium value of Ir£ will ris

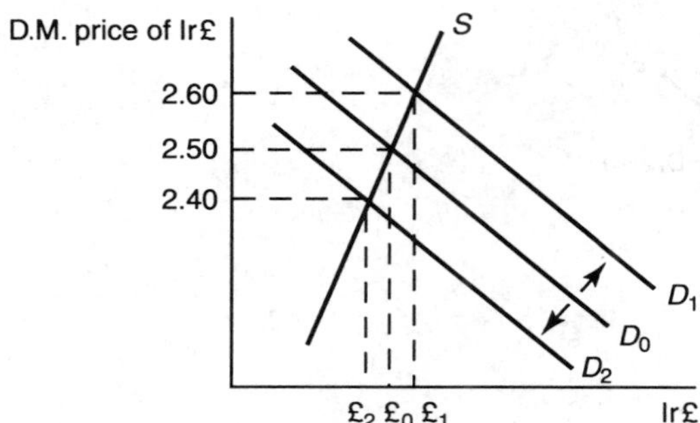

Figure 17.4: *Changes in the equilibrium value of Ir£*

vice versa. If the supply curve shifts outward (rising German interest rates causing an outflow of funds for example) the equilibrium exchange rate falls and vice versa as illustrated in Figure 17.4.

An increase in the demand for Ir£ shifts the demand curve from D_0 to D_1. The value of the Ir£ increases from, say, DM2.50 to DM2.60. A fall in demand ($D_0 \rightarrow D_2$) causes the exchange rate to fall from DM2.50 to, for example, DM2.40.

17.3 *Purchasing power parity*

Purchasing power parity (PPP) is a theory of the **long-run** determination of the exchange rate. According to PPP changes in relative prices between countries will be the most important influence on the NER in the long run. PPP predicts that countries with relatively high inflation rates will experience a decline in the exchange rate of their currency.

Using the example of the Irish and Scotch whiskies (Section 17.1) assume 100% inflation in Ireland leads to a doubling of the price of Irish whiskey i.e. from Ir£10 to Ir£20. At the original NER (I£1 = £1) the Irish whiskey loses competitiveness and whiskey drinkers in both Ireland and the UK switch to Scotch.

The switch to Scotch will mean an increased demand for sterling in Ireland, and (assuming demand in the UK for the Irish product is price-elastic) a fall in demand for Irish pounds from UK importers of Irish whiskey. Figure 17.5 illustrates these effects.

A switch in purchases from Irish to UK products implies an increased supply of Irish pounds to the foreign exchange market to buy more sterling ($S_0 \rightarrow S_1$). Assuming demand for Irish goods in the UK is price-elastic there is less demand for Irish pounds as a result of Irish inflation ($D_0 \rightarrow D_1$). The equilibrium value of the Irish pound falls from e_0 to e_1.

PPP predicts that the value of the Irish pound will fall by an amount necessary

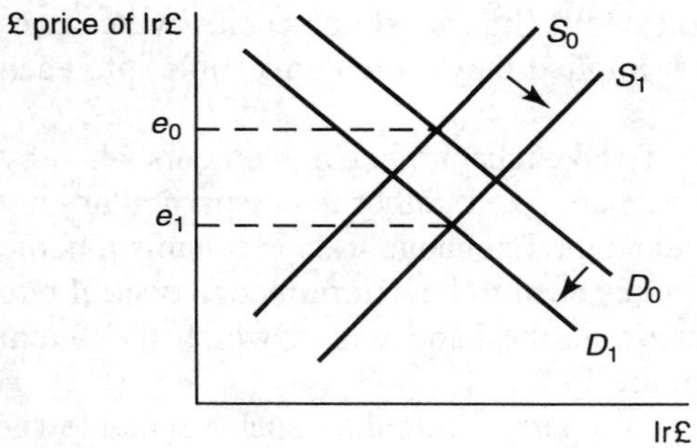

Figure 17.5: *Operation of purchasing power parity*

to restore the competitiveness of Irish products (i.e. a new NER of Ir£1 = £0.50 in our simple example). If we generalize, the prediction is that the NERs will adjust so that **in the longer term the RER remains constant**. What this means is that similar products should cost the same in different currencies. According to PPP it is current account transactions that determine the exchange rate in the long run even if capital account transactions lead to short-term fluctuations.

17.4 *Fixed and floating exchange rates*

In pursuit of their macroeconomic objectives (Section 12.1) governments must decide on an appropriate policy for the exchange rate. Three alternative policies (or exchange rate regimes) are typically available:

- free floating;
- fixed
- managed float.

A free floating system is where the government allows the exchange rate to be determined by free market forces. The currency may appreciate or depreciate depending on the relative strength of supply and demand in the foreign exchange market.

The level of the exchange rate has an important bearing on the ability of a country to trade. Fluctuations in the exchange rate can be damaging for the economy. Because of this governments may intervene to influence the exchange rate through a variety of fixed exchange rate systems.

Strictly speaking a fixed exchange rate would require currencies to be locke together at a particular rate. For example, the Irish pound had a fixed rate wi sterling (one for one) for over 150 years up until 1979. The Central Banks Ireland and the UK were committed to dealing in unlimited amounts at the rate, which meant that nobody would be willing to deal at a less favourable the foreign exchange market. Under the **Gold Standard** currencies were 'convertible' into gold at a given rate which implied they were convertible into each other at a particular rate.

However governments may enter into fixed exchange rate agreements whereby upper and lower limits to the exchange rate are fixed, rather than a particular rate. The post-war Bretton Woods agreement and the Exchange Rate Mechanism in the EU (Section 18.4) are examples. Three rates need to be determined, a central rate plus upper and lower limits which determine the band within which the actual market rate is permitted to fluctuate (Figure 17.6).

Provided the free market exchange rate remains within the upper (e_1) and lower (e_2) limits there is no need for central banks to intervene. The objective is to limit the extent of variation allowable rather than fix the rates at a particular level. The tighter the bands the greater the degree of certainty for those involved in international trade but the greater the likelihood the central bank will need to intervene.

If the equilibrium rate moves outside the band the Central Bank must intervene (Figure 17.7). The shift of the demand curve from D_0 to D_1 will result in an exchange rate of e_4 which is below the permissible lower limit of e_2. The Central

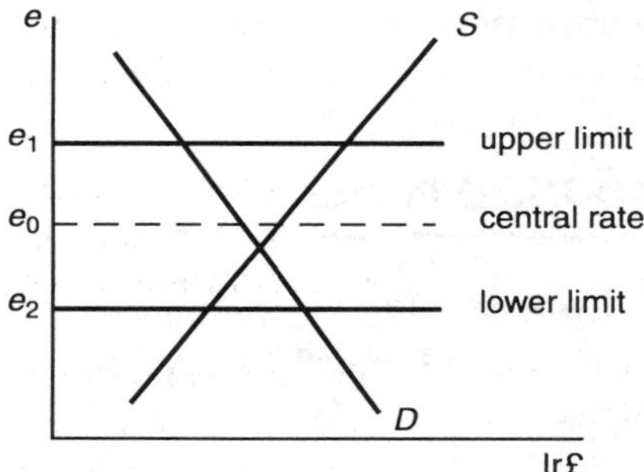

Figure 17.6: *Fixed exchange rate*

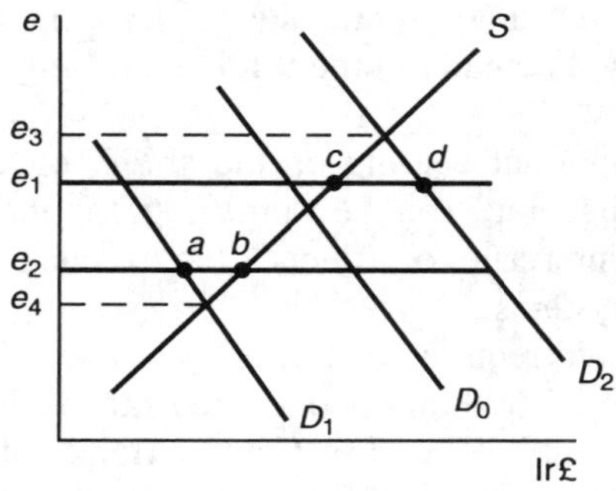

Figure 17.7: *Intervention in a fixed exchange rate system*

Bank is obliged to intervene before the lower limit is breached. The Bank will be required to use its foreign reserves to buy its own currency. The distance *ab* indicates the excess supply of the currency at the lower limit e_2 and is the minimum quantity of pounds that needs to be purchased. An alternative (or complementary) policy is for the Bank to raise domestic interest rates with a view to shifting the demand curve for the currency upward so that the point of intersection is once again within the permitted band. Were the demand curve to shift outward from D_0 to D_2 the free market rate rises to e_3 which is above the upper limit of e_1. To prevent this the Bank must increase the supply of its own currency to the market by an amount at least equal to *cd*, the extent of the excess demand at e_1. The Bank's official reserves will be rising as it purchases foreign currency. Alternatively (or as a complement) the Bank could reduce domestic interest rates with a view to shifting the supply and demand curves downwards so that the point of intersection is within the permitted band.

Operating a fixed exchange rate system imposes certain constraints on a Central Bank:

- An adequate stock of foreign currency reserves must be maintained for intervention purposes.
- Monetary policy (Section 13.4) must be subordinated to the exchange rate regime. Interest rates may need to be adjusted to strengthen (or weaken) the currency as circumstances require.

Problems arise when long-term trends – trade patterns, inflation rates etc. – create the need to realign currencies. In Figure 17.8, for example, if the shift from D_0 to D_1 reflects a longer term trend rather than a temporary shift a **devaluation** of the currency will be necessary.

If e_3 represents the *long-run equilibrium rate* then the currency has become overvalued with respect to the original band. The shift from D_0 to D_1, if permanent, is causing a continuous fall in the Bank's foreign currency reserves (*ab* per period) as it intervenes to prevent the rate falling below e_2. Furthermore, a policy of high domestic interest rates will be the appropriate monetary policy to adopt. As

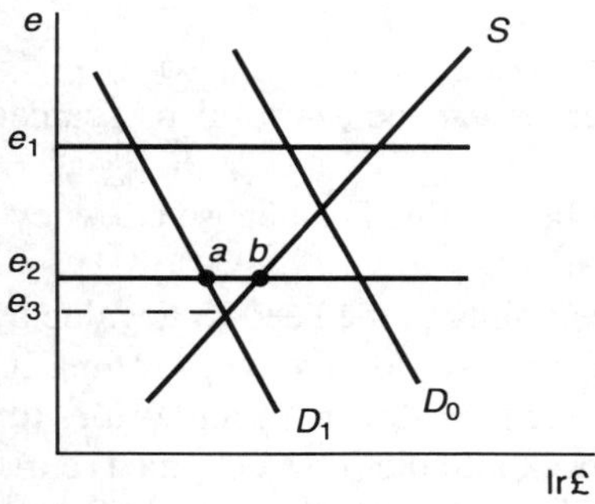

Figure 17.8: *Devaluation as an option*

foreign reserves are finite and high interest rates will undermine domestic economic activity the government will be forced to devalue the currency. Devaluation means choosing a lower central rate and therefore a new lower band which will remove the pressure on the Bank's foreign reserves and domestic interest rates.

If one country is undertaking devaluation then it follows that at least one other country must be pursuing '**revaluation**'. This requires choosing a higher band because the currency has become undervalued with respect to the original band. The ultimate freedom to devalue down or revalue up has given rise to the term '**adjustable peg**' to describe these systems. Effectively they are designed to remove short-term fluctuations rather than prevent longer term adjustments in exchange rates.

Managed float

A managed float (sometimes referred to as a '**dirty float**') is a policy whereby a Central Bank *unilaterally* intervenes in the money markets to influence the exchange rate It is not part of an international agreement requiring it to do so as in the case of fixed exchanged rate systems. The government typically sets the target for the exchange rate which the Bank pursues.

Arguments in favour of fixed exchange rate regimes

- By creating a degree of certainty regarding the exchange rate they reduce the costs and risks associated with international trade, and therefore can be expected to promote international trade.
- Participating countries will be required to pursue *prudent* macroeconomic policies that keep inflation low or face the need for frequent devaluations.
- A degree of order is achieved, particularly if the alternative is countries unilaterally seeking competitive advantage through artificially low exchange rates.

Against

- The need for stocks of foreign currency reserves can be wasteful of scarce resources.
- Periodic realignments when currencies need to be devalued can cause currency crises.
- Speculators have a one way bet. If the evidence points to the need to devalue a currency, speculators can borrow that currency simply with a view to selling it on the foreign exchange markets. This increases the pressure on the authorities to devalue after which the speculators can switch back into the (now devalued) currency to repay liabilities while leaving a profit. The now legendary George Soros is reputed to have made up to £1bn speculating against sterling in October 1992.

Arguments in favour of free floating rates

- The exchange rate continuously adjusts to bring the balance of payments into equilibrium. This follows from the fact that the Central Bank simply refuses to use reserves to intervene.
- Savings on official reserves.
- Greater freedom to pursue other macroeconomic objectives. For example, interest rates can be set to meet the internal needs of the economy rather than support the (perhaps overvalued) exchange rate.
- A flexible exchange rate can operate as a shock-absorber for an economy. For example, it is much easier for an economy to restore its international competitiveness by allowing the NER to fall than by reducing its internal price level (see Section 18.5).

Against

- Free floating rates can be extremely volatile. This increases the risks and therefore costs (in terms of hedging) involved in international trade.
- Because the costs involved rise, firms will be less likely to engage in international trade.

17.5 Exchange rates and the balance of payments

We have seen (Section 16.1) that balance of payments disequilibrium typically means a loss of official reserves resulting from a deficit elsewhere in the accounts. This deficit may be due to private outflows on the capital account. However a **'fundamental disequilibrium'** can be interpreted as a large and persistent deficit on the current account. The country is 'not paying its way in the world' resulting in falling reserves, perhaps official borrowing and very likely high interest rates in an attempt to attract capital inflows.

With flexible exchange rates this fundamental disequilibrium cannot occur. Quite simply, if the Central Bank is not intervening reserves cannot be falling. The exchange rate will adjust to equate the supply and demand for the currency for current account and capital account transactions. A fundamental disequilibrium occurs when the Central Bank refuses to allow the necessary adjustment in the exchange rate.

A current account deficit is removed by reducing the value of imports relative to exports. In the absence of devaluation, the following policies might be adopted:

- Deflate the economy;
- Import controls;
- Buy domestic campaigns.

The first implies the use of monetary and/or fiscal policy to cut the overall level o aggregate demand in the economy. While this will lead to falling demand for imports the demand for goods in general will fall with a likely increase in unemployment.

The second strategy, while it may be effective, invites retaliation. It is also likely to contravene international commitments such as EU membership or World Trade Organization (formerly GATT) agreements.

Even the third strategy will now contravene international commitments given through the Single Market Programme (Section 18.3) of the EU.

By devaluing the currency the government makes imported goods more expensive while exports become less expensive. The impact on the current account will depend on how domestic demand for imports and foreign demand for exports respond. This in turn depends on the price elasticity of demand for imports and exports.

The Marshall Lerner condition

This states that if the sum of the price elasticities of demand for imports and exports is greater than one ($PED_m + PED_x > 1$) in absolute terms then devaluation will improve the balance of trade.

There is some evidence that the Marshall Lerner condition is likely to hold in the longer term but perhaps not in the shorter term. International trade flows may be the result of contracts that cannot be quickly changed. Furthermore, it may take time for consumers in one country to adapt to changes in another country's prices. If so the demand for imports and exports may be relatively inelastic in the short term.

If the sum of the elasticities is less than one in the short term but greater than one in the longer term, devaluation will initially have a worsening effect on the balance of payments followed by an improvement. This is the **J-curve** effect illustrated in Figure 17.9.

Starting at point *a* with a trade deficit the government devalues the currency. The short-term effect is for the trade balance to worsen by going further into deficit but to improve over time.

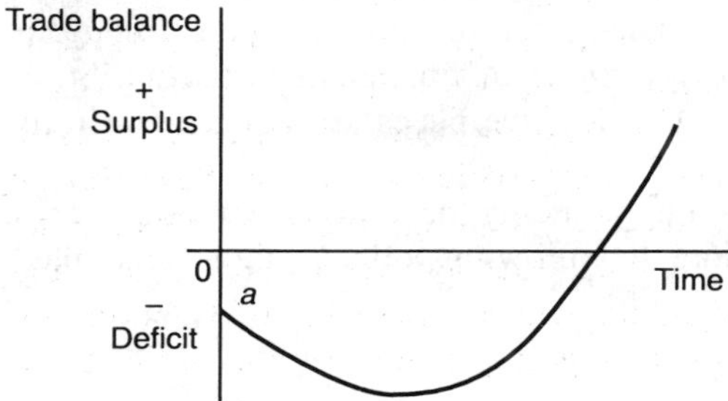

Figure 17.9: *J-curve*

17.6 Monetary and fiscal policy with fixed and floating exchange rates

Fixed exchange rate systems have a cost in terms of monetary independence. We have seen that the level of domestic interest rates will have to complement the exchange rate policy. Furthermore the domestic money supply will respond to surpluses and deficits on the balance of payments whereas with flexible exchange rates domestic money supply is internally controlled.

Assume fixed exchange rates and a balance of payments surplus reflected in rising official reserves. The surplus is the result of the Central Bank selling the domestic currency (i.e. buying foreign currency) to prevent the exchange rate rising. However the increase in foreign reserves at the Central Bank will be matched by an increase in the liquidity of the banking system as the Bank is supplying domestic currency to the foreign exchange market. A balance of payments deficit would cause the domestic money supply to contract as the Bank would be buying domestic currency with foreign currency reserves.

It is possible for the Bank to counteract this balance of payments effect on the domestic money supply. Open market operations (Section 13.4) can be used as a means of **sterilization**. When there is a balance of payments surplus which would otherwise cause the money supply to expand the Bank could sell government bonds which would reverse the expansionary effect of the surplus. With a balance of payments deficit the appropriate sterilization policy would be to purchase government bonds.

Monetary policy designed to influence the domestic economy becomes **ineffective** with fixed exchange rates when there is free capital mobility. Assume the government attempts to stimulate the domestic economy via an expansionary monetary policy. The domestic money supply expands **causing domestic interest rates to fall**. However with free capital mobility the fall in interest rates will cause an outflow on the capital account as investors seek higher returns abroad. This outflow will cause the exchange rate to fall. To prevent the exchange rate falling the Central Bank must buy its own currency and/or raise domestic interest rates, i.e. put the monetary policy into reverse.

Fiscal policy will be more effective under fixed exchange rates. Assume an expansionary fiscal policy whereby the level of taxation is cut. Increased spending leads to an expansion of the economy. As incomes rise there will be rising demand for money balances (Section 13.5) **causing domestic interest rates to rise**. This in turn will lead to an inflow of capital which will cause the exchange rate to rise. However the Central Bank must now intervene to prevent the exchange rate rising. It does so by selling the domestic currency and or lowering domestic interest rates either of which implies an increase in the domestic money supply. This expansionary monetary policy reinforces the initial fiscal policy.

The above analysis implicitly assumes that output rather than the price level increases with fiscal expansion. If the domestic price level were to rise then exports would fall and imports rise in which case the previous analysis would require some modification.

With flexible exchange rates the effectiveness of policy is reversed, monetary policy is effective whereas fiscal policy is not. We have seen that fiscal expansion exerts upward pressure on interest rates whereas monetary expansion implies lower interest rates. With free capital mobility and rising interest rates, capital inflows will cause the exchange rate to rise with the result that exports fall while imports rise. These effects of the rising exchange rate will reverse any expansionary effect of the fiscal policy. However the lower interest rates following monetary expansion result in a lower exchange rate due to capital outflows. This stimulates exports and curtails imports, both of which reinforce the effects of monetary expansion.

REVISION FOCUS CHAPTER SEVENTEEN

Key Areas

Exchange rates
→ nominal, effective and real
Foreign exchange market
→ motives for buying and selling currencies → supply and demand curves → determination of the equilibrium exchange rate → changes in the equilibrium exchange rate
Purchasing power parity
Fixed and floating exchange rates
→ intervention to fix rates → devaluation and revaluation → for and against fixed/floating rates
Exchange rates and the balance of payments
→ correcting a fundamental disequilibrium → the Marshall Lerner condition → the J-curve effect

Self Test

(1) An increase in the nominal exchange rate will improve international competitiveness T/F
(2) An increase in interest rates will cause the exchange rate to rise and bond prices to fall T/F
(3) Provided the demand for imports is price-elastic the supply curve of the currency will slope upwards from left to right T/F
(4) Purchasing power parity explains short-run fluctuations in exchange rates T/F
(5) If a country is in a fixed exchange rate system it cannot pursue an independent monetary policy T/F

(6) A devaluation of the currency is more likely to improve the balance of payments if the demand for imports is inelastic T/F

(7) All else being equal, a surplus on the balance of payments causes an expansion of the domestic money supply T/F

(8) With flexible exchange rates and free capital mobility fiscal policy will be more effective than monetary policy T/F

Discussion Topics

- Compare the advantages and disadvantages of fixed and floating exchange rates.
- Using $S + D$ curves to illustrate, indicate the factors that would cause the equilibrium exchange rate to rise or fall.
- Explain the factors that determine the international competitiveness of an economy,
- Explain the effectiveness of fiscal and monetary policy with fixed and floating exchange rates.

CHAPTER EIGHTEEN

THE ECONOMICS OF EUROPEAN INTEGRATION

18.1 *Economic integration*

All countries must devise a **commercial policy** which will govern their trading relationships with other countries. At an early stage in their economic development countries might pursue a policy of self-sufficiency with a view to cultivating home industries. The Republic of Ireland, for example, had a range of protectionist measures in place up until the late 1950s. However, there are gains from specialization and international trade (Section 16.1) and there are few countries willing to forgo these gains in the longer term.

Countries can enter into a variety of trading relationships including the following:

- Preferential tariffs: countries reduce tariffs for certain products from certain countries;
- Free trade area: participating countries agree to abolish tariffs and quotas with a view to liberalizing merchandise trade;
- Customs union: participating countries agree to free trade among themselves but also they agree to common commercial policies regarding non-members;
- Single market: as well as the elimination of tariffs and quotas members agree to the abolition of a range of *non-tariff barriers* (NTBs); allow free factor mobility and adopt a common set of rules regarding competition, etc.;
- Economic and Monetary Union (EMU): members agree to a single currency (or at least irrevocably locked exchange rates), a single Central Bank operating a common monetary policy and harmonization of fiscal policies where appropriate.

The European Union (EU) was always more than merely a set of economic relationships between members. Since its inception in 1957 the EU (then called EEC) has had a strong political dimension. 'Federalists' wish to see the EU evolve into a modern superstate with power residing in European institutions such as the European Parliament and European Court of Justice. Others ('confederalists') prefer to see the EU remain as basically a set of agreements between sovereign governments. These want power to be exercised on an *inter-governmental* basis and exercised through a Council of Ministers representing national interests.

From an **economics perspective** however, the EU can conveniently be viewed as having evolved from the stage of customs union, is currently in the single market phase and planning to proceed to the EMU phase.

18.2 *Trade creation and trade diversion effects of a customs union*

Up until the mid 1980s the economic relationship between members of the EU was largely that of a customs union with the addition of a Common Agricultural Policy (Section 3.4) financed through (a rather meagre) centralized budget.

When analysing the effects of a customs union it is important to realize that a customs union requires the harmonization of two sets of tariffs: abolition of internal tariffs but the adoption of common external tariffs. The abolition of internal tariffs can be expected to have a **trade-creation** effect. However adopting a common external tariff can have a **trade-diversion** effect in certain circumstances.

Trade-creation occurs when a change in tariffs enables consumers to buy cheaper products from more efficient producers. Trade-creation benefits consumers and efficient producers at the expense of inefficient producers.

Trade-diversion occurs when a change in tariffs requires consumers to purchase higher cost products from less efficient producers. Trade-diversion benefits inefficient producers at the expense of consumers and efficient producers. This trade-diversion effect can occur if, when harmonizing external tariffs, a country ends up with a relatively higher tariff on a product from a non-member that it was previously trading with. Figure 18.1 illustrates the trade-creation effect of a customs union.

Assume to begin with that a country prevents the importation of a particular product. If so the equilibrium in the domestic market will be determined at the intersection of the domestic supply (*S*) and domestic demand (*D*). This is at point *a* in Figure 18.1. with an equilibrium price of p_0 and an equilibrium quantity of q_0. Assume now that this country forms a customs union with one or more other countries. If the removal of trade barriers leads to foreign suppliers entering the

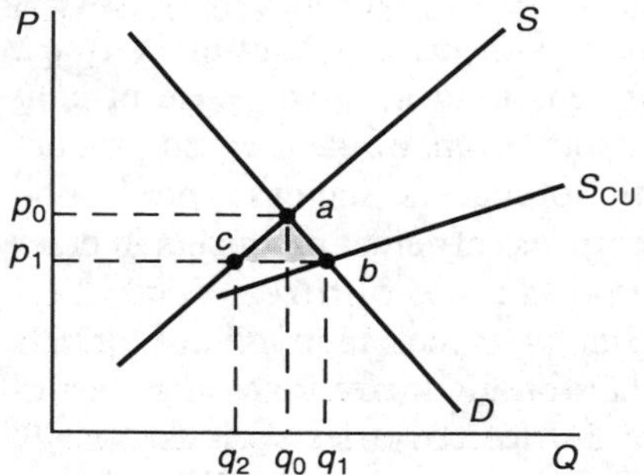

Figure 18.1: *Trade creation effect of a customs union*

domestic market, supply to the domestic market will expand. This effect is illustrated by the customs union supply curve (S_{cu}). The new equilibrium will be at point b with an equilibrium price of p_1 and quantity of q_1.

Giving foreign suppliers freedom of entry to the home market has led to increased domestic consumption ($q_0 \rightarrow q_1$) at a lower price ($p_0 \rightarrow p_1$). However at the lower price domestic producers will only supply q_2. Less efficient domestic producers have been squeezed out of the market resulting in a fall in domestic production ($q_0 \rightarrow q_2$). The country is importing $q_1 - q_2$ from foreign suppliers and this represents the trade-creation effect. Consumers' surplus (Section 3.1) has increased by p_1p_0ab while there is a loss of profits to domestic firms of p_1p_0ac. The result is a net welfare gain equal to the shaded triangle cab.

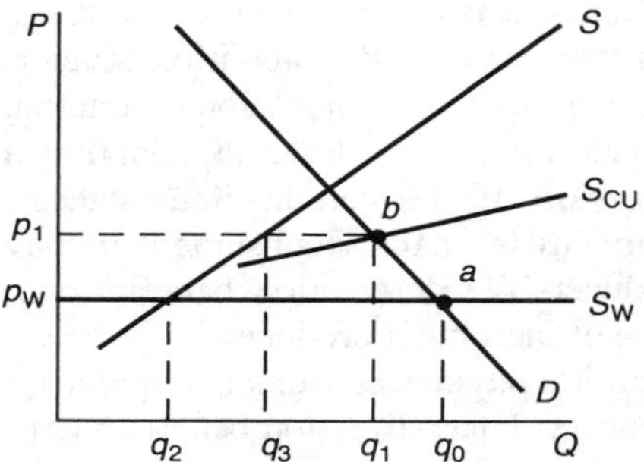

Figure 18.2: *Trade diversion effect of a customs union*

Figure 18.2 illustrates a trade-diversion effect resulting from a customs union. S_w represents the world supply of a product to an economy at a world price of p_w (see 'small country assumption, Section 3.5). If we assume that initially the country imposes no barriers to the importation of this product the equilibrium will be at point a with a price of p_w and domestic consumption at q_0. Of this, q_2 is supplied by domestic producers and $q_0 - q_2$ is imported.

If we assume that the country now forms a customs union which entails prohibitive tariff barriers for this product to non-members the relevant supply curve is now S_{cu}. There is a new equilibrium at point b with price p_1 and quantity q_1. Inefficient customs union producers are now benefiting at the expense of consumers and more efficient world suppliers. Imports from efficient world producers ($q_0 - q_2$) cease. Less efficient domestic producers increase production ($q_2 \rightarrow q_3$). The country now imports $q_1 - q_3$ from less efficient producers in other members of the customs union. Consumers surplus falls by p_wp_1ba.

The Common Agricultural Policy traditionally meant high prices for EU farmers and high tariffs on imported foods. There would therefore have been significant trade-diversion effects on joining the EU for countries such as the UK who were major importers of food from non-members. As the Republic of Ireland's trade with non-members was relatively small at the time of joining, trade-diversion effects are not likely to have been significant.

The net welfare effect of membership of a customs union will be influenced by the extent of trade-creation and trade-diversion effects. However additional economic gains are likely to arise from the removal of internal tariffs in the form of greater efficiency due to the increased competition and also economies of scale resulting from larger markets.

18.3 *The Single Market programme*

In 1987 the member states of the EU ratified the Single European Act (SEA). The SEA represented significant reform of the way in which the EU conducted its political and economic affairs. The economic dimension of the SEA was a commitment to a single market programme (SMP). Member states were given a five year adjustment period so that the single market could be in place by the end of 1992.

The background to the SMP was accumulating evidence that the EU was being outperformed economically by its major international competitors, i.e. the USA and Japan. In a range of areas such as job-creation, unemployment, international competitiveness (particularly in modern hi-tech sectors), investment in research and development, innovation, etc. the relative performance of the EU was an increasing cause for concern.

The poor performance was put down to the **fragmentation** of the EU economy. The EU represented a collection of distinct national economies that still retained a wide range of non-tariff-barriers (NTBs) to trade rather than a single integrated European economy. These NTBs had a distorting effect on intra-community trade and in many cases prevented cross-border trade altogether. The EU had succeeded in removing tariffs and quotas on merchandise trade but the NTBs remained a major obstacle to intra-community trade and competition.

The NTBs come under four broad headings:

Physical barriers – delays at border crossings resulting from the monitoring of '*imports*' and '*exports*' – excessive paperwork associated with cross-border trade.

Technical barriers – different countries having different national standards regarding health and safety, etc. with the result that goods satisfying the requirements of one member country might not be permitted into another member country.

Fiscal barriers – indirect taxes influence retail prices (Section 3.2). Different rates of tax have a distorting effect on trade particularly in border regions.

National preferences in public procurements – government contracts (roads, schools, hospitals, defence etc). represent approximately 15% of economic activity in the EU. The practice of governments was to give preference to local firms when awarding these contracts which effectively precluded cross-border competition.

The SMP is based on *the four freedoms* – free movement of goods, services, labour and capital. Firms supplying goods or services in one part of the single market should be free to supply the same in any other part. Workers from any part of the EU should be free to seek employment in any other part and on equal terms with local workers. There should be no restriction on investors from one member state transferring funds to any other member state.

The SMP has meant the abolition of border checks on goods (and within the **Schengen** group of countries on the movement of people). In the absence of the total harmonization of standards there should be **mutual recognition** so that goods or services satisfying the requirements of one member state should have unrestricted access to others. Policies for the approximation of indirect taxes have been agreed (despite the fact that national governments are extremely reluctant to give up their independence regarding general taxation). There is now a system of **compulsory competitive tendering** for public contracts with legal redress for firms who feel they are being discriminated against on the basis of nationality.

New competition rules have been devised with a view to creating a ***level playing field*** for firms competing in the single market. In particular, national governments are no longer free to subsidize domestic firms nor are they free to restrict access to domestic markets. For example the Irish government is no longer free to subsidize Aer Lingus, nor could it prevent BUPA entering the health insurance market to compete against the VHI and it must open up the whole telecommunications sector to foreign competition by the year 2000.

The SMP is designed to create a more competitive economy in the EU. Greater efficiency should result from:

- more competitive pressure as barriers to entry are removed form national markets;
- improved resource allocation through freer play of comparative advantage;
- exploitation of economies of scale as firms gain access to larger markets;
- restructuring as firms adopt pan-European rather than national strategies;
- product innovation and process innovation resulting from greater competitive pressure.

The **Cecchini Report** published by the European Commission (1988) attempted to quantify the expected gains from the removal of the NTBs (which were referred to as the *costs of non-Europe*).

Stage 1 gains would come through quickly as the removal of physical and technical barriers gave consumers greater choice by enabling firms to operate in wider markets. Cecchini estimated these ***static gains*** as being of the order of $2\frac{1}{2}\%$ of (EU) GDP.

Stage 2 gains were longer term gains as industry adapted to the new more competitive environment. Restructuring would take place as domestic monopolies were forced to compete and firms in general sought to exploit the new opportunities. Cecchini estimated stage 2 gains as being of the order of 3% of (EU) GDP.

Stage 3 gains were macroeconomic benefits which were envisaged for the longer term. Improvements in economic conditions (more jobs, rising GDP) would relax the pressure on national budgets enabling governments to further stimulate their economies through fiscal measures. The best case scenario was an overall increase in GDP of 7% with increased employment of 5m.

The SMP has resulted in increased competition in many sectors of the EU economy. However, the results do not yet add up to the expectations in the Cecchini Report. A number of explanations can be advanced for the relatively poor outcome:

- Failure by governments to fully implement SMP measures particularly in the areas of state subsidies and public procurements.
- An unfavourable macroeconomic background to SMP. Tight monetary policy resulting in high interest rates in the EU in the early phase (Section 18.4) followed by tight fiscal policies designed to satisfy EMU requirements (Section 18.5).

It is also possible that the Cecchini analysis is, at least partially, flawed:

- Overemphasis on the scope for exploiting economies of scale in the single market. Critics argue that **economies of scope**, i.e. the ability of firms to produce a flexible product mix, is of increasing importance.
- Failure to highlight issues other than NTBs which may be greater sources of inefficiency. For example, the lack of flexibility in EU labour markets or the failure of managers to adopt advanced managerial techniques.
- National preferences on the part of consumers indicates that fragmentation is at least partially the result of demand-side rather than supply-side factors.

Whatever the longer term impact of the SMP it is clear that it represents a major transfer of power from national governments to the European Commission in the economic sphere. Governments will inevitably have to adapt their industrial strategies and may be required to harmonize them in some respects. For example, as the SMP refuses to distinguish between private sector and state sector enterprises for the purposes of competition policy and as governments are restricted regarding subsidies, there is a developing trend to privatize state enterprises. In the longer term the ability of governments and regional development agencies to offer special incentives in a competitive effort to attract FDI may be open to question.

18.4 *The exchange rate mechanism*

In 1979 the European Monetary System (EMS) was established, the aim of which was to *create* **a zone of monetary stability in Europe.** Monetary stability is concerned with the *purchasing power* of currencies and has two dimensions:
(i) internal purchasing power which is linked to the domestic rate of inflation and
(ii) external purchasing power which is linked to the exchange rate of currencies.
The exchange rate mechanism (ERM) of the EMS was designed to stabilize the exchange rates of the EU's various currencies and thereby promote intra-community trade. A composite currency, the European Currency Unit (ECU),

made up of elements of all the EU currencies was the standard measure of value. All currencies were given a central rate against the ECU and a permissible range of fluctuation (±2.25% for *narrow band* currencies and ±6% for others up until August 1993).

By fixing all currencies against the ECU by implication they were fixed against each other. In practice the DM was the most powerful currency in the system which gave the German Central Bank (the Bundesbank) a large measure of influence over the monetary affairs of participating countries. If the Bundesbank pursued a tight monetary policy (which it did following the unification of the two Germanies) resulting in high interest rates in Germany, then other countries were forced to do likewise or face the inevitable depreciation of their currencies against the DM.

By the late 1980s there was a significant convergence of inflation rates and interest rates among the participating countries (see Section 17.6 for discussion on fixed exchange rate systems and monetary policy). Critics of the system argue that by transmitting a strict German monetary policy to the whole of the EU the ERM had an inbuilt deflationary bias which was costly in terms of economic growth and employment. Others argue that the strict monetary discipline was the appropriate macroeconomic framework for the longer-term development of the EU economy.

Despite periodic realignments the ERM did create a degree of stability regarding EU exchange rates. In 1992, however, the system came under severe strains. This was in part due to the tight monetary policy being pursued by the Bundesbank following German unification. High interest rates in Germany were transmitted to the rest of the EU which contributed to a severe recession in the EU in the early 1990s.

In addition, the Germans argued the case for a realignment of ERM currencies in 1992 which other countries rejected. In effect the Germans indicated that they would not be prepared to intervene in the foreign exchange markets to defend the existing rates. (Unlike the Bretton Woods system, the Central Banks of both the strong and the weak currencies were expected to intervene in defence of the weakest under the terms of the ERM). When a range of currencies came under speculative pressure their Central Banks were incapable of defending them.

Sterling was forced out of the ERM in October 1992, but only after the Bank of England spent massive sums of foreign reserves attempting to defend it. The Italian Lira was also forced out while others such as the Irish pound were forced to devalue.

On the first of January 1993, free capital mobility was introduced in the EU as part of the single market programme. The removal of controls aimed at restricting capital flows weakened the position of Central Banks in the foreign exchange markets. In August 1993, rather than abandon the ERM altogether, the permitted fluctuation was increased to ±15% about the central rates (except for Dutch Guilder and DM which remained at ±2.25%).

By widening the bands the pressure was taken off the system. Figure 18.3 illustrates with reference to the Ir£/DM exchange rate. With a central rate of

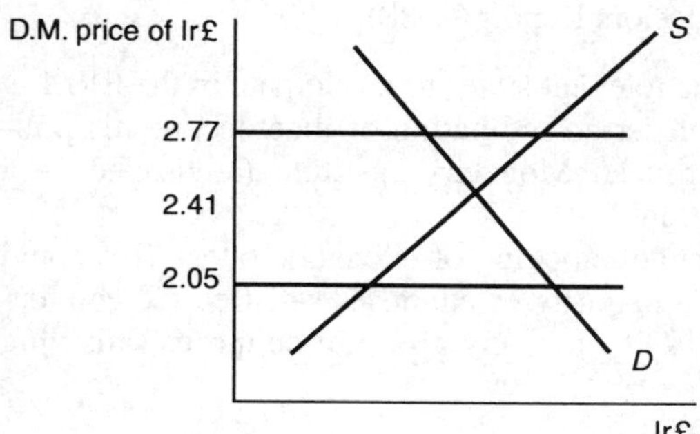

Figure 18.3: *The ERM since August 1993*

DM 2.41 the Ir£ can fluctuate between DM 2.05 and DM 2.77 without Central Bank intervention.

Widening the bands, in effect, gave rise to a system of **managed floats** within an extremely loose **fixed exchange rate** system since most Central Banks continued to shadow the DM **as if** the narrow bands still existed. For the Irish authorities shadowing the DM proved difficult due to the strength of Sterling. Given the historical association between the Irish and British currencies a change in the value of Sterling against other EU currencies has traditionally meant a similar change in the value of the Irish pound. The Irish pound was the strongest currency in the ERM for much of 1997 causing the authorities to have it revalued in early 1998 (a 3% revaluation to a new central rate of approximately DM 2.48). Economic and Monetary Union (Section 18.5), if it goes to plan and if sterling continues to remain outside, will end the long association between these currencies.

18.5 *Economic and monetary union (EMU)*

The ultimate solution to exchange rate instability is to get rid of exchange rates by introducing a single currency. The Maastricht Treaty (1992) committed the member states of the EU (excepting the UK and Denmark) to the creation of a monetary union by no later than 1999.

Monetary union can be achieved without a single currency. A *weak form* of monetary union simply requires the locking of exchange rates at a specific rate with full convertibility (as with the Irish pound and sterling up until 1979). What this means in practice is the closing of the bands in the ERM (Figure 18.3) so as to preclude any fluctuation whatsoever in the rates.

A *strong form* of monetary union would imply a single currency. The planned transition to EMU is to occur in three stages whereby a weak form monetary union will be achieved (1/1/99) followed soon after by the introduction of a single currency (2002).

The three stages are based on the Delors Report (1988):

- Stage 1 (starting 1990) required the relevant states to participate in the ERM.
- Stage 2 (starting 1994) required closer co-ordination of macroeconomic policies and the creation of the European Monetary Institute (envisaged as a forerunner to a European Central Bank).
- Stage 3 is to begin with the irrevocable locking of exchange rates. This could have occurred as early as 1997 if a majority of countries satisfied the **convergence criteria** but failing this in 1999 when any group of countries satisfying the criteria would proceed.

The Maastricht Treaty laid down **convergence criteria** which participating countries were expected to achieve if they were to be eligible to participate. The Treaty, therefore, opened up the prospect for the first time in the EU of a **two-speed Europe**, i.e. those proceeding to monetary union and those being left behind (whether by choice or exclusion).

The convergence criteria which participants were to satisfy are:

- Price stability – member states should have a rate of inflation not more than $1\frac{1}{2}\%$ above the average of the lowest three countries;
- Interest rates – long-term rates should be no more than 2% above the average of the three countries with lowest inflation rates;
- Exchange rates – should have remained, without devaluation, within the **normal band** of the ERM for the previous two years;
- Budget deficit – should be no more than 3% of GDP;
- National debt – the debt to GDP ratio should be no more than 60% (or making satisfactory progress in that direction).

The purpose behind these criteria is to give the new currency (to be called ***the Euro***) credibility as a strong currency on the foreign exchange markets. Only those countries with a good track record regarding the prudent management of monetary and fiscal policy would participate. In this way the EMU countries would represent a zone of monetary stability. The Germans were particularly anxious that strict criteria should exist, because with the DM being one of the strongest currencies in the post-war period they had most to lose if the Euro turned out to be a weak currency.

The advantages of monetary union are clearcut and include the following:

- removal of exchange rate risk on intra-community trade and therefore no need to incur hedging expenses;
- removal of transactions costs involved in changing one currency for another (in strong form case);
- facilitates the development of the single market by removing another non-tariff barrier to intra-community trade (different currencies operate as a NTB);
- facilitates **price-transparency** in the single market as ultimately all goods and services will be priced in the same currency;
- potential savings on foreign currency reserves at Central Banks;

- the emergence of a single European capital market based on the Euro. The result will be a single system of interest rates in the EMU area (of particular benefit to countries like Ireland that tend to have higher rates than, for example, Germany). There should also be greater efficiency in the allocation of investment funds across Europe.

The overall effect should be to create a European economy that is more competitive and dynamic.

However, certain **disadvantages** may emerge as a result of the loss of monetary sovereignty:

- a single currency requires a single European Central Bank and therefore represents a loss of monetary sovereignty at the national level;
- the European monetary policy pursued by the new Central Bank may not suit the needs of all member-states;
- members will no longer be able to devalue their currencies with a view to achieving or restoring international competitiveness;
- if the EMU area is subject to **asymmetric shocks** (i.e. shocks that are country-specific or disproportionately impacting on a particular region) the ability to adopt a local monetary response (e.g. devaluation) may be critical for member states.

Clearly, the greater the degree of **integration** between the economies of the prospective members of EMU the greater the potential gains. For example, the higher the proportion of an economy's GDP that is traded (degree of openness) and the higher the proportion of this that is traded with other members of EMU the greater the benefits in terms of reduced exchange rate risk, reduced transaction costs, etc. On the other hand, the less trade a country does with the EMU area the less incentive to join.

Furthermore, the greater the degree of integration, not only in trade, but also in terms of capital mobility and labour mobility, the lower the potential losses. For example, if there is a **country-specific shock** leading to high unemployment, the greater the labour mobility the greater the dispersal rather than localisation of the shock. The greater the degree of integration the greater the capacity of the EMU area to collectively absorb shocks.

Taking a typical country we can illustrate the potential losses and gains as in Figure 18.4. Potential gains (G) increase with the degree of integration. Potential losses (L) decline with the degree of integration. Beyond I^* the potential gains exceed potential losses, to the left of I^* potential losses exceed gains.

Ireland is one of the most open economies in the EU. With less than 1% of EU GDP in 1996 it accounted for 2.5% of intra-community trade. Table 18.1 gives the geographical distribution for imports and exports for the Irish economy.

With the UK included, Ireland has a high degree of trade integration with the prospective EMU area, with 68.5% of exports and 56.8% of imports accounted for. However, if the UK exercises its right to opt out, the degree of integration falls

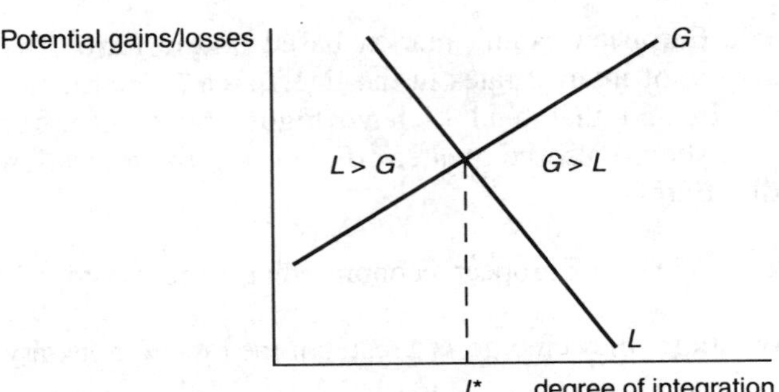

Figure 18.4: *Potential losses and gains from monetary union*

Table 18.1: *The geographical distribution of imports and exports for the Irish economy for the year 1996*

	UK	Other EU	Other Europe	NAFTA	APEC	Other
Exports (%)	24.7	43.8	6.5	10.5	7.6	6.8
Imports (%)	34.8	22	4	16.5	16.5	6.4

Source: Ireland, Trade Statistics, Jan 1997. CSO

dramatically to 43.8% and 22%, respectively. Ireland has a clear interest in the UK joining EMU.

An obvious potential asymmetric shock for the Irish economy would be a decline in the value of sterling outside of EMU. This would pose a significant threat to Irish exports to the UK, and (given that much of this trade concerns indigenous, labour-intensive industries), a significant threat to employment. As a member of EMU Ireland would be incapable of devaluing its currency and competitiveness could only be restored by a reduction in domestic prices and wages.

An ESRI report (Economic Implications for Ireland of EMU (1996)) estimates that the net gain to the Irish economy from membership of EMU minus the UK is less than half of one percent of GNP. This would place Ireland extremely close to I^* on the horizontal axis of Figure 18.4. Given that the growth rate for Irish GNP since the mid-1990s typically exceeds 5% pa the gains from membership of EMU as calculated by the ESRI seem meagre.

In May 1998 eleven countries were deemed eligible to proceed to the third and final stage of EMU as outlined in the Delors Report. It required a rather relaxed interpretation of the convergence criteria (particularly the debt to GDP ratio) to enable all eleven countries to qualify. It remains to be seen whether the EMU area represents an **optimum currency area** (Section 18.6).

18.6 *Optimum currency areas*

An optimum currency area (OCA) is one where the various regions can achieve internal balance (full employment) and external balance (satisfactory balance of payments) without needing to resort to exchange rates as instruments of economic policy. With no need for exchange rate adjustments an OCA derives the benefits without incurring the costs of monetary union.

The following conditions contribute to net gains in an OCA:

- a high degree of inter-regional trade, preferably in a wide range of differentiated products;
- a high degree of price and wage flexibility within regions coupled with a common (preferably low) rate of inflation across regions;
- a high degree of labour and capital mobility between regions.

A high degree of intra-industry trade reduces the risk of asymmetric shocks to specific regions. A high degree of labour mobility implies that any shocks that do occur can be absorbed across regions. Wage and price flexibility is important if regions are to be able to absorb shocks and maintain competitiveness, particularly when devaluation is not an option.

In reality, currency unions are unlikely to have perfect price flexibility and perfect labour mobility, etc. Therefore, in practice a further condition is likely to be required if a currency union is to have sufficient cohesion:

- A Central Budget facilitating inter-regional fiscal transfers.

For example, if one region of the United States of America suffers a shock resulting in unemployment the way the union absorbs it is by a net transfer of funds to that region through the federal budget. In addition, the relatively high level of labour mobility in the USA will tend to disperse the effects of the shock rather than keep it localized.

The EU states collectively possess some of the conditions for an OCA. Intra-community trade is highly developed and intra-industry trade is an important feature of it. Free capital mobility exists and inflation rates are currently relatively low. However cultural and linguistic differences represent major barriers to labour mobility. European labour markets may also lack the necessary level of wage flexibility to enable countries adapt to localised shocks. There are, at present, no plans to increase the central budget of the EU as part of the EMU project. Furthermore, rather than provide for fiscal transfers, plans for EMU provide for *financial penalties* if governments fail to achieve specified limits to budget deficits. This scheme is referred to as a 'stability pact'! As it stands EMU represents an unprecedented sacrifice of both monetary and fiscal sovereignty at the national level.

REVISION FOCUS CHAPTER EIGHTEEN

Key Areas

- Commercial policy
  →alternative trading relationships
- Customs union
  →trade-creation and trade-diversion effects
- Single market programme
  →background→nature of non-tariff barriers (NTBs)→effects of removing NTBs→Cecchini Report
- European Monetary System (EMS)
  →zone of monetary stability→exchange rate mechanism(ERM)
- Economic and Monetary Union (EMU)
  →strong form and weak form of monetary union→convergence criteria
  →advantages and disadvantages of monetary union
- Optimum currency areas

Self Test

(1) In a free-trade area the members adopt a common commercial policy with respect to non-members T/F

(2) Trade-diversion benefits inefficient producers at the expense of efficient producers and consumers T/F

(3) The Single Market Programme is primarily concerned with removing tariffs and quotas from intra-community trade in the EU T/F

(4) An advantage of the Single Market Programme is that it will increase the scope for the operation of the law of comparative advantage in the EU T/F

(5) Real exchange rates will be irrevocably locked as a result of EMU T/F

(6) Membership of EMU entails a greater loss of monetary sovereignty than membership of the ERM T/F

(7) Membership of EMU will increase the need for national central banks to maintain reserves of foreign currencies T/F

(8) The 'stability pact' is designed to help countries respond to asymmetric shocks T/F

Discussion Topics

- Using a diagram to illustrate, explain the trade-creation and trade-diversion effects of a customs union.
- Explain why the Irish Republic has an interest in the UK joining EMU.
- Compare the implications for monetary sovereignty of membership of the ERM with membership of EMU.

Answers to self-test questions

CH	Q1	Q2	Q3	Q4	Q5	Q6	Q7	Q8
1	F	F	T	F	F	T	T	T
2	F	F	b	T	T	F	T	F
3	F	F	T	T	F	F	T	F
4	T	F	T	F	T	T	F	T
5	F	F	T	T	F	T	F	T
6	T	T	T	F	T	T	c	F
7	F	T	T	F	F	T	F	T
8	F	T	T	T	F	a	T	T
9	F	F	T	F	F	T	F	F
10	a) 10500 b) 8300 c) 9300 d) 975	a) T b) F c) F d) T	£1.43bn	T	T	F	F	F
11	5	£250m	£40m	b	T	T	F	F
12	£2500	T	a	T	T	F	F	a
13	a	F	T	F	T	F	b	T
14	F	T	F	T	T	F	T	T
15	T	T	F	T	F	F	F	F
16	T	T	F	T	F	F	T	F
17	F	T	T	F	T	F	T	F
18	F	T	F	T	F	T	F	F

INDEX